W. T. COSGRAVE
1880 -1965

FOUNDER OF MODERN IRELAND

ANTHONY J. JORDAN

For
Those who Did and Dared,
Those who Died, and Those who Lived

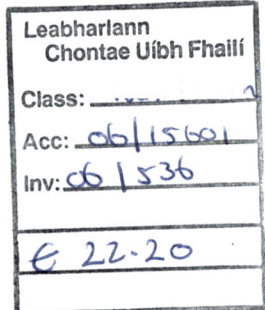

W.T. Cosgrave

Acknowledgements

I would like to thank the many archivists and librarians who have been so helpful and courteous to me during my work. I met them at the National Archives; National Library and its department of Manuscripts; Dublin City Library and Archive – Mary Clarke, Maire Kennedy, Padraic O'Brien, Eithne Massey, Eithne Shalcey; Dublin Diocesan Archive – Noelle Dowling; RDS Library - Mary Kelligher, Gerard Whelan and staff; Pembroke and Ringsend Public Libraries; Seán Cromien, Dermot Lacey, Dublin City Council, Patrick Lynch, Dr. Ristard Mulcahy, Dr. Garret Fitzgerald, Tom Garvin, Maire O'Neill. Mary Lambe and Stephen Farrell at Áras an Uachtaráin. Patrick Lynch for taking this book's most recent photographs of the various historical sites. Thanks also to: Alan L'Estrange, Paddy White, Seán Donnelly, David Bolger, Eamonn McGoldrick, Donal O'Connor, and David Lowe, of the Central Remedial Clinic's Desktop Publishing Training Unit, for their help and commitment. I want to thank Brendan Keane for reading the text and being generally supportive to the project. And lastly to my wife, Mary, who continues to put up with my various projects.

ISBN 0952444771

Graphic Design & Print Reproduction
by
The Central Remedial Clinic DTP Training Unit,
Clontarf, Dublin, 3
Ireland.
Tel: (01) 805 7400

CONTENTS

INTRODUCTION

WT Cosgrave's accession to the position of President of the Executive Council in appalling circumstances in 1922, and his understanding of that role, no doubt contributed to the equanimity with which he handed over power to the opposition, some ten years later.

While Cosgrave had a long and honourable pedigree in the national movement, including being one of the leaders sentenced to death after the Easter Rising of 1916, he had not been of the top rung of military leadership. However with the execution of the 1916 leaders, the opposition of deValera and others to the Treaty, allied to the shocking deaths of Arthur Griffith and Michael Collins in August 1922, the mantle of leadership, continually open to the possibility of assassination, fell on the shoulders of WT Cosgrave. On the day of Griffith's death, fearing assassination, Cosgrave wrote an extraordinary last testament, forgiving those who might kill him and expressing sorrow for his wife and family[1]. Succession had to be effected "quickly and uncontroversally", as he admonished the weeping soldiers at Government Buildings. saying, " This is a nice way for soldiers to behave"[2].

Even then, he was not the unanimous choice, with Kevin O'Higgins, favouring General Richard Mulcahy[3]. From the start therefore, Cosgrave "inherited a team and continued to speak in terms of cabinet rather than personal leadership"[4]. He was quite open in speaking to the Dail about his collaborative methods of choosing cabinet members, seeing himself as primus inter pares. His philosophy found wholehearted support among his Ministers, especially the dynamic Vice President Kevin O'Higgins.

Unlike many politicians Cosgrave, while admiring deValera, did not stand in awe of him. They had become close friends when deValera returned from the USA in late 1920. DeValera thought Cosgrave was at one with him after the Treaty negotiations, but was outmanoeuvred by Cosgrave on two vital occasions, both before and after the plenipotentiaries returned from London. During the Treaty Debates, he down-faced deValera. Unlike the latter, who according to Sean MacBride, almost considered himself as the embodiment of the State declared by the 1916 leaders[5], Cosgrave regarded himself, not an idealist but rather a businessman who wanted to get things done. His modus vivendi, so unlike that of deValera, whom he once accused of personal hatred of him[6], and dubbed him a 'magician of political metaphysics', was expressed thus: " In times of crisis it is advisable, - it is necessary - to make up your mind rapidly, to make it up correctly and, having made it up, to stick to it like a man and to do what you can towards preserving, improving and exalting the country, which it is our duty to serve"[7].

Cosgrave had a difficulty with party politics after his early experience within Sinn Fein, of uniting in a national movement. The recent demise of the Irish Parliamentary Party added to this concept. The constitutional founders of the Irish Free State had neither anticipated nor desired organised political parties[8]. They hoped that community groups and others would have representation in Parliament and keep a watching brief on the Government, as it endeavoured to bring the new State into calmer waters, despite extensive opposition to its very legitimacy.

Cosgrave's facility of acting as 'Chairman' rather than 'Chief' was clearly exemplified when during the Army Crisis of 1924 he allowed his Vice President handle the matter. Cosgrave himself had to manage the thorny Courts Bill of 1923 and 1924, as Kevin O'Higgins absented himself. After the murder of O'Higgins in 1927, Cosgrave's unassuming leadership was never in doubt.

Cosgrave tenaciously stood by the Treaty as an international agreement, and forced Fianna Fail to take the oath of allegiance to the King, before they entered the Dail. For this Tom Garvin has referred to him as the founder of Fianna Fail[9]. Cosgrave guided the diplomatic moves within the Commonwealth, which vindicated Collins' belief that the Treaty was a stepping-stone to independence. His governments had to continually function in the face of IRA mayhem and intimidation, and the continuing denial of legitimacy from Fianna Fail, even after that party entered the Dail in 1927.

It is generally recognised that the peaceful and orderly handover of power to the incoming Fianna Fail Government in 1932, stands as a major achievement of the leader of the outgoing Cumann na nGaedheal government, WT Cosgrave. He had led governments for the previous ten years, since the signing of the Treaty with the departing colonial power. A series of civil wars had occurred in the country, with those demanding a republic, defeated, North and South. The Nationalists of the North were, to a great extent, left to fend for themselves by their Southern compatriots. In the South the intransigent republicans had been defeated in a most bitter war by the Cosgrave Government. The republican political leader, Eamon deValera, was unable to convince his militarists that the way forward was by political means. He then founded his own political party, Fianna Fail, in 1926, and was quite successful in a series of general elections, receiving much support from his erstwhile militant faction. However, as that party refused initially to take their seats in the Dail, due to the Oath of Allegiance to the King, the assassination of Kevin O'Higgins in 1927, enabled them overcame principle, and enter the Dail. They came close to gaining immediate power, but had to wait until the election of 1932, when they were able to form a minority government, with the aid of other groups in the Dail.

The great fear of Fianna Fail, after the election results were declared, was that a group of Ministers, in association with the army and a new secret organisation, would seize power. The newly founded, *Irish Press*, the mouthpiece of Fianna Fail, reported thus on 26 February, creating a highly charged atmosphere, as the Dail met to elect a President. James Dillon, a new T.D., in 1932, found his first day in the Dail quite extraordinary. He wrote:

"A very considerable number of the Fianna Fail party arrived in the Dail on the day Mr. deValera was elected, armed to the teeth. They thought there was going to be a putsch; that if Mr. deValera was elected, Mr. Cosgrave would not hand over Government. They had a completely illusory notion of the standards and character of Mr. Cosgrave, who, of course, had brought – indeed forced - Fianna Fail into Dail Eireann, in order to establish normal political functioning in the country. So they were swaggering around the place with revolvers bulging out of their pockets. One old gentleman was assembling a machine gun in a telephone booth": Dillon added that, "far from being involved in frantic plotting", on the occasion of the vote for the President, Cosgrave was upstairs playing pontoon with the

outgoing Education Minister, John Marcus O'Sullivan, while waiting for Dail business to begin[10]. In later years, Gerry Boland and Sean Lemass gave differing views on the preparations of Fianna Fail deputies for that auspicious day[11].
In modern times, it would be difficult to envisage a political leader encouraging and welcoming a rival leader to succeed in forming a new government. However as early as 1928 WT Cosgrave had told the *New York Times*: " We have been in power too long. When one party remains in office five years, it brings upon itself heaps of exaggerated and inflated criticisms…what I would like to see before long is the present government stepping down and the other fellows taking the reins"[12]. He told the same paper just after the 1932 election that he would have "preferred as President one of deValera's lieutenants, like Sean Lemass, whom he regarded as a practical politician, rather than deValera, whom he looks upon as an impractical dreamer and a coiner of dangerous phrases"[13]. The paper added, " Only those with first-hand knowledge of Cosgrave's difficulties can appreciate the greatness of this little tawny-headed man, who has been in office longer than any other Prime Minister in Europe".
Cosgrave was essentially a very reserved family man, who when called upon, served his country in a variety of daunting ways. He rarely gave interviews. Dr. Risteard Mulcahy, who had undertaken a series of in- depth interviews with his own father, approached WT for an interview. The elderly Cosgrave declined, saying that he had taken no papers with him when he left office, and he was content to let the record speak for itself[14]. In June 1980 there was a celebration of the centenary of his birth. The main event was a mass at St. James' Church in James' Street. This was attended by the Cosgrave family, Dr. Garret Fitzgerald and members of the Fine Gael front bench and the entire parliamentary party.. President Patrick Hillery attended, but no members of Fianna Fail were invited so as to avoid any embarrassment. A plaque was unveiled on the old Cosgrave family home.
Maurice Manning wrote an article in the *Irish Times* of 5 June 1980, which captured the essence of WT's contribution to his country and explained some possible reasons why his legacy has been neglected. He wrote, " WT Cosgrave is almost certainly one of the most underrated of the major Irish political figures of this century. When he died in 1965 he had already become one of the forgotten figures of Irish politics and in the time since then, his contribution has faded even further into the background of history….In some ways this playing down of his role was of his own making. His style of politics was straightforward and unspectacular. His approach was business-like and unemotional".
Around that same time, Alf MacLoughlin, Director of the National Library, approached Mr. Liam Cosgrave for his father's private papers. The request was declined[15]. There are some personal papers of WT in the National Archive, but they are not substantial. His record and his character are to be found for the most part, in the record of the Oireachtas and Governments. It is substantial, heroic and modest. He was a conservative Catholic, a witty Dubliner from the inner city, totally devoid of any tendency towards personal aggrandisement. He was in a very real way, the founder of modern Ireland.

CHAPTER ONE

YOUNG WILLIAM THOMAS COSGRAVE

William Thomas Cosgrave's mother, Briget Nixon, came from Landenstown, Prosperous, Co. Kildare. His father, Thomas Cosgrave T. C., P.L.G., came from Castledermot Co. Kildare. Thomas Cosgrave's father was named Patrick. The Cosgraves came originally from Kilrush in North Wexford. A Cosgrave was hanged in the 1798 rebellion and the family moved to Kildare. William Nixon, Brigid's father, was a convert to Catholicism There were six children born from the marriage, Patrick Thomas, William Thomas, Thomas, May, Phillip and Joseph[1]. William Thomas was born on 6 June 1880, at the family home on 174 James St. Dublin, opposite the South Dublin Union. The family ran a grocery and public house business. Thomas Cosgrave was a public-spirited man, being a member of the Board of the Poor Law Guardians. The Poor Law was an attempt to come to terms with some of the problems arising out of widespread poverty in Ireland in the early 19th century, by providing institutional relief for the destitute. The Irish Poor Law Act of 1838 divided the country into 130 poor law unions, each with a workhouse at its centre. Each Union was administered by a board of poor law guardians, some of which were elected and some appointed from the local magistracy. As the 19th century progressed, the poor law unions were given many additional functions, particularly in relation to health, housing and sanitation. There were two Unions in Dublin, the North Union and the South Union at James' St. William Thomas [WT] attended the local primary school, run by the Christian Brothers on nearby Francis St. However at the age of eight, a catastrophic family event occurred. *The Freeman's Journal* of Monday 9th July 1888 carried notice of the premature death of his father on 7 July 1888 at the age of thirty-three. It read:

COSGRAVE - July 7 1888. At his residence 174 James' Street Dublin, Thomas Cosgrave P.L. G. Second son of Mr. Patrick Cosgrave of Castledermot, county Kildare, deeply regretted by his sorrowing wife and family. May the Sacred Heart of Jesus have mercy on his soul. Funeral for Goldenbridge Cemetery at 10.30 O'clock on this Monday morning.

After the death of Thomas, the name of Peter Cosgrave appears on the register of electors from that address, instead of the deceased. This was the case for three years until 1892 when Mrs Bridget Cosgrave's name appears alone. Mrs Cosgrave then apparently took the pragmatic step of ensuring the family's survival, by marrying the man who worked for them and knew the business so well. He was Thomas Burke, a native of Seskin in Tipperary. Two children were born from Mrs Cosgrave's second marriage, Joan Burke, born on 28 September 1892 and William Francis (Goban) Burke[2]. Thomas Burke's name alone appears on the electoral register for that address up to 1909, when the names of WT Cosgrave and Miss M. Cosgrave are added. These three names remain the registered names on the address until 1920, with the name of WT Cosgrave disappearing in 1921. His name alone appears for number 175 James's St for the three years of 1922-1924, under the title of 'purveyor'. In 1925 the property at 174 lists Patrick O'Dwyer alone, as the registered elector there[3]. Today both 174 and 175 both form part of Kenny's public house.

Thomas Burke was a very different man from his late employer, being much more garrulous and pretentious, but one who was well capable of accepting his good fortune in becoming master in the household and business. The family was very religious with the boys being regular mass servers. Thomas was known on occasion to make comical remarks about WT's penchant for horse riding and story-telling[4].

When WT finished primary school he was sent across the city, to another Christian Brothers School at the O'Brien Institute in Marino. This was a journey of nearly five miles each way. He finished school at sixteen. and for the rest of his life, regretted that he had not continued on to university. Instead he went to work for his stepfather in the family business, as did his younger brother Phillip. The brothers were very close friends.

The Cosgrave-Burkes had a good middle class standard of living and participated in a vibrant social life. A version of the life of that society was well captured in John Huston's film, *The Dead*. Dining, singing, dancing, storytelling, at which WT was excellent, and political and social conversation, were common pastimes. The nearby Phoenix Park was the setting for much of the outdoor activities of the middle classes of the area, with walking, picnics or in the case of WT, horse-riding being quite common. Moira Lysaght, a contemporary of the family, recalled her family walking in the Phoenix Park with the Burke-Cosgraves, when WT passed them on his horse. She said, " as he galloped by on horseback, his golden hair flying in the breeze, Tom Burke humorously commented "There goes John Gilpin"'. On another occasion Miss Lysaght recalled an occasion when WT was regaling them with one of his ghost stories. She noticed his impatient stepfather in the background, muttering –" Will the bloody fellow ever shut up?"[5].

Like his own father, WT took an interest in public affairs. It was an exciting period in national life, with the Irish Parliamentary Party {IPP] leading nationalist Ireland in the quest for Home Rule. This party would have been the expected natural home of a man of WT's background. There was also a publican's group on Dublin Corporation with which he would have some affinity. But he was influenced by the cultural revival of advanced nationalism and became interested in that movement.

To understand the background that led the twenty-five year old WT Cosgrave to attend the founding convention of Sinn Fein in November 1905, together with his uncle James and brother Phil, one must take an overview of what was happening in the country at the time, and specifically in Dublin city. There was a multiplicity of organisations in Dublin involved in the national movement, often with vastly different aims and methods. Some felt that a new Ireland had to be a Gaelic Ireland, while others believed that such a policy would make Ireland too provincial, if not parochial. WT would appear to have been of the former dispensation. Arthur Griffith was the leading light in the wider movement and it was he who decided to create an umbrella organisation for the disparate groups, called Cumann na nGaedheal in 1900. Its aims were:

1. Cultivate a fraternal spirit among Irishmen.

2. Diffusing knowledge of Ireland's resources and Irish industries.

3. The study and teaching of Irish history, literature, language, music and art.

4. The assiduous cultivation and encouragement of Irish games, pastimes and characteristics.

5. The discountenancing of anything tending towards the Anglicisation of Ireland

6. The physical and intellectual training of the young

7. The development of an Irish foreign policy.

8. Extending to each other friendly advice and aid, socially and politically.

9. The nationalisation of public boards[6].

NATIONAL COUNCIL

In 1903 Griffith had assembled a group to protest against the visit of King Edward VII to Dublin. The Corporation heeded the group and refused to present the usual address of welcome to the King. Some of those Councillors decided to take a more nationalist stand and work towards alleviating the plight of the working class. In June of 1905, the National Council; against the wishes of Griffith, who was sceptical of gaining success through the political process, insisted in putting up twenty candidates for the election to the Dublin Poor Law Board, thirteen of whom were elected. Ever since the debacle of running Major John MacBride in a by-election in South Mayo in 1900, Griffith remained sceptical of the political process[7].

WT Cosgrave with his brother Phil and their uncle PJ Cosgrave attended the first meeting of Sinn Fein, presided over by Edward Martyn at the Rotunda, on 28 November 1905. Also present was Oliver St. John Gogarty, who was to become a close life-long friend of WT's. Cosgrave found that Sinn Fein had a profound influence in arousing the National consciousness, and attracting not only the youth, but also men and women of all ages to its ranks[8]. Griffith had intended that the National Council would remain a Dublin based coordinating body. The Dublin members accepted Griffith's wishes, but the country members opposed it and voted to set up branches in each electoral district. However the organisation, Sinn Fein, whose official inauguration is accepted as having taken place at that Rotunda meeting, accepted Griffith's Dual Monarchy proposals, to the great annoyance of those whose aim was a totals separation from England[9]. The General Election in January 1905 resulted in a substantial Liberal victory, weakened the position of the IPP and consequently strengthened the new Sinn Féin Party.

The IPP did not appeal at all to WT. He had the option of aligning himself with the publicans who fought local elections as a group, but Sinn Fein was to be his political home. In conjunction with the General Election of January 1906, local elections also took place. The National Council, the name Sinn Fein was still known by, ran in the local elections, where WT was their candidate in the Usher's Quay area. He lost narrowly to a publicans' representative. But the Council won six seats in Dublin, where Tom Kelly became their leader. Their successful candidates included John T. O'Kelly. WT then formed a branch of Sinn Fein in his own area and worked assiduously in preparation for the next election. The branch meetings of Sinn Fein, the Craobh Éamonn Mhic Gearailt, were held in the Cosgrave-Burke public house, and Arthur Griffith was a frequent visitor.

In 1907, CJ Dolan MP resigned his IPP seat in the House of Commons, as a protest at the ineffectuality of his party and offered to fight the bye-election as a Sinn Fein candidate. This was an offer Sinn Fein could not refuse, though Griffith did not welcome it. However, at the time, Sinn Fein was a moderate party with a wide membership. Three priests, several IPP councillors and three women sat on its executive, alongside a group of IRB men. To Griffith's relief, and thanks to great work by Bulmer Hobson, Sean MacDermott and other IRB men, the party won a respectable 27% of the vote in Leitrim, spending over £700 on the campaign[10] This was to be the most successful electoral feat of Sinn Fein until 1917. Griffith's preferred policy thereafter was, if elections had to be fought, it was better to concentrate on local elections.

CHAPTER TWO

DIARY OF A DUBLIN CORPORATOR[1]

In 1908, Sinn Fein members of the Dublin Corporation numbered 13 out of a total of about 80. The next local elections came in 1909, when WT and Sean T. O'Kelly, or John T. as he was then known, were among seven victorious Sinn Fein candidates. They joined the group in the Corporation led by Alderman Tom Kelly. The Sinn Fein party policy consisted of reforms in areas of education, housing, re-aforestation, protection of Irish industry, independent civil courts, and a pledge if non-recognition of Parliament at Westminster. However it was on a social housing policy that WT concentrated early on. In 1917 he was pleased to see a local authority estate built in his own area at Mount Brown. It consisted initially of 31 houses with extensions built in 1922 and 1925. It was named Ceannt Fort, after Eamonn Ceannt, who was Cosgrave's commanding officer at the South Dublin Union during the Easter Rising. It currently contains 202 houses. WT later became an expert on public finances and became Chair of the important Estates and Finance Committee. This made him a well-known public figure in the city establishment and a great boon for his party.

Most of the work at the Corporation was naturally concerned with the very mundane operations of the local authority area. However as the Sinn Fein members worked for their local constituents, Arthur Griffith highlighted their profile in his Sinn Fein paper. Dubliners began to realise that Sinn Fein was a serious party, which delivered for its own people, mainly the poor. At the start of each year, Standing Committees were elected to look after particular functions. In his first year on the Corporation, WT was a member of the Public Health Committee. In successive years he was a member of the Waterworks Committee, the Cleansing Committee, and finally Chairman of the prestigious Estates and Finance Committee. He took the work very seriously and was an assiduous attendee at all committee and general meetings. The Sinn Fein Party made its presence felt with its clear nationalist ideology and interest in alleviating the living conditions of the working classes.

However, on occasion, matters of a wider and even national import appeared on the agenda of the Corporation. On these occasions the Sinn Fein party was to be clearly heard, with WT usually to the fore, either leading or seconding his leader, Alderman Tom Kelly. It is instructive to consider some of these items, as they give an indication of the early course travelled by WT Cosgrave, and will assist in understanding his later career.

1910

At a Special Meeting of the Council on 12 May 1910, a motion was introduced that "The Lord Mayor, Aldermen, Burgesses of Dublin City Council, respectfully tender our sincere sympathy and condolences to His most Gracious Majesty, the King, and to Queen Alexandra, and the other members of the Royal Family, in the great affliction that has befallen them through the death of His late Majesty, King Edward VII". The vote was, for the motion, 32 votes, with 7 against. The seven Sinn Feiners opposing were, Tom Kelly, Daniel McCarthy, Patrick O'Carroll, and Messers. Cregan, O'Toole, Denis D. Healy and WT Cosgrave. [375][2]

The Sinn Fein group, especially WT, who was a very devout Catholic, became very agitated concerning the Coronation Oath to be taken by the incoming monarch. They entered a motion: " that the Corporation of Dublin demands that the following declaration for the Coronation Oath, which is intolerably offensive to at least twelve million of persons in these realms- should be deleted there from". Part of the Oath was included to wit; " I do solemnly swear in the presence of God, profess and testify and declare, that I do believe, that in the Sacrament of the Lord's Supper, there is not any transubstantiation of the elements of Bread and Wine into the body and blood of Christ, at or after the Consecration thereof, by any person whatever and that any Invocation or Adoration of the Virgin Mary or any other Saint, and the Sacrifice of the Mass as they are now used in the church of Rome are superstitious and idolatrous".[376] The motion was put and carried unanimously. Some time later, on 13 June, it was proposed to send a delegation to, " the Bar of the House of Commons" concerning the recent resolution on the Coronation Oath. A Sinn Fein amendment said, " It was undignified to now beg at the Bar of the House of the English Parliament in the matter of the blasphemous declaration taken by the King on his succession". The Lord Mayor ruled the amendment out of order and the motion was passed by 22 votes for to 15 against. [443]

On the 14 November 1910, the Council passed a motion for WT as " an expression of sincere sympathy on the death of his brother Mr. Thomas J. Cosgrave". [785]

1911

As with all political parties, Sinn Fein liked to assist people with whom they might share an ideology. John MacBride was a well-known nationalist, who had become quite famous for organising and co-leading the Irish Transvaal Brigade in the Anglo-Boer War during 1899-1900. The advanced nationalists in Dublin, foremost among them Arthur Griffith and Maud Gonne, had used the Brigade as a vehicle to whip up anti-British sentiment in Ireland. MacBride had subsequently made a disastrous marriage with Maud Gonne and was a party to an acrimonious divorce case in Paris. He had sued the *Irish Independent* for libel in its reporting of the case. The paper was very aggrieved to be singled out in this way. James Campbell Queen's Counsel represented the paper and used the occasion, to ridicule MacBride and Maud Gonne, as well as nationalist Ireland. In Dublin, MacBride had some difficulty in gaining employment and became an IRB organiser for some time.

Latterly he had become an employee of the Corporation as assistant to their Water Bailiff. The latter died during 1910 and the Markets Committee recommended that since MacBride had carried on with the duties concerned successfully, he should be confirmed in the post of Water Bailiff. When the Council considered this Report in November 1910, it did not accede to the suggestion. [775] Instead the Council advertised the post and attracted eleven candidates. At its meeting in January 1911, the Sinn Fein party again, through Tom Kelly and WT Cosgrave, sought, " that Standing Orders be suspended to enable the Council to take into consideration the Report of the Markets Committee". This motion was lost and a vote was taken on the appointment from a long list of applicants It resulted in: MacBride – 32: Thos. Cahill – 24: Mr.Creaven – 3.

John MacBride was declared appointed to the post. [2]

MacBride was a noted public speaker on nationalist occasions and just two months later, the Corporation received a letter of complaint from the City of Dublin Unionist Association. It quoted from a speech he had made in Belfast espousing the view that violence was required to remove England from Ireland. The Unionist Association felt that "such treasonable sentiments in a public meeting by a paid official of the Dublin Corporation and a servant of the ratepayers and citizens of all creeds and politics, is most unseemly and contrary to the practice of all responsible officials of public bodies". The letter was discussed by the Council and a motion, put and carried stating, " that a reply be sent to the Association to the effect that the Corporation does not invite opinions from its officers, nor does it wish to impose its opinions upon anyone in the service of the Corporation".

During that year of 1911, the Council carried a motion, " that the City Hall, Council Chamber, and Members Rooms, be placed at the disposal of the Gaelic League and the Gaelic Athletic Association Carnival committee, for the purpose of holding their Ceilidh, which had to be postponed because the Mansion House was not available". [205]

1914

In May 1914, as Home Rule moved closer, a letter from Tom Kelly to the Council, which requested it to send a representative to a conference on the territorial integrity of Ireland and against the exclusion of Ulster, was considered. A motion emanated which included supporting Irish nationalism and expressing confidence in the Irish Parliamentary Party. Tom Kelly and WT tried to forestall this motion by an amendment, " that the resolution embodied in the letter be adopted". The amendment was defeated by 40 votes to 11. [364]

In November 1914, with the Irish Party apparently victorious, and understandably feeling somewhat triumphant, a motion was put to the Council, " That this Municipal Council of Dublin representing the citizens of the capital of Ireland, expresses, in union with the Irish race the whole world over, its unbounded satisfaction at the placing on the Statute Book of the Charter of Ireland's Freedom: and it places on record its appreciation of the tactics of the Irish Party so ably led by Mr. John Redmond M.P., which have resulted in the successful conclusion of Ireland's struggle for liberty". Once again Sinn Fein through Tom Kelly and WT Cosgrave, tried to forestall the motion by putting an amendment stating; "That the consideration of this motion be postponed until the terms of the Amending Bill are made known". Support for the amendment came solely from the seven Sinn Fein Councillors present, with 41 voting against. The motion was then carried.

1915

PROFESSOR KUNO MEYER

In July of 1911, the Council had unanimously elected Professor Kuno Meyer and Canon Peter O'Leary [Peadar Ó'Laoghaire] as Freemen of Dublin. However, during the course of the World War, there was great anti-German animosity. This was reflected in a motion put to the Council on 15 March 1915, urging it to expunge Dr. Meyer's name. WT Cosgrave took great exception to this proposal and as a preparatory measure, wrote to the Town Clerk concerning Dr. Meyer. His long letter outlined the value of Meyer's work as Professor of Philology in Berlin and Liverpool Universities, and as a Founder and Director of the School of Irish Language in Dublin, and as Todd Lecturer in the Royal Irish Academy in Dublin. He went on:

Perhaps the most pernicious influence which has effected this country is the denationalising of the Irish race by the absorption of the soul of the nation. Whatever may have been lost throughout the whose history of Ireland, there has always been maintained, valiantly upheld, and jealously guarded the individuality of the Nation, and no influence has been more potent, no incentive a greater inspiration, no heritage more glorious than the language of our forefathers. And in a country almost rent in twain by different schools of politics and distracted by sectarian prejudice, the Associations which have undertaken the preservation of the native language have attracted all that is best of every shade of political and sectarian thought.

Imbued with a sense of deep obligation, which Ireland owes to the greatest living authority on Old and Middle Irish, the Municipality inscribed upon the roll of Honour Freeman the name of Dr. Kuno Meyer...

The proposal now before the Council is to remove the name of this eminent Celtic Scholar from the roll of Honorary Freemen; to negative a life of work of Celtic erudition. No Continental upheaval can affect the everlasting gratitude owed to German Celtic Scholars...

In conclusion, I submit that this proposal, made at a time when passion and prejudice cloud the better qualities of the human mind and on evidence which is ex parte at its best, that in other times would not dare to be advanced for any purpose and certainly cannot appeal to the better judgement of the Council to support an attempt to degrade a scholar who loved our country and served her well.

Faithfully yours W.T. Cosgrave.

An amendment by WT was voted on, and a tie resulted in 24 votes for and against. The Lord Mayor then cast his deciding vote against the amendment.

The original motion to expunge Dr. Meyer's name from the list of Freeman was then put by Alderman McQuaid and seconded by Councillor O'Hara.

Another amendment was put, postponing Alderman's McQuaid's motion until after the war. This was voted down by 30 votes to 22. The original motion was again put, and carried by 30 voted to 17. [262]

However in April 1920, Dublin City Council voted to rescind this expunging of Dr. Meyer's name, and he again became a Freeman of Dublin. Unfortunately he had died in the meantime.

JOHN REDMOND

John Redmond sent a letter to the Council, in September 1915, thanking it for its earlier motion of support. He wrote, "the record of the achievement of the Party, during the last four years have earned us the right to expect and demand this consideration. Throughout all this time a small section of Irishmen have devoted themselves to the task of destructive criticism. They have done their very best to obstruct the movement, to break up the Party, and to render the passage of the Home Rule Act impossible... They have filled the air with their prophecies of evil and the preaching of despair...nothing can undo the enactment of the Home Rule Act by the Imperial Parliament...the highest duty and the most vital interest of Ireland, at the moment, is to do everything in her power to support the cause of the Allies." [682]

At the same meeting, a letter from Alderman Tom Kelly sought endorsement from the Council to appoint a delegate to an anti-conscription conference. This was carried by 31 votes to 7. WT Cosgrave then moved, "That Alderman O'Neill be appointed as the delegate". This was carried. [685]

In July 1915 the Council considered a motion, " That the use of the Council Chamber be granted for the holding therein of a meeting of representative citizens to consider the question of threatened conscription". 35 voted for, 24 against. [544]. During this period, the Council carried a series of motions, protesting against the imprisonment of Volunteers.

1916

In January of 1916 WT Cosgrave was again elected as Chair of the Estates and Finance Committee.

On 4 April he presented the Committee's Report to the Council.

On 19 April WT Cosgrave moved that the Poor Law Rate be adopted. [402+403]

On 5 May a Special Meeting of the Council was called to consider an application from the Guardians of the North and South Poor Law Unions for distress relief, arising from the recent disturbances in the city. The Council was also asked to nominate an additional member to the Board of Guardians of the Poor Law.

On 10 May the Council agreed a request from the North and South Dublin Unions to convene a special meeting, to receive applications to relieve distress caused by the Sinn Fein Rebellion

On 5 June the Council voted " Deepest sympathy to relatives of the citizens who lost their lives during the recent rebellion". [407]

On 17 July the Council voted "That this Council demands the immediate withdrawal of Martial Law".

On 2 August it voted for an inquiry on the shooting by British soldiers of named and unnamed prisoners in North King St.

On 4 September the Council demanded the release of interned Irish prisoners. [654]. It also considered condemning Dublin employers, who victimised their employees, who were the relatives of those who participated in the recent rising. This motion was later dropped. [574]

On 2 October Alfie Byrne M.P. moved a motion, "That in consequence of the numerous complaints received as to the treatment of the Irish prisoners at Frongoch Camp and as 38 of our fellow countrymen are now in solitary confinement for refusing to be informers on their comrades, who were wanted by the Military, we request officials of the United States Embassy, who inspected all camps in Great Britain where German prisoners are interned, to turn their attention to Frongoch and the treatment of Irish prisoners". The Lord Mayor ruled the motion out of order. [689]

A month later a similar motion was put and carried by the Council. [795]

A letter from the US Embassy said it had no grounds to interfere in the matter. [877]

In November the Council voted to overrule its officials who refused to call Noel D. Lemass of 2-3 Capel St. to resume his engineering study at its Workshops, after an absence of some months, due to his being wounded in connection with the Rising in Dublin during Easter Week. [816]

Many motions came before the Council concerning the reconstruction of buildings damaged during the Rising.

On 4 December a motion, "that 3 members of the Municipal Council visit Frongoch and report on conditions under which hundreds of our countrymen are interned there, a very large proportion of them citizens of Dublin", was put by Tom Kelly and Councillor Sherlock. [868] At this same meeting it was agreed, "that Mr. Charles Power, Secretary of the Markets Committee be appointed Water Bailiff, without salary". [844]

On 9 October 1916 the Council considered the following motion, "That we, the members of the Dublin Municipal Council are of the opinion that the time has arrived for the Irish nation to unite in demanding the release of our fellow countrymen and women interned in English prisons, without trial, and an Amnesty for those who have been sentenced to terms of imprisonment, and pending their release, we request the government to consider the advisability of treating them as political prisoners...to establish a Political Prisoners Amnesty ..in connection with the "Rising" of Easter Week 1916.. The motion was carried. [726]

1917

On 8 January, it was agreed in a series of motions that persons who were disqualified as members of the Council by reason of absence, would be co-opted back onto the Council. These included William Partridge, PT Daly and WT Cosgrave. [9,10,11,12]

At this same meeting a motion stating, " that as the continued imprisonment of men sentenced in connection with the Rebellion is a cause of great irritation to the Irish people, because men charged with rebellion in South Africa were treated in a very different manner and released after a very short detention, this Council demands as an act of justice their release". [12]

On 23 January WT was elected to the Improvements Committee. [78] The day previously the Council heard from John Dillon M.P. that a person nominated by the Council, Sir Charles Cameron, had visited Frongoch concerning the health of the prisoners and the sanitary conditions there. [59]

On 2 July WT Cosgrave reappeared at the Council.

On 13 August WT Cosgrave is identified in attendance at the Council as an M.P.

On 27 August WT seconded the Lord Mayor's motion expressing sympathy on the death of Bishop O'Dwyer of Limerick .

On 1 October WT Cosgrave seconded a motion by the Lord Mayor, " that this Corporation begs to place on record the expression of its deep sorrow at the death of the late Thomas Ashe, and that the Council adjourns until this day week". [616]

WT Cosgrave was again involved in a motion on 5 November which stated, " that this Council appreciates the action of the Lord Mayor during the tragic circumstances of the forcible feeding of the Irish political prisoners in Mountjoy Jail, followed by the lamentable death of Thomas Ashe" [684]

1918

WT Cosgrave M.P. was appointed to the Improvements Committee on 23 January.

On11 March the Council expressed its regret on the death of John Redmond M.P.

On 8 April it considered inviting John Dillon M.P., Eamon deValera M.P., Joseph Devlin M.P., and Mr. Arthur Griffith, and representatives of the Irish Trade Union Conference to a meeting, concerning an all Ireland conference on conscription. The vote was 40 for and 3 against.

The Council also protested against the arrest and deportation of 88 people, then imprisoned in English gaols.

On 7 October the Council demanded the release of Countess Marcievicz, Kathleen Clarke, and Maud Gonne MacBride from Holloway Prison [628].

1919

On 3 January the Council offered the freedom of the city to President Wilson of the USA. The motion was proposed by the Lord Mayor and seconded by John T. O'Kelly. [1]

On 8 January the Town Clerk notified the Council, by letter, that WT Cosgrave had been absent from the Council meetings for over six months and therefore, "ceases to be a member". The clerk received a letter from WT, dated 12 January. Mr. Cosgrave would have been aware that the Council was about to reconvene for the New Year, and that Standing Committees would be nominated early in January. His letter read:

Place of Internment

Reading.

Dear Town Clerk,

Explanation due.

I was arrested by police and armed soldiers on or about midnight on 17th May 1918 and brought, accompanied by police and armed military escort, in an English Army motor, to Kingstown, and subsequently here, accompanied by armed military escort. I have therefore been forcibly prevented from discharging the duties of my public office.

In the event of retaining the office of Councillor, I should like to go back to the Estates and Finance Committee, if the Council is willing to allow me to do so.

If however, my enforced absence has disqualified me, I think the earliest opportunity should be afforded to the electors of filling the vacancy.

Believe me, Dear Town Clerk,

Very faithfully,

Yours sincerely

W.T. Cosgrave

The Town Clerk consulted the Law Agent, Mr Ignatius T Rice on the matter. He wrote to the Town Clerk that the Council would have to be satisfied with the explanation for a six months absence, if it was not to declare the seat vacant. He continued, " If a member is absent through being in custody, which is authorised by the state of law for the time being, the fact that he is absent under duress, will not be sufficient to enable the council to accept the absence as satisfactory so as to prevent disqualification".

At the relevant meeting of the Council, when the matter was being discussed on January 25, Alderman Tom Kelly proposed and Councillor Doyle seconded, "That these letters be inserted in the minutes and that the seat be declared vacant". The motion was put and carried. [160]

On 5 May the Council members were invited to apply for tickets to attend the public sessions of Dail Eireann. [421]

On 3 November the Town Clerk advised the Council that Councillor John T. O'Kelly M.P., was absent from the Council for six months. The Council did not take any action. [739]

Kennys, 174 James Street, Dublin,
Birthplace of W.T. Cosgrave.

Crowds view devastation following the 1916 Easter Rising.

CHAPTER THREE

EASTER RISING

LIEUTENANT WT COSGRAVE, 4th BATTALION IRISH VOLUNTEERS

Another General Election took place in 1910, which restored the balance of power in the House of Commons to the IPP, and allowed it to force the third Home Rule Bill from Parliament. This gave an impetus to the IPP and was a negative for Sinn Fein. This was reflected in the Sinn Fein Ard Fheis, with a small attendance and an absence of people willing to sit on the executive. Griffith acknowledged the vulnerable position of his party, later telling George Russell, " If a good Home Rule Bill had been introduced, I and my party would have disappeared from Ireland. Nobody would have listened to us"[1]. As Home Rule appeared to be moving towards a political reality under Asquith's Liberal Government, with the removal of the House of Lords legislative veto, the Unionist of the North, under The Ulster Unionist Council, decided to organise themselves into an armed militia in January 1913. They would oppose Home Rule by force if necessary. The threat of civil war loomed as the Conservatives, under Bonar Law and the upper echelons of the Army, openly supported the Unionists and their Dublin born leader, Edward Carson. The latter's raison d'etre was the legislative union binding Ireland to Great Britain. For him, Ulster was essentially a device to crush Home Rule for Ireland. This was the basis of his strategy at the Buckingham Palace conference in July 1914 to exclude the nine counties of Ulster. However, John Redmond, in his foolishness, was satisfied the Statute of Westminster, the decision of the Imperial Parliament, would deliver Home Rule, as defined, in a peaceful manner.

In the South it appeared sensible to bring into being, a body, which could act as a bulwark against the Ulster Volunteers and defend Home Rule. Thus under Professor Eoin MacNeill the Irish National Volunteers came into being in November of 1913. This new body was inaugurated at a meeting in the Rotunda. The platform party, which consisted of many nationalist notables, included WT Cosgrave. He joined the Volunteers as a private and was later appointed to "B" Company of the 4th Dublin Battalion with the rank of Lieutenant[2].

While the attitude of the authorities to the Ulster Volunteers was almost benign, allowing it to import thousands of guns and ammunition unhindered, and march under arms unhindered, the National Volunteers were closely scrutinised and harassed.

The attitude of the IRB to the National Volunteers can be summed up in John MacBride's letter to John Devoy, as he wrote in May 1914, " The Volunteer Movement will be a tremendous force in national life over here, if properly handled"[3]. The IRB intended to infiltrate their members into the movement and gain the capacity for training in weapons and manoeuvres. MacBride was adamant the National Volunteers would in no circumstances be used to oppose the forces of the Ulster Volunteers. For him the British Government was the enemy. With the outbreak of the World War and the postponing of the Home Rule, the IRB, and others, were adamant that the time for a Rising against the British was nigh. This became more certain when the National Volunteers split, as John Redmond led the majority to support the British war effort. Redmond staked his political leadership and the existence of the IPP upon his conviction that Irishmen should cooperate without hesitation in the war, and be rewarded by the British government after the war, with Home Rule. He had no idea that the IRB was planning an insurrection[4]. The break away group, named the Irish Volunteers, were led by Eoin MacNeill, with IRB men to the fore. WT Cosgrave was never a member of the IRB, though Donnchadha Healy suggested in 1910 that he should join. During Holy Week of 1916, D. O'Hannigain came to see him and asked him about "giving the oath to the men". Cosgrave told him that "if they intended to turn out, they would do so without any oath". He added that later in Lewes Jail, Tom Hunter told him that he had been given two opportunities to join " and that there would not be a third"[5].

The Asgard, crewed by Molly Childers and Mary Spring Rice, had sailed from Hamburg with nine hundred rifles and twenty nine thousand rounds of ammunition aboard for the Irish Volunteers. On 24 July 1914 WT and his battalion had marched with the Dublin Brigade of the Volunteers to the harbour at Howth at midday. They awaited the arrival of a yacht, which was rounding the bar. Though tired after the march, they went at the double to meet the yacht at the pier. Eoin MacNeill and Tom Kettle distributed rifles. Heavily armed, they marched back towards the city. On the Howth Road they diverted to the Malahide Road, when they saw that men ahead of them had been stopped by the military and police. Cosgrave decided to off-load the rifles to a safe place and telephoned for a taxi. He loaded the taxi with rifles and went by a circuitous route to Alderman Kelly's house in Longwood Avenue. That night he removed the rifles to the house of Dr. Russell, MOH[6]. In all the authorities seized nineteen guns. However later that day, the King's Own Scottish Borderers fired on a civilian crowd, which had harassed them at Bachelor's Walk. They killed three people and wounded thirty-two[7].

Cosgrave's battalion had included Maurice Healy, KC., John Royane, BL., and Professor Arthur Clery. However after the split in 1914, they lost three quarters of the men. Among those who remained were George Irvine, James Kenny, Eamonn Ceannt, Cathal Brugha. The Volunteers practised regularly and were lectured to, by Officers and ex-officers of the British Army[8].

During the spring of 1916, Volunteers were asked for proposals in writing, on effective and rapid mobilisation. Cosgrave's suggestions were based on the principle of a fan and he felt that the plan adopted for the Rising was based on this. They attended the 1916 St Patrick's Day Parade having earlier attended mass at the Church of St's. Michael and John. At College Green John (Eoin) MacNeill took the salute.

WT Cosgrave had naturally allied himself with his Sinn Fein comrades against Redmond. His brother Phil and his stepbrother Goban, were also members of the Irish volunteers. However the plan for a rising remained a closely guarded secret from most people, as a conspiracy within a conspiracy, planned its course of action. On one occasion in early spring of 1916, Thomas MacDonagh spoke to Cosgrave of a rising within the next month or two. Cosgrave told him it would be little short of madness – as they lacked men and ammunitions. Cosgrave had heard earlier, during the winter, that the Citizen Army intended to rise soon. MacDonagh further pressed Cosgrave on his attitude, if the Germans defeated the British navy and landed arms and men. He replied that that would be a different situation, but he was not interested in the glamour of a moral victory. Cosgrave said that any action should leave the country in a better state than when it began, and they should press ahead only on that basis. Cosgrave did not know James Connolly. It was his impression that the Irish Citizen Army came into being more as a sectional than a national effort. However, he adds that, harmony was affected between the Irish Citizen Army and the Volunteers, with both taking part side by side in the Rising.

A major training exercise by the Volunteers took place in the Finglas area before the Rising. It was designed to accustom the men to street fighting. Cosgrave's battalion had orders to keep to the roads, while their opponents held positions on the far side of the fields. He comments in a way that echoes my own experience of manoeuvres with the FCA in the 1960s, "The operation took some two hours and gave rise to dissatisfaction, as no one was quite clear about their purpose". Another pre-Rising event Cosgrave participated in was a meeting at a house in Oldbawn. Many of those who played a principal part in the Rising were present. While the discussion went on, Captain Douglas ffrench Mullen discovered a piano and played over and over the Dead March in Saul. Cosgrave comments, "Knowing the seriousness of our enterprise, and in the light of subsequent events, it had a prophetic significance. In fact, two-thirds of those present on that evening were dead within a month".

During Holy Week 1916 a priest from Kilkenny came to see Cosgrave. He told him that the Volunteers there, were against an early rebellion, as they did not have arms or ammunition. He said that they were preparing, but needed time and equipment, and that an early rising would be fatal[9].

During that week also, Eamonn Ceannt asked Cosgrave to accompany him to Guinness's Brewery. Ceannt was surprised at how extensive it was, and suggested that barrels would make good barricades. He did not mention the rising, though he did say that if a certain report concerning him, which was under examination in the

Corporation, was not decided upon soon, it would not matter[10]. The IRB group planning the Rising hoped that they would be able to hold out for the required three days, which Germany, then the expected victor, had deemed would enable them to attend a post-war conference on a new Europe. They had also hoped, prior to the capture of arms being imported from Germany, that there might be a countrywide rebellion. In no way were they engaged on any kind of mere blood-sacrifice.

The Rising was of course scheduled for Easter Sunday 1916, but due to the action of Eoin MacNeill, who issued countermanding orders to the Volunteers, the conspirators had to postpone it to the following day.

On Easter Sunday evening, WT Cosgrave attended a concert in the Fr. Mathew Hall in Dublin, where his stepsister Joan Burke sang *The Minstrel Boy* and *The West's Awake*. Miss Lysaght recalled Goban arriving at the interval and speaking to WT, who then left the Hall. It is believed that he then may have travelled to the country with information about the Rising[11]. The Lysaght family were warned by Tom Burke not to go out on the following day.

Cosgrave did not receive any mobilisation direction or order or other communication. He comments, "Whether IRB circles had suspicions of non-members I could not say". He heard of the mobilisation on the Monday from his brothers' mobilisation instructions. He cycled to Larkfield, expecting that the Company would assemble at the battalion headquarters in Kimmage. He discovered that Pearse and the London-Irish had departed for the GPO. He heard that the rest of the 4th Battalion was mobilising at Emerald Square, Dolphin's Barn.

Eamonn Ceannt commanded the 4th Battalion of the Irish Volunteers, which had a full complement of 700 men. About 120 men were assembled, fully equipped at about 11 o'clock. Shortly after Cosgrave and others arrived, the Battalion moved out in four parties. Commandant Ceannt with about a dozen cyclists, followed by thirty men on foot, proceeded along the canal bank towards the Rialto Bridge entrance of the South Dublin Union. Another group, which included Vice Commandant Brugha, went in the front entrance at James St. This group was led by Cosgrave, with his local knowledge, through back streets to avoid notice. Other groups took over the Jameson Distillery on Marrowbone Lane and the Malt House at Mount Brown. The South Dublin Union was originally a foundling hospital, later called a house of industry, the largest in Ireland - probably in the world – it covered an area of over twenty acres. The area was so big that initially the men were spread very thinly. Brugha originally occupied a wooden structure. Cosgrave suggested to him that they should instead occupy the formidable three-storey stone Night Nurse's Home, on the west side of the main courtyard opposite the James St entrance. Cosgrave said the whole area could be controlled from the Nurse's Home. Brugha acceded to the suggestion and they occupied the large stone building. Cosgrave then thought about the defence of the building. They had 1,500 rounds of ammunition. He set up a rota for sentry duty on one-hour sessions and "an officer with some training or experience posted them"[12].

Gymnasium, Richmond Barracks, Inchicore, Dublin.

Nurse's Home, South Dublin Union, now James' Hospital, James' Street.

The strategy behind occupying that location was to prevent soldiers relieving Dublin Castle. At the initial time of occupation the Volunteers could hear an army band playing in the nearby Richmond Barracks[13]. Shortly after twelve o'clock a party of about 100 soldiers of the 3rd Royal Irish appeared marching towards the city, bayonets fixed. The Volunteers engaged them at the James St entrance and received return fire. The army then established a presence on the roof of the nearby Royal Hospital, from where they could view the surrounding area. Soon another party of soldiers arrived at the Rialto Gate and fighting commenced there. Though both commanding officers were killed, Capt. Warrington and Lieutenant Ramsay, the army overran the Rialto Gate area and the Volunteers surrendered. The army then turned their fire on other outposts in the grounds and overcame them. Volunteers Owen Traynor and Dan MacCarthy were killed at Mount Brown. Cosgrave reports that "Nurse Keogh, attached to the hospital, SDU, was killed by British fire – it was generally conceded – accidentally".

The main group of Volunteers still held the Nurse's Home back on James St. But now they came under fire from the rear also. During this action one of the fatal casualties was Goban Burke, WT's stepbrother. He was shot through the neck while firing from a window in the Union. WT was called but Goban had died instantly. It was a shattering experience, as he contemplated his own influential role in bringing Goban to that moment. This remained with WT for the rest of his life. WT described the death of Goban thus:

"One of the sentry posts was in the corridor of the Nurse's Home, commanding a view of the open space, the rectangle of the Protestant church and dining hall. He was a section commander, C/Company – Frank (Goban) Burke – and particularly keen on his work and duty as a Volunteer. Across the road from where he sat on duty, a wing of the hospital was on about the same level. An enemy soldier got into the hospital, saw young Frank Burke, took aim and shot him through the throat. He died immediately. R.I.P. ("Goban" Burke was brother of Joan Burke, the Irish contralto). He was one of the best Volunteers in the battalion, energetic, untiring and devoted to his comrades with whom he was most popular. This was the only fatal casualty we sustained since our occupation of the Nurse's Home"[14].

Cosgrave mentions that three officials in the South Dublin Union cooperated and rendered assistance to the garrison. He names them as Laurence Tallon, Smith and William J. Murphy.

As night fell, the action stopped as each side tried to get some sleep. The Volunteers said the Rosary. On Easter Tuesday morning a sentry heard suspicious noises coming from outside the boundary wall of a small yard, attached to HQ, and the noise of digging, which he had heard since 3 a.m. Cosgrave investigated and pointed out that the noise of digging came from behind the window blind, caused by a broken window pane. At daylight they discovered that the trench was a path in the garden of a small house on a nearby housing estate, beside the sentry.

The next morning, the Volunteers erected a flagpole, out of a top window, bearing a flag with an emerald harp on it. They stood to attention and sang *A Nation Once Again*. This drew intensive fire from the top of the Royal Hospital, which killed a woman in her home on James St and a visitor from Belfast on South Circular Road. There was little action on Wednesday. However they received a despatch from the GPO to say that there were 680 men 'out'. Ceannt was satisfied with this message, which Cosgrave believed came from Connolly. This was the sole message received by the garrison.

On Thursday however, the British launched an attack on the Nurse's Home from front and rear. They were very careful, as they had little idea how many Volunteers were inside. In fact there were only 27. During the engagement, the plaster was shot off the walls and ceilings. Holes were breached in the walls from one room to the next, to permit of more freedom of movement, when the attack increased in severity. Explosions went on repeatedly and every now and then a shower of bricks would fall from the Nurse's Home. Brugha was on the top floor, while Cosgrave occupied the ground floor. In the evening Captain ffrench Mullen came down to tell Cosgrave that Brugha was wounded; that the British were in; that they were to retire. Cosgrave knew that the information was incorrect, but retreated as ordered along an outside passageway. They reached the point then being defended by Ceannt. Cosgrave informed him of the situation and Ceannt suggested that they return to the Nurses' Home. On the way they heard Peadar Doyle whistle or sing and they searched until they found him, Ceannt and Cosgrave each took alternate rooms, demanding surrender of anyone in possession. There was not a single soldier in the Home. An explosion at a barricade enabled the British to attack the Nurse's Home, but Brugha, though wounded, held them back with rapid fire. Volunteer Dolan and Cosgrave tended to Brugha's wounds for five or six hours, as he became delirious. The next day Rev. Fr. Gerhardt, O.Carm., wearing a stole, led a procession carrying the Vice-Commandant, to the Union hospital. Friday was an uneventful day apart from the sight of burning buildings in the city centre[14a].

On Low Sunday, Commandant Thomas MacDonagh, who regarded himself as Commander-in- Chief, since Pearse's earlier surrender, arrived with a flag of Truce, and under military escort to inform Ceannt of the surrender at the GPO. Fr's Augustine and Aloysius accompanied him. James Foran and Willie Cosgrave went out to meet them and escort them inside. They discussed the situation, which was that they had three hours in which to surrender, or else General Lowe intended to shell their positions. MacDonagh indicated that he intended to surrender. Ceannt initially disagreed.

A conference took place and while they believed that leaders might receive scant consideration, there was at least the prospect of the lives of the general body of the Volunteers being saved. Eventually there was a general acquiescence to surrender. Captain Rotherans accepted the surrender. Ceannt accompanied by WT Cosgrave, then walked with General Lowe to the nearby outpost of Jameson Distillery to convey the news to the garrison there[15].

Memorial Plaque to 1916 Garrison, James' Hospital Dublin.

The men from the South Dublin Union marched with guns slung over their left shoulders and their hands swinging freely at their sides. They wore no look of defeat, but rather of victory. It was as if they had come out to celebrate a triumph and were marching to receive a decoration in St Patrick's Park. Later, together with the Jacob's garrison, they marched to Bride St. A large force of British military and Army lorries met them. At Bride Road a British Officer and a Junior Officer came to record the names of each Volunteer who was unarmed[16]. This list was to prove of crucial importance at the later court-martials, where it became prosecution evidence. After a while, all bearing arms and equipment were instructed to place them at their feet. Then soldiers came and collected them in handcarts and brought them to the lorries. They were marched from Bride St. up Werburgh Street, Christchurch, through Thomas St. and James St, past the Cosgrave home, towards Kilmainham and eventually into Richmond Barracks. There were occasional non-complimentary observations from by-standers but no evidence of hostility[17]. Lieutenant Wylie was one of the commissioned officers in charge. In the square they saw a group of Cumann na mBan women. They had been well treated up to that by the military. Suddenly they were split into groups indiscriminately and roughly hustled by the barrack staff into rooms with space for about twenty persons in each. Doors were locked and guards placed. Cosgrave found himself in a barrack room, with no furniture and no ventilation, with sixty others[16]. The British Sergeant on opening the door was almost overcome by the atmosphere.

For breakfast a bucket containing tea and a basket with hard biscuit rations were brought in. The biscuits were tumbled out onto the floor; empty corned beef tins were used as tea containers. Later, prisoners were marched to the Gymnasium, and put sitting on the right hand side of the floor. They were under armed guard and not permitted to move or stand. A tall staff-officer came in, looked over everyone and directed most of the younger prisoners to "fall out". They were taken away later in the evening, marching down from the Barracks to the city. While passing the South Dublin Union outpost, they were singing the *"Soldiers' Song"*[17].

About midday a number of plain clothes police, belonging to "G" division of DMP, entered the gymnasium, walking from one end to the other, studying the prisoners, calling out certain Volunteers to the far side of the hall. Among these were Ceannt, John MacBride, the two Cosgraves, Corrigan, Hunter, Peadar Doyle, Downey. This selection, and others made in Richmond Barracks, completed the list of Volunteers from Dublin and the Fingal Battalion for trial by Field General Court Martial. Court martials, as well as John (Eoin) MacNeill, the only non-participant, also tried volunteers from Wexford, Galway, Kerry and Cork. Among other Volunteers to be brought to Richmond were the wounded Noel Lemass, Tom Ashe, the Lawless brothers, Dr. R. Hayes, Paudeen O'Keeffe, Gerald Crofts, Norton and Wilson. Non-combatants included J. Quigley, County Surveyor, Meath, Alderman JJ Kelly, Kelly's Corner, Edelstein and William O'Brien.

On 1 May the General, Commanding the Forces in Ireland, JG Maxwell signed a "Form For Assembly and Proceedings of Field General Court Martial on Active Service: Proceedings" because " it appears to me, that the persons named in the annexed schedule have committed the offences in the said schedule mentioned. And I am of opinion that it is not practicable that such offences should be tried by an ordinary General Court Martial, nor is the offence one of a minor character". He nominated Brigidier-General CJ Blackadder DSO as President, with Lt. Col G. German and Lt. Col. WG Kent.

On 1st and 2nd of May, some Volunteers were paraded under guard before a military officer to receive formal notice of pending court-martials. The Rev. T W Ryan, CC Golden Bridge visited the prisoners in the Gymnasium. He heard confessions and blessed the men with the Blessed Sacrament.

The prisoners were locked up at 8 o'clock. They then recited the Rosary and settled down for the night. Thee were no beds or bedclothes, rugs, or blankets. During one of these long nights John MacBride told Cosgrave that his life-long prayer had been answered. He said he recited three Hail Marys every day, that he should not die until he had fought the British in Ireland.

On Tuesday morning at nine o'clock, a group of prisoners including, Ceannt, T. Hunter, Hanrahan Brothers, Jas. Hughes, Jas. Mallin, Corrigan, the two Cosgraves, Peadar Doyle and John MacBride were brought to a guardroom immediately outside the Gymnasium. They were held there overnight and in the morning got one tin of beef with some biscuits for their daily ration. Cosgrave was afforded an opportunity to send a message to Alderman Corrigan that his son, Section Commander W. Corrigan, who had been captured early on Easter Monday after a British officer, Lieutenant Ramsay had lost his life, was about to undergo court-martial for his life. Cosgrave was later to hear of the attempts Alderman Corrigan made to have his son's life spared.[18].

Thomas MacDonagh was the first to be called into an office and the deposition of Major Armstrong was read to him and he was asked for corroboration. Then Major Armstrong read the depositions to the prisoners as a group. Ceannt asked if it was a court and was he required to answer questions. Armstrong answered 'no' to both questions. Ceannt reserved his position. Armstrong's deposition to Ceannt was to the effect that "E. Kent was in a party which surrendered at St. Patrick's Park on 30 April at 5 o'clock, which had come from Jacobs, from which shots had been fired at His Majesty's troops causing casualties. That Kent was armed".

It was then stated that Ceannt's name was on the Proclamation, though no evidence was adduced to his acquiescence to it.

The Volunteers were informed that no person was allowed to appear and speak on behalf of a prisoner, but each prisoner would be permitted to bring a friend with him, whom he could consult and who would be free to advise the prisoner, but not address the Court. They could object to any member of the three-man court, but could not object to the court itself. When they asked about legal representation, the Court appeared surprised, particularly Lieut. Wylie. The prisoners marched out again to a green sward and were directed to sit down. Sean McGarry and Dick Davis had just arrived from Kilmainham Gaol. Their Court-martial had already taken place and there was some surprise at the sentence – McGarry and Davis got eight years penal servitude. Cosgrave's information was that Davis was in the Red Cross, a non-combatant.

Cosgrave records that all the men from the South Dublin Union were mistakenly charged with being at Jacob's Factory. He also reports that Captain Rotherans, who had taken the surrender at the South Union and marched with them to Bride St., declined to give evidence of identification. Rotherans had been the best polo player in Ireland and "one of the most popular sportsmen of the County Westmeath", until he had to quit the game due to bad sight. Rotherans told the court that he had seen the men yesterday, that he did not know them, not having seen them before, that he would not know them again; that he would not feel justified in giving testimony. Cosgrave adds that Rotherans was reprimanded and received no promotion subsequently

WT Cosgrave and Major John MacBride spent a lot of time talking together at the barracks. MacBride, evidently initially, thought he was facing a term of imprisonment, as he told Cosgrave that his position as an official of the Dublin Corporation would be there for him on his release and also for those Volunteers who were officials or employees of the Municipality.

Cosgrave records that the group, later realising the precarious position they were in, agreed that messages be sent to a Solicitor and a Barrister. J. Roynane BL and the most influential member of Dublin Corporation, Dr. L. Sherlock arrived, together with the Lord Mayor, Sir James Gallagher. Cosgrave makes the point that some solicitors who were sent for did not appear. He got Ceannt and MacBride to discuss their defence with Roynane. He writes that, "MacBride did not appear to be keenly interested in his own case. MacBride had been on active service with the Boers in the South African war. He was as cool and collected, we heard during Easter Week as if he were walking to church, even when receiving warnings of impending attacks, and when there were such, he was as steady as a rock, he had a soldier's mind on prisoners. There was no more unconcerned prisoner in Richmond Barracks either, as to his fate or to the discomforts prevailing. Roynane's interview with MacBride did not last long and his court martial did not last long"[19].

Cosgrave records the essence of his own interview with Roynane:

Roynane: What do you propose to say?

Reply: There is no truth in the German charge. I accept responsibility for being in arms. A long term of imprisonment is not attractive.

Roynane: That will get you a long sentence. You will not get a firing squad. If you want to shorten your sentence, admit nothing:-

The Lord Mayor and Lorcan Sherlock came to speak on your behalf.

Reply: Very well.

Cosgrave admitted nothing at his court-martial, denied conspiracy with the Germans and said there was no truth in the charges against him. The prosecutor WE Wylie had been surprised to find that the prisoners did not have any defence counsel, and he took the matter up with the Attorney General James Campbell. The latter turned down Wylie's suggestion. Wylie was surprised to find WT Cosgrave among the leaders.

He wrote;

"I got a shock when I saw him standing there in the green uniform of the Irish Volunteers, with a sergeant's stripe on his arm. I opened the conversation by asking him if he had any idea of the position he was in, and he said he had not, and asked if it was serious. I told him that the last three men who were tried had all been condemned to death and would be shot in the morning, and that shook him up a bit".

Unlike John MacBride who was quite content to die, having refused to take safe passage out of Jacob's Factory, while it was available, WT had no desire to die for Ireland and wanted desperately to live, and acted accordingly. Wylie continued:

" I asked him if he had any defence and he said that he had never heard of the rebellion until he was in the middle of it. He assured me and I believed him, that when he marched out on Easter Monday morning, he thought he was merely going out on a route march, that he was suddenly told to take men into a hut in the South Dublin Union and hold it and before he knew what happened he was in the middle of a battle. The Royal Irish from Richmond Barracks had rushed the hut and captured him with the others.

I told him that he would have an opportunity of making a full statement and he then asked me if he could call evidence of character. I said certainly and that I would adjourn the case to the next day and have his witnesses present. If I remember correctly he asked for Mr. James Gallagher, Lord Mayor, Surgeon McArdle and Mr. Lorcan Sherlock. I told the police sergeant to have them at court at 10 a.m next morning and they duly arrived".

After the evidence had been heard, Wylie told the court that the accused wanted to make a statement and call witnesses.

I turned and asked Cosgrave to say whatever he wished. "I would rather you did it for me " he said. And so I launched out into a speech for the defence and then examined the three witnesses as regards Cosgrave's character. It seems rather a strange procedure when written down, but none of us thought it in the least peculiar. I have always believed that in prosecutions, that it is the prosecutor's duty to present the case as fairly as he can and I stuck firmly to that rule. There should be no such thing as "witnessing a prosecution. Let the jury understand that they are the guardians of the peace and the upholders of the law of the land and give the prisoner a perfectly fair run". The trial lasted ten or fifteen minutes. WT was told his sentence would be promulgated.

Cosgrave summed up the evidence against him as, "of a policeman who saw him in uniform one hour before the Rebellion. Result – found guilty; sentence – death"[20].

General Blackadder, the President of the Field Court Martial, realised from the evidence of the eminent persons called by WT, that he was not at all typical of the Sinn Feiners. He therefore questioned Wylie about WT's position, asking, " Is that a decent man and was he in your opinion rushed into this". Wylie replied, " Yes, sir". Blackadder then replied, " thank you. We will recommend a reprieve"[21.].

Cosgrave wrote,

" The trials were conducted upon the same plan as those of '98, the DMP and Constabulary taking the place of the Yeomen and informers. The members of the court-martial were pleasantly polite. Their knowledge of law was most elementary, so much so that the Crown Prosecutor had on several occasions to insist on prisoners' rights. Shawn MacDermott complained bitterly of being cooped up in a small room with 63 others – 64 in all. Sanitation laws were suspended. 10/- was paid for a few articles of clothing to use as blankets, which had to be returned at 5 0'clock a.m. The following morning one officer asked Ceannt for a souvenir. The Germans could not learn anything from the standard of culture, education or civilisation from the officers in Richmond Barracks in May 1916".

Like Cosgrave, Eamonn Ceannt was not willing to face his fate, without seeking to defend himself. His trial was adjourned several times. When he informed Cosgrave that much of the evidence against him was deemed "faulty, inadmissible or unsubstantiated", Cosgrave advised him that he should challenge this at the next session. Ceannt asked Cosgrave to accompany him as a "soldier's friend". However the court rejected this request, on the grounds that he had not availed of it on the first day of the court-martial. Ceannt told Cosgrave that he had not in fact signed the Proclamation, though he subscribed to his name being on it. He had been unable to attend the time the signatures were being put to the Proclamation.

Cosgrave wrote that there was probably not one "innocent" man brought up for Court Martial. He adds that those court-martials are historical, in one respect, up to the time he left Richmond Barracks – all persons charged were convicted; there was not a single acquittal.

Already there had been executions of the leaders. Pearse, Clarke and MacDonagh were executed on 3 May, with Daly, Willie Pearse, Plunkett, O'Hanrahan on 4 May. Because of the censorship, definite news of events was difficult to come by. The politicians of the Irish Party realised that the policy of the military could signal the end of the constitutional path in Ireland. On hearing that Courts Martial were being held in Dublin, John Redmond, marooned in London, wrote desperately to Asquith on 3 May, "I would most earnestly beg of you to prevent any wholesale trials of this kind - wholesale executions would destroy our last hopes. The precedent of Botha's treatment of the Rebels in South Africa is the only wise and safe one to follow"[22].

Cosgrave and the others heard on Wednesday 3rd May that some executions had taken place. His main concern was that there was no information available, concerning religious rites being available to Catholic prisoners. He spoke to MacBride, or "The Major" as he refers to him. The Major also had concerns over church rites. WT., MacBride, Ceannt, Phil Cosgrave, Peadar Doyle had been in close collaboration from Monday 1 May until Thursday 4 May. On that day MacBride, the last of the group, save for Ceannt, had been court-martialled. Just after his trial, he told Sean T. O'Kelly, " Nothing will save me Sean. This is the end. Remember this is the second time I have sinned against them"[23]. MacBride had called one witness to his trial, Clara Allen the woman he loved and who loved him. After his death, she converted to Catholicism, to be closer to him. WT Cosgrave remained close friends with her for the rest of her life, attending her funeral to Deans Grange in 1937.

The group then got the ominous news, that they were being transferred to Kilmainham. Before they left Richmond Barracks on 4 May, Fr. Augustine arrived and they asked him to attend them at Kilmainham, "should the necessity arise; that we had no knowledge of what was going to happen"

The group arrived at Kilmainham at 8 p.m. and each prisoner was locked in a separate cell. Phil Cosgrave was on his brother's left and the Major on his right. Cosgrave describes what happened; "At daybreak on Friday morning I heard a slight movement and whisperings in the Major's cell. After a few minutes there was a tap on his cell door. I heard the word "Sergeant", a few more whispers, a move towards the door of the cell, then steps down the corridor, down to the central stairs. Through a chink in the door I could barely discern the receding figures; silence for a time; then the sharp crack of rifle fire and silence again. I thought my turn would come next and waited for a rap on the door, but the firing squad had no further duty that morning".

Fr Augustine came to Cosgrave's cell in the afternoon and told him " Major MacBride was shot at daybreak. He had prepared him and was with him at the last. He died like the soldier he was, R.I. P. Father Augustine later told me he had done the same for James Connolly, R.I. P. Fr. Augustine anointed him before life was extinct".

On 5 May Blackadder told WE Wylie that when in South Africa, he had regarded MacBride as about the lowest thing that crawled, but " damn it", I'll never think of him now without taking my hat off to a brave man! "That, commented Wylie, was the effect his statement had on a not very imaginative Major-General. Blackadder was overheard in the officer's mess, by Charles Wyse-Power, the barrister son of a Sinn Fein family, saying that all the men he had tried had behaved well, but the most soldierly was John MacBride. " He, on entering the court, stood to attention, facing us, and in his eyes I could read: "You are soldiers, I am one. You have won, I have lost. Do your worst". [23a]

The local Catholic curate, a good friend of the Cosgrave family, Fr. Eugene McCarthy, later visited WT. He expressed surprise that they had asked for a Franciscan to attend them, instead of the parish clergy. It appeared that Kilmainham Gaol was traditionally supplied with Catholic chaplains from the Parish of St. James's. He told WT that the death sentences on his entire group, except for the Major, had been commuted. He also told him that they would be released after the war. Fr. McCarthy then went to the Cosgrave home and brought a change of clothes for the Cosgrave brothers. WT Cosgrave writes that his uniform survived until 1920, when the Black and Tans took it during one of many raids on their home in James' Street. Fr. McCarthy later visited the brothers at Portland Prison.

Shortly afterwards, three officers came to WT's cell and announced that the verdict, "You William Thomas Cosgrave, have been found guilty and have been sentenced to death and to be shot". The officer paused for effect. WT did not comment. The surprised officer continued, "The sentence has been commuted to penal servitude for life". WT's reaction, to the surprise of the officers, was to inquire as to when he could see his solicitor.

They spent the two days in Kilmainham before being transferred by Black Maria to Mountjoy Jail on Saturday evening. Grey uniforms were provided, and on Thursday they departed the North Wall, and from Holyhead by train to Portland. On the journey, they were glad to read in the newspapers of John Dillon's denunciation of the court-martials and executions[24]. The Cosgrave brothers' stepfather, Thomas Burke was also arrested and interned at Frongoch[25].

At this period WT sported a fashionable heavy moustache, curled up at the extremities[26]. Eoin MacNeill wrote to his wife Margaret on 26 March 1917 from Lewes Jail, describing the various leaders. Of Cosgrave he wrote, "is as much interested in the housing of the working classes, as if he was at home in Dublin"[27].

The Rising was seen popularly and so described by the authorities as a Sinn Fein Rising. Redmond saw it as a German plot, due to the abortive attempt to import German arms and the arrival and capture of Casement from a German submarine[28]. It was so described by the *Irish Times* on 28 April and by Asquith on 3 May, with that newspaper demanding blood. Thus the hitherto non-violent and somewhat moribund organisation of Sinn Fein, was labelled as having been responsible for action carried out by the IRB, the Irish Volunteers, Cumann na mBan and the Irish Citizen Army. Military censorship was introduced on the day of the Rising itself and for the next three months, the army controlled Ireland, with the civil authorities mere spectators. John Dillon met General Maxwell on 2 May. The latter denied that any persons had been executed without trial[29]. On 3 May Redmond saw Asquith who confirmed that, "Some few executions are necessary, but they would be very few"[30]. The Irish Attorney-General, James Campbell, told Redmond in London that there may be up to 30 or 40 executions. Campbell told Redmond that the matter was entirely in the hands of the military. Campbell was an ally of Carson and a figure despised by all Irish nationalists[31].

The lack of preparedness by the British was strange, as it was subsequently revealed in 1921, that since January 1916, the Admiralty had been intercepting a series of coded messages from John Devoy in America. These referred in detail to the plans and even the date on an impending insurrection in Dublin[32].

However General Maxwell was in control in Ireland and the executions continued, even after Asquith's intervention. Eamonn Ceannt was executed on 8 May, together with Michael Mallin and Con Colbert. The previous day, Ceannt made a written statement from Cell 88 in Kilmainham, saying:

"...I wish to record the magnificent gallantry and fearless calm determination of the men who fought with me. All, all, were simply splendid. Even I knew no fear or panic and shrunk from no risk even as I shrink not now, from the death that faces me at daybreak. I hope to see God's face even for a moment in the morning. His will be done. All here are very kind."[33].

In January 2006, President Mary McAleese described 1916 "as a fighting world where war is glorified and death in uniform seen as the ultimate act of nobility, at least for one's own side. Planet Earth was a world of violent conflicts and armies. It was a world where countries operated on the principle that the strong would do what they wished and the weak would endure what they must. There were few, if any mechanisms for resolving territorial conflicts. Diplomacy existed to regulate conflict, not to resolve it"[34].

John McBride

CHAPTER FOUR

SINN FEIN MEMBER FOR KILKENNY

When the internees were released back to Ireland, they returned in triumph to their welcoming families and communities. Internment had transformed them by its injustice, into formidable radicals, intent on continuing the struggle, but this time to a successful conclusion. They were still Volunteers, not Sinn Feiners, but it was via the latter body, which they regarded with some disdain as being too moderate, that they would gradually turn down the political road. Their initial entry into politics was motivated by their desire to defeat the IPP, rather than with any long-term coherent plan. Fr. Michael O'Flanagan had been a member of the Sinn Fein executive since 1910. He was a radical Sinn Feiner, barely tolerated by Church authorities. A by-election was pending in Roscommon, early in 1917, and he decided that the moment was ripe to seek to put Sinn Fein policy of abstentionism into practice by fighting the election, winning it, and refusing to occupy the seat at Westminster. He chose Count George Plunkett, father of the executed Joseph Mary, as the candidate. The Volunteers worked vigorously on his behalf and won the seat. This was a shattering defeat for the IPP, but worse was to follow quickly, as a prisoner, Joseph McGuinness, was successful in Longford, though by a tiny majority. A bye-election in East Clare saw the leader of the 1916 garrison of Boland's Mills, Eamon deValera, take the seat, caused by the death of Major Willie Redmond at Messiness on the Western Front in Belgium. That was where many of the Volunteers who had followed John Redmond met their fate. Tim Pat Coogan remarks upon the absence of Collins from that by-election campaign as possibly of some significance[1].

In August, a by-election in Kilkenny city saw WT Cosgrave, become the first member of Sinn Fein stand for the party. This was a more challenging election than the earlier ones, as it was in an urban area, where Sinn Fein was not necessarily as strong as in rural areas. The Volunteers again were behind the campaign, with Dan McCarthy, who had managed the 1908 Leitrim election, in charge. The newly elected MP Eamonn deValera was closely involved, as was Eoin MacNeill, the leader of the Volunteers, as well as Arthur Griffith, Countess Marckievicz, Count Plunkett, Sean Milroy, and other leading members of Sinn Fein. Indeed Griffith's wife commented at the time that her husband had not been home for a weekend for over nine months. WT was proposed by Mr. E.T. Keane and seconded by Mr. P. O'Meara. The *Kilkenny Journal* gave lengthy coverage to the campaign and at the early stages wrote editorially, " Whether it is to be Sinn Fein or the old policy, is not for us to dictate but for Kilkenny to decide"[2]. It carried an advertisement, which indicated how sophisticated the Sinn Fein publicity team was. The advertisement on 25 July stated:

COSGRAVE BADGES

IN CELLULOID TRICOLOUR

PRICE... 3d.

THE GAELIC PRESS, 30 UPPER LIFFEY ST. DUBLIN.

THE LARGEST WHOLESALERS OF SINN FEIN NOVELTIES IN IRELAND.

Kilkenny saw itself become the centre of political action with mass meetings and parades. One report said; " Kilkenny turned out en masse on Thursday night in support of the candidature of Willie Cosgrave for the representation of Kilkenny city. The Irish Volunteers and Cumann na mBan, numbering over 3,000, marched in procession through the city to the Parade, where an immense gallery representing Kilkenny and surrounding districts assembled and where stirring addresses were delivered by prominent members of the Sinn Fein Movement. Arthur Griffith, Editor of Nationality and founder of Sinn Fein was among the speakers".

A later editorial, just before polling day stated, "This election is a deep and far reaching issue, that requires deliberation and honesty of purpose and we have no reason to think that the voters of this city will be deficient in giving effect to their feelings on this issue, in a manner worthy of their manhood and with the straightforward belief, entitling them to call themselves men of principle and Irish Nationalists in the only sense of the term – An Ireland unfettered and free of foreign rule and domination as England is, as Germany is, or America or any other country is. Any policy falling short of that may call itself by whatever name it pleases, but it cannot call itself a Nationalist policy"[3].

The electorate numbered 1,300 and between 1,100 and 1,300 votes were cast. Eleven votes were spoiled, 5 for Cosgrave and one for Magennis. There were two blanks.

The result was;

WT Cosgrave   Sinn Fein   772

Mr. Magennis   U.I.L   392

When the result was announced by the Mayor in the Council Chamber, WT returning thanks, said that he had received testimony from many sources as to the orderly manner in which the election had been conducted. They had shown the world, that however high their political feelings might run, or their interest in the different sides, they could exercise the national self-restraint, which, was typical of the Irish race. Kilkenny had given expression to the opinion of complete and absolute control of their own affairs in Ireland. "They had put the hallmark of their approval on the conduct of the men who did and dared".

The defeated candidate, John Magennis, termed Cosgrave's victory by 772 to 392 votes, "as a victory for intolerance, low, mean, lying and scurrilous abuse, terrorism and intimidation of the grossest type". Eamon deValera also addressed the gathering.

WT and the other Sinn Fein leaders then appeared from one of the windows of the Victoria hotel to the cheering crowds assembled below. He addressed them, to continuous cheering and laughter, in a fashion that demonstrated his political expertise.

"I again take this opportunity to thank you on my own behalf and on behalf of my friends, for the signal honour you have conferred on me today. I have to thank the Sinn Fein committee which has put me up as their candidate, the Cumann na mBan, who participated in many of the demonstrations we had in the city; the Volunteers of Kilkenny, the members of the Corporation who supported my candidature; those who sent motor cars from all parts of Ireland; the electors, some of whom came hundreds of miles to record their votes for a free and independent Ireland; the women and girls generally of Kilkenny and the representatives of the rural districts, who at great trouble and great inconveniences worked hard night and day, to secure a victory against English influence in Ireland. I thank you on behalf of the many families that were bereaved in Ireland fifteen or sixteen months ago, because your answer at the polls was to them, a message of thanks, and a message that their sacrifices were not in vain.

We have been charged with intimidation. I know very few Irishmen who would allow themselves to be subject to intimidation, and I think that you may rest confident, that whatever we have lacked in confidence, we have pulled up for it in the principle for which we stood and the principle which you approved of, and we hope that when the time comes to give an account of our stewardship, you will be equally enthusiastic in the same cause, for which you have recorded your votes.

Only last week we were told that while certain people who were on our platform were enjoying comfortable positions, those who were on our opponent's platform, were on plank beds. The man whom they referred to above others, the President of the Volunteers, was sentenced to death and one of the charges against him, was that he had opposed recruiting in Ireland? I think it would be rather difficult to answer. We never asked anyone to make sacrifices that we were not prepared to make ourselves. To the credit and honour of Kilkenny you will be pleased to know – we had 780 promises and 776 voters came to vote for us. That is the answer we make to any charges of intimidation that have been made against us.

We have been told that they are going to meet us in every corner of Ireland. Why do they say that? Because they know that we are going to be there first, and they know what that means to them. We are determined to drive any Party out of Irish life, which subjects itself to English influence in Ireland. In the name of the men who fought and died for Ireland, I thank you for having recorded your approval of the sacrifice that they made".

The main group of the Sinn Fein leaders travelled back to Dublin by train that same evening. The next day, Sunday, WT was escorted to the station to catch the evening train by a massive procession of supporters. On arrival at Kingsbridge Station he was surprised to find only two people waiting to meet him. These were Mr. Tom Burke, his stepfather and another relative. The gates of the station had been fully closed and over one hundred policemen guarded the approaches to Kingsbridge. He was informed that the proposed meeting in Westmoreland St at the Sinn Fein HQ. was prohibited. However, a meeting would be allowed at Beresford Place, Harcourt St or James's St.

A large crowd had already assembled in Westmoreland St. A force of between two and three hundred policemen under Assistant Commissioner Quinn, Chief Superintendent Dunne and several inspectors had drawn a cordon across O'Connell Bridge and Fleet St. A large number of "G" Division, under Superintendent Quinn were also present. The crowd sang national songs and cheered for Kilkenny and WT. They offered little or no resistance to the police, who kept moving them on.

A decision was made to hold a meeting at James' St. Mr. Dan McCarthy spoke to a large crowd outside the Sinn Fein hall. He said the Kilkenny result was the answer to John Bull and the Convention, and to the Irish Party who had cheered the executions.

WT received a rapturous welcome as he spoke. He said that the Kilkenny result had struck a resounding victory for Irish freedom..."they had no quarrel with the English people...they had a quarrel with the British government and they would deal with the Government in their own methods and in their own time. Under the policy of the Irish Party, pauperism and emigration had increased so much, that in the city of Dublin, there were 80,000 people living in hovels, which were a disgrace to civilisation. They had the largest workhouse, not only in this country, but also in the British Empire". He appealed to them to preserve the order, which had been so, creditably a feature of the Kilkenny election, and which had met with Episcopal approbation that day, in one of the churches in Kilkenny[4]

The British authorities decided that they had better take some action to stem the advance of Sinn Fein. They again carried out widespread arrests and internments. Among those held were Austin Stack, Fionan Lynch and Thomas Ashe. They resorted to hunger strike and the resultant force- feeding led to the death of Ashe in the Mater Hospital, on 25 September. The resultant funeral attracted 30,00 people, with the Volunteers mounting a guard of honour. It was felt that Ashe's body should lie in state in City Hall and representations were made to WT Cosgrave on the matter. He directed the Secretary of the Finance Committee to hold a meeting for the purpose of granting the necessary permission to occupy City Hall. At the meeting of the Committee, it was suggested that the Lord Mayor should approach the authorities to facilitate the Lying-in-State. The Lord Mayor met with an absolute refusal. Meantime the cortege was en route to City Hall. Mr. Eyre asked Cosgrave whether he should go over to the Castle and see General Sir Bryan Mahon, GOC. Cosgrave thought it an excellent idea. Sir Bryan returned with Mr. Eyre to inspect the Hall Guards and general layout. He then said he would withdraw the military, pending the Lying-in State, which he did.

During the period of the Lying-in-State, the Chief Secretary issued an order to the GOC, forbidding the holding of processions and the carrying of arms, in connection with the funeral, which was scheduled for Sunday 30 September. Meanwhile the Chief Secretary left for England. Sir Bryan Mahon, acting on his own initiative, confined troops to barracks, and the funeral took place, as arranged, without interference[5]. The President of the Volunteers, Eamon deValera strangely did not attend the funeral[6].

A postscript to WT's action in the South Dublin Union occurred in 1917. Sir Richard Vane, who had been in charge of the attack on the Union on the Thursday of Easter Week, sought an interview with him. Vane told him that it had been reported to him that the Nurse's Home was impregnable, and he called off the attack. He congratulated WT on their defence. WT was disappointed to read later in Vane's book, that the South Dublin Union had been reduced to silence on Easter Thursday and surrendered the following day. WT is clear that the surrender took place on Low Sunday at 3 p.m. and in accordance with the direction from head quarters, GPO. He emphasises that Brugha and ffrench Mullen were the only casualties on the Thursday's engagement. He was proud of the fact that during their occupation of the Union, no British troops passed to or from the city by Mount Brown or James's St.

Count Plunkett thought that he could become leader of Sinn Fein, though Arthur Griffith was still president. However the Volunteers and the IRB men thought otherwise. Since the name of that party was synonymous with their tide of victory, it had to come under their control, and be wrested, even from its moderate President. At a meeting in the Mansion House in April 1917, called by Plunkett, a coordinating committee was widened to include such activists as Michael Collins, Rory O'Connor, Eamon deValera, Countess Markievicz and WT Cosgrave. These formed a temporary executive to prepare for an Ard Fheis in October, when a new constitution would emerge. Griffith realised that a take-over had occurred by the militants, and he did not contest the Presidency against deValera at the Ard Fheis. When the 1,700 delegates gathered. it had already been agreed at the executive, that while a Republic would be their official aim, there would be a subsequent referendum between that and Griffith's Dual Monarchy policy Thus the republicans took control of a vastly expanded party, with Griffith and Fr. O'Flanagan becoming Vice Presidents. The Volunteers thus became the army of Sinn Fein.

The Conscription Bill introduced in January 1916, had not been extended to Ireland. Irish people in general, felt that John Redmond would acquiesce in extending it to Ireland, as recruiting fell heavily in Ireland after the initial war euphoria. On 6 December, Lloyd George succeeded Asquith as Prime Minister and proved a loyal friend of the Ulster Unionists. On 9 April 1918 he brought in a Military Service Bill, which became law on 18 April, extending conscription Ireland. All of nationalist Ireland had long opposed this plan to send Irishmen to be slaughtered on the continent. This included the IPP, which by then was seen to be obsolete, even at Westminster. Sinn Fein ran a huge political campaign opposing conscription. The Catholic Church, and the trade unions, which called a national strike, also opposed the matter. The Volunteers began to consider further military operations, as the RIC withdrew from isolated barracks in the southwest. A raid on a barracks in Kerry saw the first deaths of Volunteers since the 1916 Rising.

The British response was to see a German Plot afoot, and on 17 May arrested up to 73 Sinn Feiners. These included DeValera, Griffith, Count Plunkett, Kathleen Clarke, Countess Marckievicz, Maud Gonne and WT Cosgrave. They were interned in England and were later to be followed by a total of 1,319 prisoners. The immediate reason for these arrests was the capture of Joseph Dowling on an island off Galway, after being dropped there by a German submarine - shades of Roger Casement's earlier action. – Dowling was one of the few prisoners of war to have enrolled in Casement's Irish Brigade.[7] Most of the military leaders of the Volunteers escaped arrest, including Collins, who had foreknowledge of the arrests. He had warned those attending an executive meeting of the Volunteers not to go home on the night in question. These included Harry Boland, Cathal Brugha and Richard Mulcahy. In a real sense, the most moderate leaders in Griffith, DeValera, Plunkett and Cosgrave were removed from the scene, which was hardly in the interest of the British or a peaceful settlement. Cosgrave was taken to Reading Jail where he was held until March 1919. There with him were, Walter P. Cole, Richard Davys, Frank Fahy, John Hurley, and Dr. Richard Hayes[8].

 Collins then became the undisputed leader in the country as he prepared to organise for a campaign of violence. He surrounded himself with like-minded radical men, some of whom would become candidates for Sinn Fein in the coming election. Collins was later to realise that his life would be forfeit to some of these very same men.

A bye-election in Offaly was avoided in April when the IPP decided not to run a candidate against Dr. Patrick McCartan of Sinn Fein. Another bye-election was pending in Cavan East. Though the IPP had withdrawn from Westminster, in protest against the Military Service Act, it felt forced to leave the field clear again for Sinn Fein and its jailed candidate Arthur Griffith. While these moderate leaders were incarcerated, Collins had become kingpin of the party, with Harry Boland and Sean T. O'Kelly as secretaries. Collins regarded the Volunteers as his shock troops to take whatever action was required. He advised the Volunteers to join Sinn Fein, while at the same time instructing them that."The principal duty of the executive is to put the Volunteers in a position to complete by force of arms, the work begun by the men of Easter Week. The Volunteers are notified that the only orders they are to obey are those of their own executive"[9]. Not content to control an organisation within Sinn Fein, Collins also made the running on the manifesto for the upcoming general election, and its list of candidates. The manifesto was a hard line republican document, with its elected members promising to boycott Westminster and set up a local constituent assembly. At that point the referendum on a republic or Griffith's Dual Monarchy, would take place.

FIRST DAIL 1919

MINISTER OF LOCAL GOVERNMENT

Sinn Fein prepared assiduously for the election and succeeded in persuading the Labour Party not to run candidates. It wanted a huge mandate to go to the upcoming post war Peace Conference, which would recognise the right of countries to independence, through national plebiscites. The IPP, under John Dillon, discovered that half of its M.P's would not run again, and it had such difficulty in getting new candidates that Sinn Fein had no opposition in 25 constituencies. The harassment by the police only reinvigorated the Sinn Fein election workers. Sinn Fein won 73 seats, Unionists 26, of which 23 were in the North with the Nationalists getting 6. Those elected Sinn Fein T.D's, and not in jail, assembled on 21 January 1919 in Dublin's Mansion House, as Dail Eireann.

Cathal Brugha was nominated as pro-tem President, in the continued absence of the senior men of the organisation. Four Ministers were nominated, Richard Mulcahy at Defence, Count Plunkett at Foreign Affairs, Eoin MacNeill at Finance and Michael Collins at Home Affairs.

On that very same day an ambush, credited with being the start of the War of Independence, or as some term it, a civil war, took place at Soloheadbeg, when Dan Breen led an ambush, which resulted in the death of two RIC policemen. This shocked many people, as it was evidence that Volunteers would perpetrate brutal violence against those who served the Crown in the ongoing struggle. This sort of activity by the Volunteers spread around the country, or as they began to term themselves, the Irish Republican Army. The British saw no difference between the IRA and the politically active members of Sinn Fein. This was very far from the reality, as the IRA consisted essentially of independent local units, fighting their own war. They were certainly not susceptible to any political control.

When deValera escaped from Lincoln Jail on 3 February another meeting of An Dail was called for 1 April. Many of those arrested had been released by that stage, as deValera became President of the State, as distinct from the national organisation of Sinn Fein[1]. deValera intended the government and Sinn Fein to remain separate, by ruling that only himself and the Minister of Home Affairs, should be members of the party's Standing Committee, and T.D's could only comprise one third of it[2]. His cabinet consisted of Robert Barton at Agriculture, Brugha at Defence, Collins at Finance, and Cosgrave at Local Government, Griffith at Home Affairs, MacNeill at Industry, Marckievicz at Labour with Plunkett retaining Foreign Affairs. Sean T. O'Kelly was sent to Paris, with Dr. McCartan posted to Washington[3].

Of course it was due to his experience in the Corporation, and his contacts in local authorities that led to Cosgrave getting his particular portfolio of local government All the Ministers had to be careful to avoid being arrested, with a series of disguises de rigeur. Cosgrave in particular dyed his hair in different colours, much to the amusement of his family and friends.

MARRIAGE

It was at this time that WT married Louisa Flanagan of Portmahon House, Rialto. She was the daughter of an Alderman colleague of his on the City Council, but who belonged to the IPP. The Flanagans were wealthy. A brother of Louisa's was nicknamed the 'Bird Flanagan' and described as "an elaborate practical joker, with a rich father who could afford to pay for his son's exploits, who rode a horse into the Gresham through the swing doors"[4] In his Diaries, Ulick O'Connor writes of a friend of his, Desmond Gorges, whose "Aunt was married to WT Cosgrave. The white Anglo-Saxon Protestant strain of his ancestor Admiral Gorges, whom he claims as one of the founders of the English navy, mixes merrily with the anarchic Flanagan genes...Desmond regales us with stories about his Uncle Willie. He married the immensely rich but somewhat plain daughter of a Dublin rancher and market gardener, Miss Louise Flanagan. Desmond spent much of his early boyhood in the embattled house of President Cosgrave which was constantly under threat from post civil war opponents"[5]. O'Connor continues " The 'Bird' Flanagan got his nick-name after he had gone to a fancy-dress ball on roller-skates, dressed as the Holy Ghost, and assisted by two disciples, laid an egg (a painted rugby ball) on the floor in front of a large audience, who chased him out of the arena. He escaped however on his roller-skates, ably assisted by his disciples"[6] After his marriage WT bought a property called Beechpark, in distant Templeogue, which remained his home and the centre of his life. His first son, Liam, was born on 13 April 1920.His second son Michael, born in 1922.[6a]

On 12 April 1919 Collins proposed a motion in the Dail, saying;

"The elected Parliament and Government of the Irish Republic pledge the active support of the Irish Nation into translating into deeds the principles enunciated by the President of the U.S. at Washington's tomb on 4 July 1918. We are eager to enter a World League of Nations based on equality of rights...We are willing to accept all the duties, responsibilities and burdens which inclusion in such a league implies" Collins ever the pragmatist added, "The principles enunciated by President Wilson, would damage only the very allies they were issued to save. It was going to be a great diplomatic tug-o'-war between Lloyd George and the French "Tiger" on the one hand,

and President Wilson and the democratic forces of the world on the other hand. If President Wilson got the support he desired the hypocrites would be dished". WT Cosgrave seconded the motion.

President Wilson knew of the Irish attempt to be heard at the post war Peace Conference in Paris. He sent a delegate, George Creel, to Ireland to meet members of the government. A three-man delegation of Irish Americans arrived on 3 May 1919 for a ten-day visit[7]. It consisted of Frank Walsh of Kansas City, Edward Dunne, a former Mayor of Chicago and Michael Ryan of Philadelphia. They were met by WT and Richard Mulcahy and escorted around the country. A session of the Dail met to honour the delegation on 9 May. On that occasion, soldiers seeking to arrest Collins surrounded the Dail, but failed to arrest him. This was the start of his reputation as something of a mystery man, difficult even to identify. This was deValera's last public appearance before his departure on 1 June for America, where he was to spend the period of the War of Independence, returning in late December 1920. The Irish-American delegation met President Wilson in Paris on 11 June, but the Irish did not get a hearing at the Peace Conference, despite the war rhetoric about the right of small nations to self-determination. This disappointed and angered the Irish-American community[8]

deValera's extended period in the USA was mainly concerned with raising funds for the Irish Republic. However he caused havoc amid the Irish-American community, causing splits among a variety of Irish-American organisations, as he sought to take control of policy and finance. The Irish-American organisations were very complex, with many owing first allegiance to America. In addition, it also mirrored the complexity of the wide political situation within Ireland. deValera thought that as he was the President of the Republic, Irish-Americans would take their lead from him. He tried to bypass the leading figures of John Devoy and Judge Daniel Cohalan, in favour of Joseph McGarrity, making lifelong enemies of the former men. Eventually he brought his own man, James O'Mara, over from Ireland, to run a new organisation called American Commission for Irish Independence. deValera succeeded in raising several million dollars in Republican Bonds, which would later become another battleground between the anti-Treaty forces and the Irish Free State[9].

Soon after the Versailles Treaty, the British proscribed the Dail, Sinn Fein, the Volunteers, Cumann na mBan and the Gaelic League. Despite this, Griffith, in deValera's absence conducted a Sinn Fein Ard Fheis. However the party again became a shadow organisation, though acknowledged as the nation organised, when required for political purposes. The Dail, meanwhile, developed its own structures and bureaucracy to affect its own policy, with the IRA conducting a guerrilla war. All the disparate groups contained some common membership, each operating independently, though none constituted a totally united body. To complicate matters, the effective leader of the IRA, Collins, was also the leader of the secret IRB This could not go on, as tensions and rivalries were bound to cause splits within each group. The centre, wherever it was, could not hold. This situation was personified in the persons of WT Cosgrave, Michael Collins and DeValera, as well as a multitude of others. By August 1921 WT Cosgrave spoke of, 'the almost complete disappearance of the Sinn Fein organisation'[10].

LOCAL ELECTIONS

Cosgrave wrote that Arthur Griffith had frequently laid stress on the potentiality of the general council of county councils, in the event of a national conflict with the British Government. That was then imminent.

WT's role as Minister was to persuade local councillors and councils to transfer their allegiance to the Dail. He advised all councils to continue to use all the benefits, grants and subsidies, accruing from the established bodies for local development. Local elections for urban areas occurred on 15 January 1920 and were held under the old electoral system. Cosgrave wrote that having observed the " Sinn Fein candidates had such a victory at the Parliamentary elections in 1918, the British Government in 1920, imposed a system of proportional representation in Irish local elections. But legislation was out of date in dealing with public opinion in Ireland at the time. Sinn Fein control of local government was complete, directly the local government elections took place"[11]. However despite this assertion, the British move proved successful, to the extent that the vote for Sinn Fein, did not match its overwhelming success of the previous general election. Independents won 269 seats (14%), the IPP won 238 (15%), Labour won 394 (18%), Sinn Fein won 560 (27%), and the Unionists 550 (26%). The country was more radical and in the county council elections in June Sinn Fein won control of 29 of the 33 councils. WT had delivered reasonably successfully overall. As councils declared for Sinn Fein, the British ceased paying the annual grants in aid, payable to augment local authorities' income, if the councils did not fully accept the authority of the British Government and recognise the authority of the Local Government Board[12]. In September WT stated that, " The stoppage of grants in aid of local taxation by the enemy government is a last despairing attempt to bribe the people of Ireland"[13].

At this same time, WT was also Chairman of the Finance Committee of Dublin Corporation. He felt that if Dublin Corporation failed to maintain public services, he as Minister for Local Government, would find great difficulties in supervising County Councils and other Corporations in their administration and financial problems. Dublin Corporation needed money. WT approached the Munster and Leinster Bank, which was regarded as the most national of those institutions. He was met with a blank refusal to give any accommodation. He consulted Mr. E W Eyre, the City Treasurer, who arranged for him to meet two Directors of the Bank of Ireland, Henry Guinness and Andrew Jameson. That bank gave the accommodation so urgently required for the Corporation[14]. Among the early schemes considered by Cosgrave for local government were a municipal milk run and the purchase of the *Freeman's Journal*[15].

Shortly after the birth of his son, in April 1920, WT was again arrested and detained for several weeks. Through the intervention of a friend, he was released on parole, on the clear understanding that he would not indulge in politics. When released he had to keep a low profile for several weeks. He wrote that at that time it was necessary for him to have further dealings with the Bank of Ireland. The Governor of the Board of Directors said that the Bank and its business had nothing to do with politics. In his understated style WT found this reply "interesting", as the Bank's objection to an overdraft, was based on the refusal of the Corporation to strike a Criminal and Malicious Rate. He adds, "that of course it must have escaped their observation. Eventually the Directors agreed to grant the usual overdraft".

The Bank of Ireland had accepted Collins' invitation to become the financial agent for the new State. Andrew Jameson felt the other banks to be " quite out of touch and sympathy with Free State affairs"[16]. Early in 1923, Cosgrave, as Collins' successor, approached the Bank of Ireland for accommodation for £500,000. The Bank of Ireland's monopoly of government business rankled with the other Irish banks. If the bank's top men were Unionist by sentiment, they worked hard at relations with Free State Ministers[17]. Andrew Jameson became a Senator and played an important role there, and with Senator James Douglas, would act as go-between Cosgrave and deValera in a futile and dangerous attempt to end the civil war.

Diarmaid Ferriter writes, "The Minister for Local Government, William T. Cosgrave and his assistant, Kevin O'Higgins, presided over the new regime, one which was fraught with danger, but remarkable for its resilience and concrete achievements"[18]. However in a later book, Ferriter illustrates how Cosgrave, desperate for financial rectitude, raised the possibility of encouraging a particular group of deprived citizens to emigrate. Cosgrave wrote to Austin Stack, Minister for Home Affairs, "As you are aware, people reared in workhouses are no great acquisition to human society. As a rule, their highest aim is to live at the expense of the ratepayers. As a consequence, it would be a decided gain if they all took it in their heads to emigrate. When abroad, they are thrown into their own responsibilities and have to work whether they like it or not"[19].

Writing about local government Cosgrave said, "British prestige was the most powerful asset of British authority in Ireland. British supporters never tired of saying "she was never beaten". Police, courts, civil servants and some local authority officials had their national pride, if they had any, discounted by this complex. But doubts began to affect them as the struggle proceeded and they accepted the new situation, if not with grace, with a growing conviction… At the time of the Truce sixty five persons comprised the staff of the Local Government Department of Dail Eireann – just one quarter of the number of the officials in the British Local Government Board. In effect Cosgrave was running a local government system, under the noses of the Castle and the Custom House. A secret postal system facilitated this operation[20]. Tom Garvin adds "WT Cosgrave's role in the extraordinary achievement of taking over bodily the

British local government system in the south, was central and deserves more examination than it has hitherto had"[21].

During this period, Cosgrave developed the sense that all the people had to be served and treated with respect by public representatives and officials, irrespective of their politics. He had particular trouble with both Meath and Westmeath county councils. While the Truce was on, he criticised Meath county council heavily for dismissing a nurse because she was a Redmonite, and looked down on Sinn Feiners[22]. Cosgrave was well aware that the Local Government system run by him had to be successful, or else it would rebound as a failure on a wide political stage. He admonished Monaghan council for not keeping him apprised of its severe financial difficulties, telling it that if necessary, the Dail could organise a loan. Though he added, "You will please keep this item of information to yourself. I mention it to show you, how absolutely vital it is considered that the public stand firm"[23]. Some local bodies such as one in Manorhamilton in Leitrim, wanted reorganisation proposals shelved 'until the National question is finally settled'. Cosgrave replied in a forthright way:

"I have to point out that if this was the spirit of the people Dail Eireann would not have set up civil departments and proceeded to take over the administration of the country. It has, however, done so, and in doing so has acted strictly on the mandate it received from the electors. The 'great National question' would never be finally settled, if those who were elected to act in the name of the people simply sat down and waited for the enemy to evacuate, and yet in substance that is what the resolution of your Board recommends. You quote English statutes ignoring the fact that the sole legislative authority in this country is Dail Eireann, and that Dail Eireann in adopting the English local government Act and regulations therein did so 'subject to such modification and alteration as might from time to time be promulgated by the Dail Local Government Department'[23a]

British Ministers of State confessed in London – after the Truce - that the fatal blow to British authority in Ireland, was the loss of civil control, which they conceded in the case of local government, was complete in effect"[24].

Cosgrave had offices successively at Clare St., Rutland Square and Exchequer St. Among his staff were Kevin O'Higgins, Alderman Tom Kelly, Dr. Hayes, Dr. J. Ryan, JJ Clancy, Frank Fahy, A. O'Connor, F. Lawless, JJ Walsh, J. Dolan and J. McGuinness[25].

W.T. Cosgrave addresses 1918 Election Meeting.

*W.T. Cosgrave (right) with Mr. Justice W.E. Wylie
who prosecuted him after the 1916 Rising.*

The first Dáil sitting in the Round Room of the Mansion House, Dublin 1919.

British auxiliary forces Cork, (the so-called Black and Tans) 1921.

CHAPTER SIX

ANGLO-IRISH WAR

'VIOLENCE UPON THE ROADS'

WT Cosgrave described the expansion of the British forces in Ireland: "For eighteen months now the Royal Irish Constabulary had been challenged by the Irish Volunteers and had been so hard pressed that a military addition had been made to the 'Force', in the uniform of a dark tunic and a kaki trousers. Some of these recruits had courage – most of them were bullies, and none of them had any morals – A further addition had been made by the British Government to the police and military in the state, of a body called 'Auxiliaries'. They were called 'Auxies'. Among other sources combed to recruit these forces were English gaols. These three bodies had this in common, they had no discipline: they murdered, they burnt; they looted and they drank..."[1]. This force was recruited at Winston Churchill's initiative, while chairing a cabinet committee on Ireland. When General MacReady complained about their reprisal policy, Churchill refused to hear any criticism of them, regarding them as honourable and gallant officers[2].

The Foreign Secretary, Lord Curzon, expressed the British view of the situation in Ireland in the House of Commons. In October 1920, he said, "What is going on in Ireland at the present moment? You have a desperate and malignant conspiracy known by the name of Sinn Fein, which is endeavouring by every means in its power, seldom fair, usually foul, to sever the connection with this country and to set up an Independent Republic in Ireland. They first tried to affect this end by open rebellion in April 1916. That attempt ended in failure, and is, I think, not likely to be repeated. They have now passed to a different method of – firstly by passive resistance and secondly, they pursue, what I will not honour by describing as guerrilla warfare. It is not guerrilla warfare. It is the warfare of the Red Indian, of the Apache"[3].

The guerrilla war by the Volunteers then called the IRA, at first targeted RIC men, but later all three British forces. The situation gradually got more vicious, with cruel reprisals common currency[4]. Munster and Cork in particular, was the scene of much of the IRA activity. On 20 March the Lord Mayor Tomas Mac Curtain, was murdered by the RIC at his home and in front of his wife. On 21 October, his successor as Lord Mayor, Terence MacSweeney, died from force-feeding in Brixton Prison after a 74-day hunger strike that attracted international condemnation. Later that year, British security forces combined to burn much of Cork city centre and murder several people.

WT Cosgrave, whose source for the following statement was Bishop Fogarty of Killaloe, wrote that during the early stages of the Black and Tan war the leading personalities of Dublin Castle were summoned to a meeting of the British Cabinet at Downing Street. They were questioned generally on the situation and invited to express their opinions. Mr. Wylie, K.C. was one of the last to make a contribution, and he was opposed to a continuance of the terror pogroms. There was and had been a request for another month to be allowed the Government to suppress the national movement. Mr. Wylie said he understood that after suppressing the national movement it was proposed to make a settlement of the Irish question. If that were so, and he believed it was, he advised an immediate settlement. Further repressive measures made a final settlement more difficult. Bonar Law is alleged to have inquired if Wylie was a papist. Wylie replied that he was the son of a Presbyterian minister.

In Dublin, the British had set up an active intelligence service organisation, called the 'Cairo Gang', due to their previous experience in the Middle East. This group proved quite successful. Michael Collins planned an early Sunday morning attack on a variety of addresses where they lived, and shot the intelligence men dead. Several IRA men were captured.

That same afternoon a football match between Dublin and Tipperary was scheduled for Croke Park. The Auxiliaries and Black and Tans surrounded the venue. While the match was in progress, they opened fire on the crowd and on the players, as a reprisal for the events earlier in the morning. One of the Tipperary players, Michael Hogan, was among the fourteen civilians killed, with hundreds being wounded. Some hundreds of spectators were detained in Croke Park for several hours. The Hogan Stand at Croke Park is named after Michael Hogan. Later that night the prisoners captured earlier, Peadar Clancy, Dick McKee, Conor Clune, were tortured and shot dead.

A feeling of terror permeated the city, as they waited for the next atrocity. Collins had a spy working in Dublin Castle named David Neligan. He kept Collins informed on the plans of the intelligence unit there. Word came that among those on a list to be arrested was WT Cosgrave.

As the workload extended, WT had got an assistant Minister, in the person of Kevin O'Higgins. Their office was in the General Office of the County Councils in Parnell Sq. They had a clerk, a typist and an office messenger. Cosgrave and his Assistant did not get on well and there was constant friction between them. DeVere White has written that they were, " diametrically opposed to one another in temper, intellect and outlook". WT was wont to instruct O'Higgins to answer all abusive letters saying, "Here, Higgins, you're a cross-grained devil, you had better deal with this fellow – and for God's sake work off some of your spleen on him, instead of me".

O'Higgins had a background in the Volunteers and had been jailed briefly. Earlier he had been a clerical student both at Maynooth and Carlow, but had been expelled from both institutions for minor misdemeanors. He declined an invitation to join the Jesuits and studied law at UCD. When Cosgrave heard from Collins that he was again likely to be arrested, he decided to close the Department for a time. He left a note to this effect for O'Higgins. However the brash young man refused to do so, and took the opportunity to demonstrate his own organisational capabilities. O'Higgins believed that a certain type of person was required to stage a revolution, and he also believed that it was then up to people of his professional class to take over and run the country. He was to promote the careers of his fellow classmates at UCD, including Paddy McGilligan, even though they had not been engaged in the national struggle[5].

Kevin O'Higgins, like Ernie O'Malley[5a], had been quite affected by the execution of Major John MacBride and wrote a poem to commemorate that event:

"HOW HE DIED"
By
KEVIN CHRISTOPHER HIGGINS

"I never was greatly a friend to John MacBride
But he caught my heart in the end by the death he died.
Rich be his sleep and deep
By Kilmainham side.

For when they called him out, the cold last tryst to abide,
The cheeks of some of the men, though their hearts were stout
Had marked the ebb of the tide.
And – set your lips as you can
To riddle a smiling man is not, on the present plan
So perfectly cut and dried,
But it takes a bit of stiffening out of a soldier's pride.

Then in a cheery voice
As to friends at his side
"Lads" said the rebel, " I know that if you had the choice
You'd let the thing abide
For you see, though my hands aren't tied,
I'd be giving away too much, if 'twas fighting I tried.
But the business has to be done
Though it isn't good fun.
Let you rest well o'nights, myself will do it for one!
And tell them that nobody cried…[6].

There is some confusion as to precisely what happened during the episode of WT going underground. In his book *Revolutionary GOC in Ireland*, Arthur Mitchell writes,........ "According to one account Cosgrave had ceased going to his office to avoid arrest. Upon receiving complaints, Collins sent a message to Cosgrave to open the office. Cosgrave told the messenger "Tell Collins that I am not going to be shot for him"[7]. Collin's master spy, David Neligan has written that William T. Cosgrave found sanctuary with the Oblate Fathers in their house in the Wicklow Hills. He dressed as one of them and was never betrayed. Kevin O'Higgins, his assistant, also found shelter with another Order"[8]. Tim Pat Coogan described Cosgrave as one of the steadiest men ever to come into Irish public life. Cosgrave was not acting unwisely. Anything might have happened at the time. General Boyd GOC ordered Arthur Griffith arrested without consulting the Chief Secretary"[9]. The British offered a reward of £3,500 for the capture of Cosgrave. One week later, an ambush at Kilmichael saw the IRA, under Tom Barry, kill seventeen victims.

Joe Lee has written that Collins was capable not only of boisterousness but of immature behaviour[9a]. He never hesitated to interfere in a colleague's department if the need arose. He hated slackness and inefficiency and did not hesitate in berating those he felt could do better. He is reputed to have said to Austin Stack, " Austin, your department is a bloody joke". During an important meeting of the cabinet immediately after the truce, Cosgrave fell asleep and later woke up to be told by Collins: "It does not matter a damn whether you are asleep or awake". On another occasion, when exasperated by Cosgrave, Collins referred to him as "the bloody little altar-boy"[9b]. Arthur Griffith set the scene for one arrest of Cosgrave in 1920, in a hand-written note:"On Thursday a Municipal bye-election was held in the Usher's Quay Ward, where Alderman Cosgrave, member for Kilkenny is senior Alderman. The Sinn Fein candidate was Mr. Lynch, his opponent a Mr. Kelly. Alderman Cosgrave took an active part in the election which resulted as follows:

Lynch (Sinn Fein) 2,492
Kelly   168

A majority of 15 to 1 for the candidate supported by Alderman Cosgrave. On the morning following the election, Alderman Cosgrave's home was surrounded by the armed forces of the English crown and he himself seized and imprisoned! It is the Castle's reply to the vote of the people"[9c].

Kevin O'Higgins wrote an unflattering, though amusing estimation of his superior to his future wife Brigid Cole, that same year. "Things is wuss instead of better with C. back - he really gives very little attendance, messing about to Coporation meetings etc. - other when he does blow in he'll take up some business at random, give some wholly outlandish ruling on it and blow out again most complacently, feeling that he has saved the state sufficiently for one day, So my attendance now has the positive side of getting through work and the negative side of stopping old C. from doing things hopelessly reactionary ... the man is only fitted to drive his wife about the countryside in a smart pony and trap and return the salutes of the peasantry with the proper mixture of graciousness and bonhomie. His Corporation reputation is the kingship of the one-eyed man amongst the blind."[9d]

DeVALERA BACK FROM USA

In December 1920 deValera returned from the USA after a long stay, to find Collins was in the ascendancy. deValera began to reassert his primacy almost immediately, with an early cabinet meeting on 9 January. Cosgrave resumed his work as minister that same month of January 1921. He and DeValera worked closely. DeValera told Frank Gallagher that WT was "nearer to me in a personal sense than anybody in cabinet"[10]. Tim Pat Coogan writes "Cosgrave was the one who called at deValera's office to take him to lunch and performed other small, necessary services such as ensuring that he got his hair cut"[11]. deValera acknowledged this closeness on the occasion of Cosgrave's death when he said, " Before the division on the Treaty we were very close friends and it has always been a regret of mine that political differences should have marred our personal friendship"[12].

The War of Independence continued with all its brutality throughout the country, as the British attempted to coerce the people. Lloyd George was determined to " pluck the last revolver from the assassin's hand"[13]. He was reluctant to negotiate with the activists saying, " The question is whether the British people would be willing for me to negotiate with the head of that band of murderers"[14]. However the British were under pressure to come to a political solution to the Irish question. Lloyd George had decided that the partition of Ireland was the only practical way forward. In late 1920 he introduced the Government of Ireland Act, under which two parliaments, in Dublin and Belfast respectively, would sit. The Unionists, after a careful headcount to ensure their electoral supremacy, decided to abandon three Ulster counties, and accept a six county parliament[15]. Lloyd George feared that making an offer of Dominion status would not be acceptable to the South, which he felt, would make him look ridiculous to the War Party in England.

Several approaches from the British came to deValera, during the early months of 1921, with visits from Lord Derby, James Craig and General Smuts of South Africa.

Mark Sturgis, a leading British civil servant in Dublin Castle, recorded in his Dairy on 7 May 1921, after speaking to the wife of Sir Hamar Greenwood, " Another bar to a Truce in the lady's mind is that under it, Cosgrave, for instance, would expect to come home, unmolested, to his wife. Personally I have always regarded this aspect as a pro; not a con: as I can't but think that men on the run, who under a truce could get home again, in many cases for the first time in months, would be loath to take up the role again, of the hunted hare"[16].

deValera explained his position to Collins thus: " This particular peace move business has been on for some time. The reply I have sent through other channels is that if they send a written communication addressed to me directly, and not through intermediaries they will get a reply"[17]. Pressure grew on Lloyd George, as his military leaders in Ireland informed him that the troops in Ireland must be relieved by October, and that it would take a hundred thousand new troops to take control of the country[18].

At the general election in May 1921 Phil Cosgrave joined his brother as a member of the Dail. DeValera told the people that Sinn Fein stood for "the legitimacy of the republic and for the right of the people of this nation to determine freely for themselves, how they shall be governed and for the right of every citizen to an equal voice in the determination"[19]. None of the seats were contested and Sinn Fein took 124, with the remaining four going to Independents in Trinity College. As the Second Dail met on 16 August, all the elected prisoners had been released to attend. Each took an Oath of Allegiance to the Republic, as DeValera was re-elected President. He said, "I was not a doctrinaire republican and never cared for forms of government as such". He had understood the Republic as the symbol of Irish independence and he interpreted the Oath, as meaning that, "he should do his best for Ireland"[20]. As John Regan writes, " this was an admission that the republic of Easter Week 1916, reiterated in the 1919 Declaration of Independence, had been a rhetorical and an aspirational device, not descriptive fact. In this, arguably, there was a denial of both the legitimacy of the 'existing republic', which Dail Eireann purported to represent and the validity of the political sentiment which enabled it to do so"[21]. deValera's new smaller cabinet, designed to chart the country through the difficult times ahead, consisted of Barton at Economic Affairs, Brugha at Defence, Collins at Finance, Griffith at Foreign Affairs, Stack at Home Affairs, and WT Cosgrave again at Local Government. Brugha and Stack were limited militant revolutionaries, antagonistic to Collins' brilliance. Cosgrave thought Brugha a fighter but nothing more.

Wedding of Kevin O'Higgins and Brigid Cole.
Eamon deValera on his right, Rory O'Connor his best man, on his left.

CHAPTER SEVEN

TRUCE AND TREATY

COSGRAVE'S VITAL VOTE

When the King opened the Northern Parliament for six counties, on 22 June 1921 in Belfast, which had been set up by the Government of Ireland Act, he said, " I appeal to all Irishmen to pause, to stretch out the hand of forbearance and conciliation, to forgive and forget and to join in making for the land they love, a new era of peace and contentment and goodwill". The next day Lloyd George came under pressure from the King to do something so that, "the effect of the King's speech will not die away. There is not a moment to be lost". With the knowledge that the Conservatives also supported action, and under severe pressure from America and Commonwealth countries with large Irish populations, and under pressure from Churchill at the Colonial Office[1], Lloyd George wrote, inviting deValera:

(1) to attend a conference in London in company with Sir James Craig and to explore to the utmost possibility of a settlement.

(2) to bring with him for the purpose any colleague whom he might select.

deValera called a Conference in Dublin on 4 July insisting that there must be a truce first. Lloyd George agreed very reluctantly and a truce commenced on 9 July. The Irish delegation of deValera, Griffith, Barton, Stack, Childers travelled to London on 12 July where they were greeted by a massive Irish gathering at Euston Station. deValera and Lloyd George met alone on four occasions, 14, 15, 18 and 21 July. deValera reported on his discussion to his colleagues, who did not participate directly. deValera learned clearly that a republic was not available from the British. As expected, Dominion Home Rule was on offer, but was rejected, though Griffith told Stack that he thought the terms acceptable[2]. Austin Stack reports that at the cabinet meeting, " MacNeill and Cosgrave did not give themselves away one bit"[2a] T. Ryle Dwyer writes that at cabinet Griffith and WT Cosgrave said the British offer was better than they expected. MacNeill welcomed it. Collins found it a step forward. Both Stack and Childers opposed it[2b]. The British terms were officially rejected on 10 August. The Dail met on 16, 17, 18, 22, 23, 25 August and unanimously confirmed this stance. Stack and some others were perturbed to hear deValera say on 16 August that the interpretation he put on the oath was "that he should do the best for Ireland" and that he made use of the expression that he was not a doctrinaire republican as such. Stack did not believe that deValera "had in mind the abandonment of the republic- as is charged by his enemies"[2c]

deValera later agreed to appoint plenipotentiaries if, "consent of the governed", was accepted as the basis of the peace, as, "our nation has formally declared its independence and recognised itself as a sovereign state", and that, "it is only as the representatives of that state that we have any authority". Lloyd George read this as being disloyal to the King and Empire and refused. deValera then proposed that the conference would be free, "and without prejudice". Lloyd George issued an invitation to a conference on Tuesday, 11 October, which would consider, "How the association of Ireland with the Community of Nations, known as the British Empire, may be best reconciled with Irish national aspirations". There was no agreement that Ireland would acquiesce in remaining within the Empire, and no agreement that England would accept anything less.

The choice of delegates to the London conference rested initially with the seven-man cabinet. The cabinet was surprised to hear of deValera's resistance to going as Chairman, and his insistence that Collins should go. The latter was completely reluctant to go, arguing that it was a politician's job. Collins also argued that as the British saw him as the hard military man, the delegates could argue that any agreement would have to be acceptable to him.

There was great rivalry between these two very different men, as Collins had been exercising almost independent authority given his different roles as politician, intelligence supremo and military leader, as well as leading IRB man. Brugha and Stack ruled themselves out absolutely. They along with Barton, backed deValera, who used his casting vote in the cabinet to get his way over not going. Cosgrave was very strongly of the view that it was essential that deValera go as Chairman, because of his extraordinary experience in negotiations, and the advantage of being in touch so recently with Lloyd George. It made no sense to Cosgrave that the Irish team should be, "leaving their ablest player in reserve". Cosgrave proposed this formally again in the Dail despite it having been agreed by the cabinet. Dr. Patrick McCartan accused Cosgrave as being out of order. However Cosgrave insisted that deValera should go. Cosgrave's position was, surprisingly, opposed by his junior colleague Kevin O'Higgins.

deValera was insistent that he would not go and he espoused many reasons for this, including that he was 'the symbol of the Republic', that it was necessary, "to keep the Head of State and the symbol untouched and that was why he asked to be left out". Cosgrave's motion was defeated[3]. Collins had agreed, very reluctantly to go, and Barton and Gavan Duffy, with Erskine Childers, as secretary and Griffith as Chairman went. Collins was second in command; Barton was the economist and both Duggan and Gavan Duffy were lawyers. Griffith distrusted Childers.

Stephen Collins says that at that stage Cosgrave became very suspicious of deValera, as he knew that he was working on his 'External Association' proposal. Cosgrave felt that deValera was expecting that Griffith would move Lloyd George towards the Irish position. Cosgrave tried to forewarn Griffith that deValera might be creating a scapegoat. But Griffith knew what he was doing[4].

The cabinet drew up credentials for the delegates, which were ratified by the Dail on 14 September.

> The terms given to the Plenipotentiaries, over the hand of deValera were; as envoys Plenipotentiary from the elected Government of the REPUBLIC OF IRELAND to negotiate and conclude on behalf of Ireland with the representatives of his Britannic Majesty GEORGE V., a Treaty or Treaties of Settlement, Association and Accommodation between Ireland and the Community of nations known as the British Commonwealth.

> TO ALL TO WHOM THESE PRESENTS COME, GREETING:

> In virtue of the authority vested in me by Dáil Eireann, I hereby appoint

> Arthur Griffith, T.D., Minister for Foreign Affairs, Chairman;

> Michael Collins, Minister for Finance;

> Robert C. Barton, T.D, Minister for Economic Affairs;

> Edmund J. Duggan, T.D.

> George Gavan Duffy, T.D.

> IN WITNESS WHEREOF I hereunto subscribe my name as President.

Done in the City of Dublin, this 7th day of October, in the year of our Lord 1921, in five identical originals.

However, the cabinet also gave them apparent contradictory Instructions, under which, "the complete text of the draft treaty be submitted to Dublin and reply awaited".

As the delegates met the British across a table on 11 October, only Lloyd George shook hands with the Irish delegation[5]. The Treaty negotiations went on for almost two months[6]. At one difficult stage, Collins remarked , "Have Cosgrave with his oil-can sent over here immediately"[7]. Some of the negotiators returned to Dublin each weekend, and cabinet meetings were held and progress or otherwise was discussed. On 25 November, the cabinet agreed unanimously that, " Ireland shall recognise the Crown for the purposes of association, as symbol and accepted head of the combination of associated States and that an annual sum be voluntarily voted to the civil list". In each case the unanimity represented an advance towards compromise. Ideas originating and developed in London, were now stamped with the assent not only of deValera and Cosgrave but of Brugha and Stack[8]. However it was clear to the negotiators, that compromise was necessary as breakdowns occurred. They also realised that those who had refused to go, would not agree with compromise.

Lloyd George led his team brilliantly, while deValera sought to introduce a new element by bringing forward an External Form of Association between Britain and Ireland, outside the Empire. deValera 'coerced' the plenipotentiaries to return to London on 25 November and again on 3 December, to negotiate on this as a basis for settlement with an unwilling Britain.

Austin Stack has said that deValera had asked the remaining cabinet members to meet regularly in Dublin to consider reports from the plenipotentiaries. He says that O'Higgins was also in attendance, " the President had invited him to attend cabinet meetings, as he was Cosgrave's assistant minister, and the abler and stronger man of the two"[8a]. Joe Lee has said that O'Higgins was the "most formidable personality, apart from Collins himself, thrown up on the Free State side"[8b].

On 30 November, as deValera was down the country, a despatch from Griffith in London, was sent to Cosgrave. Anthony Gaughan writes that this was significant[8c]. It contained the draft Treaty and a request for a cabinet meeting on 3 December at 11.00. Cosgrave went to Stack with it. Anthony Gaughan writes that deValera regarded Stack as second in command in his absence. Cosgrave asked Stack did he mind that Griffith had sent the draft to him. Stack says he replied, " Of course I did not"[8d]

When the delegation presented the draft treaty to deValera and the cabinet on 3 Dec, deValera continued to act as if his External Association was possible, despite the fact that a majority of the delegation told him External Association was a non-runner at the negotiations. That cabinet meeting lasted for seven hours and many of those present differed on the detail of what was agreed. The plenipotentiaries travelled back to London that same night.

Eventually and under the threat of, "war within three days",[9] the plenipotentiaries, who were not willing to gamble on the threat, signed a Treaty on 6 December 1922. As Griffith's final message to deValera said, " We were on the point four times of breaking on the Crown, which I told the cabinet I would not break on. The issue was peace or war. We decided our course and they gave in on fiscal autonomy and other matters"[10]. This was to be a point reiterated by Cosgrave when as President of the Executive Council, he addressed the Dail for the first time. He insisted that Griffith, "honest man that he was", kept his word to cabinet, and had signed on a new set of proposals[11].

The Treaty gave Ireland Dominion status, equivalent to Canada, with Britain having the right to certain military facilities. At British insistence, T.D's would have "to swear an Oath of Allegiance to the Irish Free State Constitution and to the crown, in virtue of the common citizenship between the two countries and as head of the Commonwealth". If the Northern Parliament refused inclusion in the Free State, a Boundary Commission under a British nominated chair, would "determine in accordance with the wishes of the inhabitants, so far as may be compatible with economic and geographic conditions, the boundaries between Northern Ireland and the rest of Ireland". A Governor-General in Ireland would represent the crown.

The Irish wanted to come to an agreement, because they realised that there was a strong possibility of Bonar Law and the Tories coming to power. This could have spelled disaster for Ireland. Lloyd George knew this, and misled the Irish into believing that the Boundary Commission was certain to leave Northern Ireland unviable. This made the Irish delegation focus on sovereignty as the main issue, and not on the possibility of a partitioned Ireland. The British strategy was to render each part of Ireland more acquiescent to self-government than an independent all-Ireland might be. The British hoped that the two parts of Ireland would, in time, come to peaceful terms with each other, within the Commonwealth. Britain, represented by the cream of experienced imperial politicians, saw the Treaty as a solution to an Irish problem that had dogged British politics for too long.

It is sometimes overlooked in Ireland that the Treaty was met with great hostility in the House of Commons, with Churchill put to the pin of his collar defending it and getting it agreed to. He thought that eventually the North would unite with the South. He said in the Commons, " It is no longer possible to say that Ulster is barring the way to the rest of Ireland, that Ulster is forbidding the rest of Ireland to have a government. That is all past. Ulster has said, 'Have the government you choose, we will do our best to make things go right and as long as you stay within the British Empire, we close no doors in the future'. That, it seems to me, is what Ulster has said, and I repeat the debt to her is great"[12]. He wrote of the final hours of negotiation thus, "This was an ultimatum delivered, not through diplomatic channels, but face to face, and all present knew and understood that nothing else was possible. The British representatives were in their places at nine o'clock, but it was not until after midnight that the Irish delegates arrived…it was nearly three in the morning before we separated" [13].

deValera, Brugha and Richard Mulcahy were staying in the home of Mr. O'Meara of Limerick when the details were phoned there. deValera made no reply and refused to take the call personally. Mulcahy believed that deValera was favourable to the terms. The next day, all three travelled by train back to Dublin, but deValera and Brugha sat alone in a carriage, as Mulcahy was otherwise engaged[14.]. Frank Pakenham has Austin Stack saying they travelled by car[15].

It became clear shortly that deValera would totally oppose the Treaty.

COSGRAVE INTERVENES CRUCIALLY, TWICE

On that same day, 7 Dec, deValera called a cabinet meeting attended by Brugha, Stack, O'Higgins and Cosgrave. They considered a proposal for arresting the delegates on their return, but decided against. Brugha and Stack wanted the immediate sacking of the delegates, and a public repudiation of the Treaty. WT Cosgrave 'interceded for them persistently' in Pakenham's phrase[16]. He felt that it was vital to buy time and avoid a knee jerk reaction by the militants, without giving the delegates a hearing. Finally, deValera decided to be cautious, partially in order to keep Cosgrave onside, and agreed that Cosgrave's position was reasonable[17]. However a statement was issued which indicated that the cabinet was against the Treaty. When this was pointed out to de Valera by Desmond Fitzgerald, he replied, "and that is the way I intend it to read. Publish it as it is". Fitzgerald commented to Stack, " I did not think he was against this kind of settlement before we went over to London"[18]. Stack replied, " He is dead against it now anyway". The statement read:

"In view of the nature of the proposed Treaty with Great Britain, President De Valera has sent an urgent summons to members of the cabinet in London, to report at once, so that a full cabinet decision may be taken. The hour of the meeting is fixed for 12 o'clock, noon, tomorrow. The date of the meeting of the Dail, to which the cabinet's decision has to be submitted has not yet been fixed"

Whatever about the machinations about choosing the delegates and the ongoing contacts between them and their colleagues who remained at home, de Valera still believed that he had the majority of the cabinet with him. Brugha and Stack were militant republicans like himself. de Valera knowing that Cosgrave had expressed objections to the oath at the earlier cabinet meeting, believed that Cosgrave was also with him, giving him a 4-3 majority in cabinet.[19] This was a serious miscalculation by de Valera. Though they had much in common, such as having been sentenced to death, awaiting execution, only to have that commuted to life imprisonment, they were very different men.

Cosgrave was practical, direct and straightforward. He saw a task, made up his mind and took action. He had been a loyal colleague in cabinet and had been particularly concerned with de Valera since his return from America. But Cosgrave went back to the beginning of Sinn Fein. He saw how it had developed. He was a long time colleague of Arthur Griffith. He was as much concerned with housing and social matters as with constitutional affairs. He was in public life to better the lot of Dubliners. His public record made him feel subservient to no man. He had been among those who had, "done and dared", as he said after his victory in Kilkenny. It was part of his character, that he would not make a great play about his momentous decision in cabinet, then or afterwards. There was his vote and that was that. He realised like Griffith and most of the people, that this was a major step forward, one which the men and women of 1916, would scarcely have believed possible, in such a short time span. It was only on the very next day, 7 December, when the cabinet met that de Valera discovered that Cosgrave was not with him[20].

Next day's cabinet meeting at the Mansion House, which went on all day and late into the night, was attended by the seven members, with Erskine Childers and Kevin O'Higgins also present. The vote in cabinet was four to three for the Treaty. The matter then had to go to the Dail for ratification. de Valera issued a statement that same night saying, " …I feel it is my duty to inform you immediately that I cannot recommend the acceptance of this treaty either to Dail Eireann or to the country. In this attitude I am supported by the ministers of Home Affairs and defence…".

deValera realised within a week that a majority of the population, would support the Treaty, though in his estimation, unlike Cosgrave, under duress[21]. However deValera as usual had an answer for that, as he said that, "the people have never had a right to do wrong"[22]. It became clear to most TD's during the Dail recess over the Christmas break that a majority of the people were for the Treaty[23].

The first Article of the Treaty stated:

"Ireland shall have the same constitutional status in the Community of Nations known as the British Empire, as the Dominions of Canada, Australia, New Zealand, the Union of South Africa, with a Parliament having powers to make laws for the peace, order and good government of Ireland, and an Executive responsible to the Parliament and shall be styled and known as the Irish Free State".

W.T. Cosgrave and Michael Collins,
flank Arthur Griffith (centre front row) at the Dáil, August 1921.

18. This instrument shall be submitted forthwith by His Majesty's Government forthe approval of Parliament and by the Irish signatories to a meeting summoned for the purpose of the members elected to sit in the House of Commons of Southern Ireland, and if approved shall be ratified by the necessary legislation.

Signature page of the Anglo-Irish Treaty,
British delegation signed on left, Irish on right.

CHAPTER EIGHT

TREATY DEBATES

"IS THIS A BARGAIN OR IS IT NOT ?"

The Treaty Debates are particularly important for this study, because they furnish one of the rare opportunities, when WT Cosgrave speaks quite candidly about himself and his beliefs. As he said to Michael Hayes before the debates began, " everybody wants to lap the milk but nobody wants to recognise the cow"[1]. Though, like most of his colleagues, he admired deValera as a great leader, he was nor averse to challenging and breaking with him, as he had already demonstrated, when he felt the occasion required it. He made two substantial interventions, one on the Treaty itself and the other on the extraordinary attempt to re-elect Eamon deValera as President of Dail Eireann, just after the acceptance of the Treaty. In his contributions, despite the gravity of the occasion, Cosgrave displayed a unique lightness of touch; he was witty, drawing regular laughter from all sides. He mocked himself, though particularly, "the little Deputy from Monaghan", as well as several other members of the Dail, including President deValera. He spoke as an elder, chiding younger members for not following his good example for order and brevity in debate. He also made a number of interventions, guiding the Speaker with points of procedure. He portrayed himself as a bargain-maker, a businessman, not an idealist, rather one concerned with practical matters, like the fact that 20,000 Dublin families lived in one room tenements. He was well respected by all sides. His record, like many of the other participants, spoke for itself.

The Dail met on Wednesday 14 December at University College Dublin on Earlsfort Terrace, where deValera was Chancellor. The session continued after the Christmas recess to the vote, on 7 January 1922. There were, not surprising, some very bitter and acrimonious speeches, with those intent on only settling for a republic, accusing those willing to accept the Treaty, as traitors. There was no agreement on the length of speeches, so that some, like that of Miss Mary MacSweeney, lasted for close to four hours. WT. Cosgrave's first intervention, which was on a point of order, indicated that the debate was not as orderly as on the Dublin Corporation. He said,

"May I respectfully draw your attention to number eight of the rules of debate by members, which states that the subject under discussion should be kept to, and another rule is that a member is not allowed to speak more than once".

THE MAN IN THE STREET

The Oath to the King exercised many of the TD's. WT addressed this, on 21 December; He said;

We have been listening for some days to various and varying opinions – legal opinions, I should say – from both sides of the House and as to what this means and what that means. And latterly these opinions have been centring around the relative distinction as between faithfulness and allegiance, and we have heard today that faithfulness is from a slave to a master, and that allegiance is only from a subject to a King. That is not the interpretation the man in the street puts upon it, and that is not my interpretation. A doctor of divinity in explaining this matter to me in connection with the oath, points out that one can be faithful to an equal and it is in this sense that I interpret this oath, and I believe I gave expression in the cabinet to the opinion that the oath could be interpreted in whatever way you looked at it. If you were sufficiently prejudiced on one side, to say that it was an oath of allegiance, you were entitled to do so, and if that were the interpretation of those who are against ratification of the treaty, I make them a present of it. My interpretation of it is that, in those Commonwealth or Association, each of the members is equal, and that if that were wrong, I think that we will find ourselves in the company of some distinguished constitutional lawyers. Now practically every possible phrase of the Treaty has been discussed, and there is very little for those who are taking part in the debate now to deal with, except statements or interpretations of this instrument or that has been made before. I concern myself with one or two of these.

We were told that if we of Dail Eireann, should approve and ratify a Treaty, we are deliberately relinquishing and abandoning the Declaration of Independence...Well everybody who has taken part in this struggle knows what it means, and knows what it involved and what it cost the people of this country. It means the arresting of every national development in this country. It means the English Parliament has got the power that it has of sixty thousand troops behind it, to put its authority into practice. We have resisted it magnificently and some of the best of those who resisted it, are in this house for the ratification of the treaty...

The Minister for Finance has said, " in my judgement, it is not a definition of any status that would secure that status: it is the power to hold and make secure and to increase what we have gained". Does any man who is against ratifying take exception to that statement? Is he in honour entitled to make that statement? He is, and in my opinion the people who are for this treaty are entitled to carry out to the letter, every syllable that is in the Document. I listened with great patience to some very long speeches this afternoon, but you have set the examples yourselves.

Now I think we have examined the Declaration of Independence that was given to us...we are told that we did not make it plain at the elections that we were standing for Dominion Home Rule. Was it made plain to the people that we were standing for External Association within the Commonwealth of Nations, and to associate that with the national aspirations of the Irish people...?

Now this Treaty has been criticised, belittled, and I believe, slandered to the extent that certainly surprised me. It represents work that has been done in five years: greater than what was accomplished by Emmet, O'Connell, Mitchell, Davis, Smith O'Brien, and Parnell, down even to Mr. Redmond, with a united country behind him.

GRATTANS' PARLIAMENT

References have been made of Grattan's Parliament. Did those people who spoke of Grattan's Parliament think that it was an injustice to this country to be deprived of it, and did the honourable and gallant – and I believe he has some claim to the title of Rev. – Deputy from Wexford think it when addressing this Congress here yesterday. I recollect that when I was very young in the Sinn Fein movement, he was in it, and I believe that our Ambassador in Paris was in it too. But I think that the basis of the Sinn Fein movement at that time, was the restoration of that Parliament of the King, Lords and Commons of Ireland. The gallant Deputy was at that time evidently a Royal Republican. A Republican from his boyhood, I believe he told us...

For over two and a half years this Cabinet has worked loyally and well together and I should say that the two men who typified the best type of Irishmen I have ever known, are the President and the Minister for Finance. The Minister of Finance speaks of the peaceful penetration of the enemy in the country. It is typified in every walk of life. The best colleges play the foreign games. The President can bear me out in that. At the race meetings one sees the Union Jack. I believe the Minister for Home Affairs can bear me out in that. I don't know what the Minister for Defence does in his idle moments. I cannot get him to hear me out in anything. All I know him to be interested in was in shooting: and even in the rifle clubs that were established before the Volunteers, the Union Jack floated over them...

NORTHERN UNIONISTS

This instrument gives us the opportunity to capture the Northern Unionists. They are great citizens of this nation even though they differ from us...

One question that has not been put at all is this: If you could have a choice of a Republic with twenty-six counties, would you have it or a dominion for the whole of Ireland?

The economy of this country is not such at the moment that would justify us taking the risk of precipitating war. Here in this city, there is something like twenty thousand families living in single room tenement dwellings, and are these the people you are going to ask to fight for you? It is not fair, I submit. There are potentialities in this instrument undreamt of in this country up to this time...

When the plenipotentiaries went back to London on that fateful Saturday, four remarkable improvements took place in the document they brought back. The first is: absolute and entire control over the taxation of commodities coming into this country.

The second item was in connection with the oath. As an ordinary common or garden man – may I accept that interpretation of it? I have not got the constitutional lawyers mind, the solicitors mind, or even the mind of an idealist, but an ordinary businessman's mind, and I see nothing objectionable in it absolutely. I believe I heard the President on one occasion say if you were prepared to make a bargain, why would you not be prepared to be faithful to it.

President: Hear, hear.

WT COSGRAVE: *Very well. Is this a bargain or is it not? It is a bargain.*

PRESIDENT: *It is not.*

WT COSGRAVE: *Very well, then , the objection is not to the oath at all, but to the bargain. I am fair at making bargains myself...*

I believe sir, the loss of the President to the Irish Free State, should this instrument be approved, would be a terrible loss. I believe the loss of the Minister for Home Affairs and the Minister for Finance would be equally irreparable. I know the Minister for Defence. My own conviction is that except for war, he is not worth a damn for anything else; but he is a great man for war. I bear witness to that, because even as the spark of life was going out of him, he was full of fight as when he was going into it... Whether or not I have a case for signing the treaty or not, I think Dail Eireann is in better humour now than when I started, and I now formally approve, recommend, and support this Treaty.

At the start of the debate on 5 January, WT Cosgrave was first on his feet, on a point of order. He said: " I would like to bring this matter before the House. Yesterday I was informed that one of the principal business houses in this city received this letter.

Sinn Fein Headquarters   Jan. 3rd 1922
6 Harcourt St.

Dear Sirs,

We have found that it will not be possible for us to obtain a Union Jack of sufficient size in the event of it being necessary for us to display one at the end of the session of Dail Eireann when the treaty will, in all probability, be ratified. We are anxious to comply with all necessary courtesies, and propose to hoist the Union Jack beside the green flag on the University building, as soon as the result of the discussion is known. We would be grateful if you would give the bearer your largest flag. We will, of course, return it to you, as soon as the one, which we have ordered, arrives.

We are, dear Sirs,
Yours faithfully
Mr. Whelan, Secretary,
Decorating Committee
Irish Free State.

Mr P. O'Keeffe intervened immediately to say that he was the Chief Executive Officer for Harcourt St and that the letter was forgery. After some discussion an adjournment was agreed.

When the session resumed again that evening at 8.35 p.m. WT Cosgrave was again the first speaker. He said;

"I have not consulted my friends about the leading article that appeared in the Freeman's Journal, but I wish to express my own regret that an Irish journal would publish such a leading article, as that which appeared in a Dublin morning paper today. I think that the Dail has the highest respect for and confidence in the President, and I believe that the people of this country have the highest respect for the President also, and it is not in the interest of the ratification of the treaty that such an article as this should appear in an Irish journal."

Much condemnation of the *Freeman's Journal* resulted, with various suggestions of retribution. However Arthur Griffith intervened to say:

"I condemn the reference to the President as in the worst taste...the Press has a right to say what it likes about us. I must say the Press must be free to say what it pleases. President DeValera and Erskine Childers agreed with Griffith. WT Cosgrave then intervened again to say:
"A protest has been made and I think the matter ought to end. I beg to move that leave be given to withdraw it.

JAN 6th

WT Cosgrave questioned the Speaker's ruling that the suspension of Standing Orders be allowed, to introduce a motion on the resignation of the President. He argued that the business in hand, consisted of one entire sitting, during which ordinary business or one to suspend Standing Orders be heard, should not be put.

The cause of demand to suspend Standing Orders was to debate DeValera's announcement that he was resigning as President of the Dail. DeValera had said,
"What I do formally is to lay before the House my resignation, definitely as Chief Executive Authority. I resign and with it goes the Cabinet...This house has got my document Number Two. The new Cabinet that will be formed, if I am re-elected, will put it before the House. We will put down that document. It will be submitted to the House".
The strategy appeared to abort, stop or postpone the debate on the Treaty.

WT Cosgrave added during the debate:

"The position is this; that the document has been under consideration since the 5th or 6th of December last, and this 'matter of urgent national importance' has lasted up to the 6th of January of the following year. The 'matter of urgent national importance' is as urgent now as then. We are within, at most, forty-eight hours of a decision on the matter and on the orders of the day, it can be decided here and now. That settles the point and I claim that this is not a matter of national importance, within the meaning of the words, and that the debate should be continued without interruption."

The motion was withdrawn and the discussion on the Treaty continued.

JAN 7th

The vote on the Treaty was taken and resulted in sixty-four votes for approval and fifty-seven against.

deValera then said t that it will be his duty to resign his office as Chief Executive but that he was unsure that he should do so immediately. Michael Collins interjected, saying "No".

JAN 8th

A major upheaval began when those who had lost the previous day's vote, proposed that DeValera should be re-elected as President of the Dail. WT Cosgrave objected, saying::

" The latest interpretation of constitutional practice, is that a minority in an assembly, is to form the government and to carry out the various functions of the government in the country."

DEVALERA: Remember, I am only putting myself at your disposal and at the disposal of the nation. I do not want office at all. Go and elect your President and all the rest of it. You have sixty-five. I do not want office at all.

COSGRAVE: We are here now an hour, and the President has spoken four times, and the little Deputy from Monaghan twice.

MACENTEE: Once on the resolution.

COSGRAVE: And the first thing he has stated was that we have got to take great care that England will honour the Treaty. And he himself is making the greatest possible case that we will not honour it...now this is certainly the most unconstitutional procedure I have ever known. I am getting old: I am thirteen years in public life: I have never heard the likes of a proposition, which has been put before us this morning, and it is certainly the most exceptional procedure ever proposed. I think the President realises it too, and appreciates it – that the minority of this House takes over the Government of the country and takes over the resources of it.

DEVALERA: Select your President.

COSGRAVE: The President dictates to the House. The minority is to regulate whether a decision of this House is to be put into operation or not...

DEVALERA: This is deliberate misrepresentation and you know it.

COSGRAVE: Let us have the exact representation.

DEVALERA: I resigned. The majority can go and take over the machinery of the Republic. I do not ask you to elect me. I am quite glad and anxious to get back to private life.

COSGRAVE: As an ordinary man who has been in public life and who has generally managed to understand what people have said in public, it is this way:...The President does not want to be in this position, where his advisers want to put him.

DEVALERA :   *I said I was not consulting anybody.*

COSGRAVE: *It may be my own stupidity in the difficulty of understanding this. But the position appears – that the advisers of the President seek to take advantage of his personal popularity and the respect on which the people of this Assembly hold him – they desire to establish an autocracy. Last week the vilest abuse was poured upon us. We were held up to public scorn and hatred. We were described as only babes could be described. This morning we are getting cheap advice...*

Well we are just as anxious to do the best for the nation as the loudest spoken among you...I made it a point at the commencement here not to interrupt anyone. And I regret that those young people here have not been able to appreciate that good example. I have shown you an excellent example...

The people who do not want this Treaty, desire to have the resources of the Republic, and the Army and the finances – that and you can blaze away. I submit that the resolution to re-elect the President is out of order...Under the Treaty the Irish people are Irish citizens and not British subjects.

BRUGHA;   *Prove it.*

COSGRAVE: *The Dail understands it. There are sixty-four sensible people in the Dail and the Dail realises that, and if you are the apostle of constitutional government, you will accept their decision, because it is a majority decision. I did not interrupt the Minister for War. I know it is not fear but the sense of the people that made them favour the Treaty....the one fact remains, that we have the destinies of the country in our hands, and that we are responsible for restoring normal conditions. The enemy are now willing and anxious to clear out, and I believe making preparations to clear out...And if the government of this country is to be maintained, it will be done by an established majority rule...I am not interested in a Republican form of government. I don't care what form it is, so long as its free, independent, authoritative and the sovereign Government of the people, and that it will be respected...the world is looking at us now, having approved of this Treaty, and is expecting ordered government from it, and you cannot have ordered government if you re-establish and reconstruct the government of the minority.. Therefore I submit to you that it is not in order to receive the motion for the re-election of President DeValera.*

A vote was taken on the re-election of President DeValera. Fifty-eight voted for, and sixty against.

ARTHUR GRIFFITH: *I want the Deputies to know and all Ireland to know that this vote is not to be taken as against President DeValera. It is a vote to help the Treaty and I want to say now that there is scarcely a man I have ever met in my life, that I have more love and respect for than President deValera.*

DEVALERA: ...   *now I think the right thing has been done, that the people who are responsible have done the right thing. I hope that nobody will talk of fratricidal strife. That is all nonsense. We have got a nation that knows how to conduct itself...I tell you now, you will want us yet.*

COLLINS: *We want you now.*

DEVALERA: *I am against you on principle. and I believe that to get the best out of that Treaty, you will need us in a solid compact body. We will not interfere with you, except when we find you going to do something that will definitely injure the Irish nation...*

Some time after the Debate, the *Irish Times* wrote of Cosgrave's contribution. "One day the whole assembly was bored to mental paralysis...Then Mr. Cosgrave got up and in a moment the whole atmosphere was changed. A reply of half suppressed mirth greeted his opening sallies and in a twinkling his apparent flippancy had the whole Dail laughing without restraint. Even Mr. deValera could not resist the well pointed witticisms of the jocular gentleman from Kilkenny, as Cosgrave was nicknamed half an hour later by Cathal Brugha, and when his speech was finished, not only had several new supporters been gained for the Treaty, but the danger signals had disappeared and everyone was in good humour again"[2].

W.T. Cosgrave (centre) enters UCD January 1922, for vote on Treaty.

CHAPTER NINE

DESCENT INTO CHAOS
1922-1923

"WE HAD FED THE HEART ON FANTASIES,
THE HEART'S GROWN BRUTAL FROM THE FARE"

All T.D's supporting the Treaty gathered at the Mansion House on 10 January, to formally accept the Treaty. Arthur Griffith, in his capacity as Chairman of the Treaty plenipotentiaries, summoned members of the House of Commons of Southern Ireland, and a transitional government was established, to which the British Government and the Dail could transfer powers. The Provisional Government consisted of Collins as Chairman, WT. Cosgrave, Eamonn Duggan, Patrick Hogan, Fionan Lynch, Joe McGrath, Eoin MacNeill, Kevin O'Higgins. That was the sole meeting of that parliament.

When Arthur Griffith was being elected President of the Dail on 10th January, replacing Eamon deValera, the latter walked out in protest, followed by his anti-Treaty supporters. They later returned to he Dail where an adjournment debate took place. Griffith, still calling deValera 'President', requested an adjournment for about one month to allow the Provisional Government to function. Griffith said, "Give us a chance. We cannot work as it is.". deValera replied, "We ought, I think, to take that as reasonable. The only thing we are anxious about is the army..."It was aggreed to adjourn for about a month. The Dail reassembled on 28th February with a full attendance. It met and conducted business on fifteen occasions up to the 8th of June.

On that day a motion of censure on President Griffith, who was absent, was tabled by Cathal Brugha and seconded by Madame Markievzcz. Bitter exchanges occured on Giffith's criticisms of Erskine Childers, before, at deValera's request, the motion was withdrawn. The last item of business was a technical measure by Cosgrave from the Department of Local Government. When amendments were put in, he explained that on legal advice he could not accept any amendments. deValera replied "We are anxious to help the work of the Department in this matter but we cannot make fools of ourselves". Eventually Austin Stack seconded the adoption of the Decree and it was passed unanimously. Cosgrave was the last speaker as the Dail adjourned to Friday 30th June 1922.

An extraordinary meeting of three thousand delegates of Sinn Fein was scheduled for the Mansion House on 22 February. As it became apparent to the Standing Committee that a majority of the delegates were anti-treaty, the Ard Fheis was adjourned to May. This afforded the Provisional Government a breathing space, during which it was able, by taking control of a variety of institutions, as the British withdrew, to build up its civil and military power, and gain a wide majority support among the people. Divisions on the Treaty began to become apparent in many quarters of public life. Most Sinn Fein clubs became anti-treaty as did Cumann na mBan.

The army, which was of course crucial to progress, was riven with division as the IRA flexed its muscles countrywide, with lawlessness widespread. An army convention was demanded, and with Mulcahy's initial approval though against Griffith's orders, took place on 26 March. This resulted in a major split on the Treaty, resulting in at least two armies. The anti-Treaty force took over the Four Courts complex in central Dublin in defiance of the Provisional Government. Their comrades occupied other installations countrywide.

deVALERA-COLLINS PACT

All this did not bode well for the holding of a general election to allow the people to vote on the Treaty. However Collins and deValera entered into a pact, to the consternation of the British, which was intended have the general election replicate the electoral situation in the Second Dail, and avert a vote on the Treaty, per se. Stephen Collins writes, "Neither man appears to have understood the working of proportional representation because such a pact was simply not feasible in multi-seat constituencies, with other parties and Independents involved"[1]. Churchill wrote to Collins, "I think I had better let you know at once, that any such arrangement would be received with world-wide ridicule It would not be an election in any sense of the word, but simply a farce, were a handful of men who possess lethal weapons deliberately to dispose of the political rights of the electors, by a deal across the table". Lloyd George summoned Collins, Griffith and WT Cosgrave to London on 31 May[2]. In London they met Lloyd George, Churchill, Birkenhead, Austin Chamberlain and Hamar Greenwood. The Irish told them that a successful election needed republican approval, but assured that they would win and implement the Treaty. The meeting was tense, until Cosgrave lightened the apprehension by asking Churchill how he was after a recent fall. Churchill later accepted their assurances, but told them that there was fierce scrutiny of what was happening in Britain, adding that, "You will find that we are just as tenacious on essential points – the Crown, the British Commonwealth, no Republic – as deValera and Rory O'Connor, and we intend to fight for our points"[3]. Lloyd George insisted that the Free State Constitution conform to the Treaty. Griffith replied that 'in so far as it can be shown that the draft constitution is in conflict with the Treaty, we are prepared to insert such amendments as will reconcile its terms with the Treaty'[3a]. During this period came the disquieting news that Pettigo and Beleek had been taken over by forces from the South[4]. Churchill later told the Commons he hoped that the election would lead to a Constitution linking Ireland firmly to the Crown and Empire.. He said, " I do not believe that the Provisional Government are working hand in glove with their republican opponents, with the intent, by an act of treachery, to betray British confidence and Ireland's good name. We have transferred the powers of government to the Irish Parliament on the faith of the treaty…This great act of faith on the part of the stronger power, will not, I believe, be brought to mockery by the Irish people. If it were, the strength of the Empire will survive the disappointment, but the Irish name will not recover from the disgrace"[5].

The deValera-Collins pact was ratified at the reconvened Sinn Fein Ard Fheis on 22 May 1922, with the election scheduled for 16 June 1922. Tom Garvin has written: "Despite massive personation and intimidation in some areas, the common people heavily favoured the pro-Treatites, the Labour Party and the Farmers party with their votes…The voters essentially were rejecting the assertion by the IRA, in seizing the Four Courts on 25 April that the Public Band (IRA) was morally superior to the Dail[6].

Thirty-eight of the 128 seats were uncontested, mainly due to the disturbed nature of the countryside. Sinn Fein had agreed that 65 pro-Treatyites and 59 anti-Treatyites would run. Other contestants numbered 52.

The result of the contested seats was:

Treayites   41

Anti-Treatyites   19

Labour   17

Farmers   7

Independents   6

Labour, Farmers and Independents supported the Treaty. This meant a majority of the T.D's supported the Treaty. deValera and his supporters felt that they had been tricked by the Election pact and refused to take their seats in the Third Dail.

The civil war really began at this juncture and was to last until April 1923.

The Government was divided on how best to deal with the IRA. Collins was most reluctant to begin action against the occupation of the Four Courts, realising that such a move would almost formalise a civil war around the country. However the civilians in government wanted action. The British were pressing the Government to take decisive action, against what they saw as a coup d'etat. deValera was their great bogey man, whom they feared might stage a return to power and repudiate the Treaty.

The assassination of Sir Henry Wilson outside his Eaton Place home in London, raised tensions in England and Ireland. It occurred on the same day as the election results were coming in. Collins was suspected of being behind it. Mulcahy was outraged and threatened resignation[7]. O'Higgins was also aghast[8]. The British blamed the supporters of the Four Courts element for the murder and threatened an all out assault on that garrison, unless the Provisional Government took decisive action[9]. The Provisional Government met on 25 June 1922 and considered the IRA activities in the South and in the North, where there was a possibility of another front opening. Churchill had decided to assist the North to expand its BSpecials to 48,000. The British army increased its numbers in the north to 9,000. Churchill told the cabinet, "We could do no less...the ferocious steps against Ulster...Collins having joined with avowed republicans"[10]. Another complication was the fact that the Second Dail, was due to meet on 30 June, and become the Third Dail, after the recent general election. On 27 June the IRA in the Four Courts kidnapped General Ginger O'Connell. With guns eagerly provided by the British, through the aegis of Winston Churchill, the Four Courts was shelled on 28 June. This lasted for two days until an unconditional surrender occurred on 30 June. Further action continued in Dublin for a week with much destruction and deaths, including that of Cathal Brugha. The Republicans claimed that the Government had started the war, and they retreated particularly to the south and attacked forces loyal to the government. At that point a women's delegation, including Maud Gonne, who knew Griffith so well over so many years, met Cosgrave, Collins and Griffith to act as go-betweens. However they were told that there could be no truce until the anti-Treaty forces surrender arms[11].

COSGRAVE TEMPORARY HEAD OF GOVERNMENT

On 12 July 1922 Collins became Commander-in-Chief of the national army, with Mulcahy as Chief of Staff and Minister for Defence. WT Cosgrave was appointed acting head of the Provisional Government and Minister for Finance. Peter Hart writes that the reason for this, was that Cosgrave was most unlikely to do anything that would go against Collins[12]. Army numbers were rapidly increased as Collins and Mulcahy worked closely together[13]. They endeavoured to keep the cabinet informed of events, but matters were so hectic, that this often did not materialise. This was tolerated while Collins was in control, but civilian members of cabinet would not tolerate the same treatment from Mulcahy, when he succeeded as Commander-in-Chief.. This caused great conflict between the army and the cabinet, with Mulcahy caught in the middle.

GRIFFITH AND COLLINS DEAD

On 12 August Cosgrave heard of the death of Griffith. He was devastated and realised that his own death could also be imminent, as the Irregulars had so recently threatened to shoot government ministers. He composed a last testament that same day, in case of his death, in which he declared that his own place would easily be filled. He undertook to forgive those who might decide to shoot him. He felt sorry for his own people, his wife, his children, his mother and family. It is a remarkable document, which he placed in the files of his Department. It reads:

"Now under the shadow of the great national calamity, the death of President Griffith, comes the news that members of the government are on the list to be shot. This is

Michael Collins with Arthur Griffith.

Michael Collins left, bearing Arthur Griffith's coffin, August 1922.
He was killed in an ambush in Béal na Bláth, Cork, the same Month.

misguided patriotism on the part of those who have been unequal to the shock of war. The people who so act are irresponsible and must not be allowed to cow or awe the people of Ireland. Even if the members of the government are shot and die, others will be found to take their places. None of us could be indispensable. The country has not yet discovered the true worth of our successes. The people must discover them. I believe General Collins is one of the greatest men Ireland has produced. A statesman and a soldier – and there are others also in the government and in the Army. My place will be easily filled. I am sorry for my people, my wife, my children, my mother and family. They all suffered during the late war and did not grumble – others suffered too and did not grumble. They did not suffer in vain. Hard times are coming, but they – the people of Ireland – will endure, but they must prevail against any minority seeking to order their will or their life, save under the laws which the people's government pass. I willingly forgive those who think I should be shot, and those who take part in such shooting, and I ask forgiveness of all those I have offended. I thank all who helped me and without whose help, any work in which I was engaged, would have been valueless. I thank all who prayed for me and helped me, whom in life it was not possible to even thank. I thank the Archbishop and all his priests and all my colleagues and friends and acquaintances, and if it can do any good, I ask those who are in arms against the government, to consider if it be not possible to come to agreement with the nation. No member of the government wished to continue any war on any nation. I ask for obedience to the Parliament of the Irish nation, and may God in his infinite mercy forgive me my sins and pardon my shortcomings. 12.8.22. Liam T. Mac Cosgair"[14].

On 15 August Griffith was laid to rest in Glasnevin, after a lifetime of self-denying struggle on behalf of the nation. Cosgrave gave the graveside oration to his old friend. He compared the straightforwardness of Griffith to, "those magicians of political metaphysics, who say one thing and mean another…His signature was his bond for the honour of the nation…He died a sorrowful man, and if it were not for the greatness of his heart and the magnificence of his mind, he would have died a broken-hearted man, for within the last few months of his life, he looked out upon the moral desolation…of reckless murder and general insincerity, in a blindly dishonest outlook and attitude towards the national position and the effect on the nation's Treaty of Peace".

Despite shocking public events, social life went on in Dublin. The Countess of Fingal in her autobiography illustrates this. She writes, "Arthur Griffith had died on August 12th. At the weekend I was one of that memorable party to which John Dillon had been invited. The Bernard Shaws were staying at Kilteragh. On Saturday morning Hazel Lavery telephoned me from the Salthill Hotel in Monkstown, where she and Sir John were staying. ' Do you think Sir Horace would like me to bring Michael Collins over to supper tonight? Horace and the Shaws were much interested at the idea of meeting a rebel leader. And that evening they came, Sir John and Hazel, and Michael Collins who signed the Visitors Book in Irish, Micheal O'Coleann. Mr. WT Cosgrave was also in the party"[15].

'THE BULLET FOUND HIM WHERE THE BULLET CEASED'

By August the national army was in the ascendancy with a series of victories. The IRA held Cork City and Collins planned an attack from the sea. He went south to assess the situation. On 22 August 1922 he was shot dead in an ambush at Béal na Bláth in county Cork. Mulcahy issued an immediate statement to the army, least any reprisals take place: " Stand calmly by your posts. Bend bravely and undaunted to your work. Let no cruel act of reprisal blemish your bright honour. Every dark hour that Michael Collins met since 1916, seemed but to steel that bright strength of his and temper his gay bravery" [16].

Military lorries carried the news to Cosgrave, who was staying with his mother at number eight Lansdowne Road that night[17]. Frank O'Connor wrote about the aftermath of Collins' death in *The Big Fellow*:

"In the early morning a middle aged man was knocked up in a house on Lansdowne Road. Two or three men stood on the steps with faces like death. They had come to tell the middle-aged man that it was left to him to carry on the task their chief had begun…There was a crowd in Government Buildings, where the Provisional Government was isolated behind sandbags and barbed wire. A door opened and two young men came in, O'Reilly and Cullen. O'Reilly, still half asleep and unable to take in the news, was ready for any trick they might lay on him. When they saw the grey frightened faces, the two lads burst into loud, unrestrained weeping. Cosgrave stepped forward, his index finger raised, "This is a nice way for soldiers to behave!"[18].

At the hastily organised meeting, which rook place throughout the night, were WT Cosgrave, Patrick Hogan, Joe McGrath, Kevin O'Higgins, Desmond Fitzgerald, Ernest Blythe, Michael Hayes, Hugh Kennedy, Kevin O'Shiel, assistant Law Officer, Richard Mulcahy, Commandant-General, Gearoid O'Sullivan, Commandant-General, Diarmaid O'Hegarty,[19].

WT Cosgrave, aged 42, emerged as the favoured Chairman of the Provisional Government. He was an obvious choice from many points of view. His credentials were second to none. His record of moderation had been respected during the treaty debates. He was a conciliator, a man who wanted to get things done, not an idealist who might mislead people. He was a businessman, who with another T.D. Joe MacDonagh, had set up an insurance business in 1919[20]. Mulcahy was too close to the military. O'Higgins had a short fuse and was fundamentally untested. Though O'Higgins had his differences with Mulchay, he suggested to him before the cabinet meeting which copper fastened Cosgrave's position, that he should be the successor. He remarked snobbishly to Mulcahy, " Dublin corporators would make this land *'A Nation Once Again'*…"[21].

Cosgrave had been Collins' temporary successor since July.
Mulcahy proposed Cosgrave as President and Eoin MacNeill seconded[22].

As early as 24 August Churchill wrote to Cosgrave, " ...the death of the two principal signatories, the retirement of another and the desertion of the fourth, in no way affect the validity and sanctity of the settlement...between the two islands which was the life-work of the dead Irish leaders, and with which their names will be imperishably associated... for our part we hold ourselves bound on the Treaty basis and will meet good faith with good faith and goodwill with goodwill to the end...You as acting Chairman of the Provisional government, and your civil colleagues and your military officers, may count on the fullest measure of co-operation and support from us in any way that is required"[23]. Churchill also wrote to Alfred Cope in Dublin saying that it was vital that deValera remain " a hunted rebel", and that Cosgrave, Mulcahy realise that the only hope of a friendly settlement with the North and ultimate Irish unity, lies in a clear line being drawn between the Treaty Party and the republicans"[24].

Churchill later remarked that, " we have found Irishmen whose word is their bond". Lloyd George's government lost out to the Conservatives and Bonar Law, and Churchill was suddenly out of office. He wrote a final letter to Cosgrave on 25 October saying, "No one knows better than I, the unceasing, tormenting struggle which was forced on Mr. Arthur Griffith and General Michael Collins, from the moment when the treaty between the two nations was signed". Cosgrave replied, "The valedictory message which you have sent me on leaving office, touches many chords. Hitherto the departure of a British cabinet from power, has meant for us in Ireland but another milestone, on the long dark road of alien government imposed on our nation, shadowed with futility in rule on the one hand, and utter bitter resistance on the other. But in our day and generation,, we have found the turning in the road"[25]. Churchill later wrote to a friend, Pamela Lytton, "Ireland is going to save itself. No one else is going to. They are a proud and gifted race and they are up against the grimmest facts...It was interesting to see how when their Parliament met on Saturday, there was no oratory or enthusiasm. Responsibility is a wonderful agent when thrust upon competent heads"[26].

Churchill was to add, "The void left by the deaths of Griffith and Collins was not unfilled. A quiet potent figure stood in the background...In Cosgrave, the Irish people found a chief of higher quality than any who had yet appeared. To the courage of Collins, he added the matter-of-fact fidelity of Griffith and a knowledge of practical administration and state policy all his own". Cosgrave pooh-poohed this tribute, in embarrassment.

Some Ministers had been critical of Collins' almost total control of government through Cosgrave, and directly in the army. Collin's departure weakened the independence of the army, and Mulcahy became isolated within cabinet. The majority were very different ideologically from those who, like Mulcahy were associated with the traditional national movement[27]. This was compounded to an extreme degree, when his colleagues discovered that he had met secretly with deValera, on 5 September 1922 to try and broker a settlement. Mulcahy held deValera responsible for the civil war and thought he was going to recant[28].

Frank O'Connor in writing of the aftermath of Collins' death, writes astutely, that, "Mulcahy, rightly, interpreting the dead man, resumed negotiations where his death had broken them off. But he did so unknown to his colleagues. The day of lofty ideas was over. An evil twilight full of storm and sinister shadows succeeded that long day, too long and bright for Lilliput's cross and weary eyes". O'Connor, while in awe of Collins' charisma and wondering what might have occurred had he lived, realised that charisma could not continue to run a government[29].

The Constitution said that, "The Irish Free State is a co-equal member of the Community of Nations forming the British Commonwealth of Nations".

It could be held that the agreed Constitution was a marked improvement on the Articles of the Treaty, and an early example of the validity of Collins' 'stepping stones' theory. The 'British Empire' was replaced by the 'British Commonwealth', as the organisation to which Ireland adhered. Articles One and Two stated:

> All powers of government and all authority, legislative, executive and judicial, in Ireland, are derived from the people of Ireland, and the same shall be exercised in the Irish Free State, through the organisation established by and under, and in accord with this constitution.

The article which caused offence to some of Cosgrave's friends, and all of de Valera's, was Article 17 which stated:

"I —— do solemnly swear true faith and allegiance to the Constitution of the Irish Free State, as by law established and that I will be faithful to HM King George, his heirs and successors by law, in virtue of the common citizenship of Ireland with Great Britain and her adherence to and membership of the British Commonwealth of Nations".

An example of Cosgrave's low-key, yet effective style of leadership, occurred, while the civil war was still in progress, and prior to the enactment of the Constitution. It was due to come into force at the end of 1922. In the event, some of the pro-Treaty T.D's got cold feet about swearing the Oath of Allegiance to the King at the enactment of the Constitution. They felt that they would have to withdraw from the Dail. This was a shattering blow to the Government.

The group could not be persuaded and made preparations to withdraw from the Dail. Cosgrave then announced that, though he had no personal objection to the oath, he had also decided not to take it and leave the Dail too. The cabinet and particularly O'Higgins, were aghast and furious with Cosgrave. WT and the dissidents withdrew to a separate room to discuss matters. After some time, the entire group returned, having changed their minds on the oath. O'Higgins, who was not aware of Cosgrave's strategy, remained very angry with him[30]. Ernest Blythe described Cosgrave as, "a very level man, who was never rushed unduly into anger and he was never terrified by any problem He was a splendid helmsman for the country, at the time he was head of the Government"[31].

As Brian P. Murphy writes, "This final denouement also confounded the best hopes of Cosgrave and his supporters for some form of united Ireland. Some had hoped that unionists would actually vote to join the Free State on 7 December. Certainly Cosgrave, in recommending the Free State Act on 6 December 1922, had fully expected the Boundary Commission's recommendations to be implemented. While denying any intention of coercing Ulster, he identified himself with the sentiment and the very words of Lloyd George, made during the treaty negotiations, that "although I am against the coercion of Ulster, I do not believe in Ulster coercing other units"[31a].

On 12 December 1922, the Constitution had come into force, and the Dail received a message from the King, through the Governor General:

"With the final Enactment of the Constitution the self-governing Dominion of the Irish Free State comes into being.

The Constitution is itself founded on the Treaty that was framed a year ago between the Representatives of Great Britain and of Ireland.

It is my earnest hope that by the faithful observance on all sides of the Pact so concluded, the peace and prosperity of Ireland may be secured.

It is in the spirit of that Settlement that I have chosen you to be the first Representative of the Crown in the Irish Free State.

With all my heart I pray that the blessing of God may rest upon you and upon the Ministers of the Irish Free State in the difficult task committed to your charge."[32].

The Irish Times wrote of Cosgrove on 9 August 1922, as he was elected to the Presidency of the Executive Council: " Mr. WT Cosgrave is a man who has succeeded very well in keeping out of the limelight of publicity. That perhaps is his best title to fame, but he has other qualities in addition to his modesty and is regarded by those who know him, as one of the soundest men in Ireland today. It would be hard to imagine anyone who is less true to what we used to consider the Sinn Fein type than Mr. Cosgrave. It is not that he does not dress in the regulation way – trench coat, leggings and slouch hat and the rest of it; but he has a thoroughly conservative face. He is neither a wild-eyed revolutionary nor a lank haired poet. He dresses usually in sombre hues, wears a bowler hat and looks rather like the general manager of a railway company. His hair is his most striking feature. It is very fair, turning now to grey and he wears it straight up on his head a la Pompadour…he has a knack of spicing his remarks with a dry and somewhat pawky sense of humour, which incensed some of his opponents hugely, in the Treaty Debates. A few of his speeches were delightful".

John Regan characterises Cosgrave as an elusive political figure and very much a family man, where his home became as important as Dail Eireann for political manoeuvring. He writes of him, "as genial and witty, on even some of the dourest occasions in the Dail he could be humorous. Possessed of a mercurial personality, he was skilled in a school of politics where affability counted on occasion as much as affirmation….On party-executive relations, civil-military relations, the Irish language, protection and free trade, Cosgrave danced in the middle of the floor.. On occasions he preferred not to attend contentious cabinet meetings. At other times he would take impromptu holidays, outside the country, succumb to sudden illness, and even disappear in order not to be drawn into a definite line on divisive issues."[33].

EMERGENCY POWERS

Even as the Dail reassembled on 9 September 1922, without the presence of the anti-treaty T.D's, a T.D. named Laurence Ginnell, who had not taken the oath, created a disturbance. As the Dail tried to elect a Ceann Comhairle, Ginnell kept interrupting, asking was it a Parliament for all of Ireland or a Partition Parliament. Eventually Cosgrave was forced to move that Ginnell be removed, as he had not taken the prescribed oath. Ginnell had been one of the Irish Parliamentary members who had valiantly defended the 1916 leaders in the House of Commons in May 1916..

As the civil war grew more vicious, the Government on 27 September 1922 introduced the Army Emergency Powers Resolution, where prisoners could be sentenced to death at military courts. Speaking in the Dail, Cosgrave said of the rebellion in progress:

"It restricts trade, it attempts to destroy the industry of the nation, it delays the progress of public administration, it destroys life, damages public and private property, it shakes public security, it defames our nation, injures the people's health, and endangers the future generation as it helps to destroy the people's peace… the absolute disregard of life and of suffering that is evidenced by the continuance of the irregular attacks, plainly indicated to the government that protection is due to their soldiers…Those who persist in those murderous attacks must learn that they have got to pay the penalty for them, a penalty greater than internment"[34].

As the ex-minister of local government, Cosgrave was well aware that during the past year the real local authority power in very many areas, was the Public Band i.e. the IRA. He and his allies "were to steel themselves to the task of eliminating it and ensuring that Dublin's writ, would run everywhere, in practice as well as in theory. For that, military force was to be required and blood was to flow; the characteristic Irish combination of extravagant farce and hideous local tragedy had to recur"[35]. The Government offered an amnesty to the IRA to lay down arms before 15 October. The Catholic Church issued a pastoral letter condemning and excommunicating those who bore arms against the government. Four men from Cosgrave's James' St area were the first to be executed under the Special Powers Act, .on 17 November. They were, Peter Cassidy, James Fisher, Richard Tuohig, John Gaffney.[36].

On 17 November Cosgrave replied to Archbishop Byrne's plea for the release of Miss Mary MacSweeney who was on hunger strike in Mountjoy Gaol. The Archbishop feared that " her death, by voluntary abstention from food, will have more harmful affect than her continued internment". Cosgrave thanked Byrne for his " mature advice on the innumerable and complicated issues that confront us daily in our trying and difficult task.

Now with regard to this issue may I say that my Government have given it the most profound and anxious thought; we have weighed it in all its bearings and considered it from every angle, including in particular Your Grace's weighty opinion and I very much regret to have to inform Your Grace that we cannot see our way to revise or alter our decision".

Cosgrave then goes on to tell Byrne " of the prominent and destructive part played by women in the present deplorable revolt against the definitely expressed will of the majority of the Irish People.. If she persisits in her present indefencible attitude until death, she may regret it, but she will do so of her own volition. She is receiving from our hands the greatest care and consideration and the best of food is near her should she choose to eat it.

We are at a crisis in the history of our beloved Country when we, as the Government of Ireland, directly responsible to the Irish People for our administration of their affairs and for the very security of their Nation have most reluctantly and painfully been forced to a decision which may involve the carrrying out of many stern but we hope, just actions.

Before God and Man we must take responsibility for all these actions…

Liam T. MacCosgair[36a].

One year later the General Officer Commanding the Army reported that his men had raided 23 Suffolk St at 12.35 a.m. and arrested Miss Mary MacSweeney, Mrs K. Clarke and Miss Barry. A clergyman named Fr. Perry of Maynooth was also arrested, 'due to his unpriestly abuse' of the soldiers. A large number of extremely seditious papers were found with the party. The GOC was writing to Archbishop Byrne to ascertain the exact identity of 'Fr. Perry of Maynooth'[36b]

Erskine Childers was executed at Beggar's Bush Barracks on 24 November for having a small gun, which had been a present from Michael Collins. Childers said before execution, "I was bound by honour, conscience and principle to oppose the treaty by speech, writing and action, both in peace, and, when it came to the disastrous point, war. For we hold that a nation has no right to surrender its declared and established independence, and that even a minority has a right to resist that surrender in arms"[37]. He also wrote " I die loving England and praying that she may change completely and finally towards Ireland"[38].

Cosgrave defended the execution of Childers in the Dail, saying:

"What do we want? We want simply order restored in this country. We want all arms under the control of the people who elected us and who can throw us out tomorrow if they so desire. We want that the people of this country only, shall have the right to say who are to be armed and who are not; and we are going to get the arms, if we have to search every home in the country. People who rob with arms are going to be brought before military courts and found guilty. Persons robbing at the point of a gun will be executed without discrimination. This is going to be a fair law, fairly administered and administered in the best interests of the country, for the preservation of the fabric of society. We are going to see that the rule of democracy will be maintained, no matter what the cost and no matter who the intellectuals that may fall, by reason of the assertion of that right"[39].

Erskine Childers' wife, Mrs Mary A. Childers wrote to Archbishop Byrne of Dublin on 27 November, saying that her husband's body would be released the next day. Though Childers was a Protestant, she asked permission for his remains to be received at Whitefriars St Catholic Church. While acknowledging that her husband had not spoken about becoming a Catholic, he had asked for one Catholic priest first and then another before his execution. She said that she believed his intention was clear and she wished to see it carried out She asked to meet Archbishop Byrne so that she could convince him. [39a]

It was clear that deValera himself could become a civil war casualty. Earlier in August, Cosgrave had told Collins of a plot to kill deValera who was fortunate to be jailed for a year on 15 August 1922[40]. Archbishop Byrne of Dublin, a close friend of Cosgrave's wrote to him about the reprisals saying that they were, "not only unwise but entirely unjustifiable from the moral point of view. That one man should be punished for another's crime seems to me to be absolutely unjust. Moreover, such a policy is bound to alienate many friends of the government, and it requires all the sympathy it can get"[41]. deValera had responded politically by convening a meeting of the Second Dail and forming his own shadow republican government[42].

In response to government actions, Liam Lynch, Chief of Staff of the IRA, drew up fourteen categories of persons whom they would assassinate. Among them were T.D's who supported the Treaty. The Irish Free State came officially into existence on 6 December 1922. The next day saw the assassination of one T.D, Sean Hales and wounding of another, Padraic O'Malley, both on their way to the Dail. This caused great fear among their colleagues. The army immediately sought government permission to execute four IRA prisoners. This was given after a cabinet meeting, where McGrath alone questioned the policy, and Kevin O'Higgins hesitated momentarily at the prospect of executing the friend, who had been 'best man' at his wedding.

The following morning, Dick Barrett, Liam Mellows, Joe McKelvey, and Rory O'Connor were handed a notice saying: "

"You....are hereby notified that, being a person taken in arms against the Government, you will be executed at 8a.m. on Friday 8th December as a reprisal for the assassination of Brigadier Sean Hales T. D. in Dublin on the 7th December, on his way to a meeting of Dail Eireann, and as a solemn warning to those associated with you who are engaged in a conspiracy of assassination against the representatives of the Irish people"[42a] Mulcahy as army leader signed the notice.

The four prisoners were summarily shot in Mountjoy Jail. They had been captured six months earlier in the Four Courts. This shocking and illegal act, did however stop any further attacks on politicians or civil servants and allowed the Government the opportunity to continue to function.

On 11 August Rory O'Connor had in a message from Mountjoy, begged Ernie O'Malley to, "beware of the compromising mind of the diplomat". He suggested the burning down of Provisional Government Departments, adding, "Cosgrave can be easily scared to clear out"[43]. On 10 September deValera had written to Joseph McGarrity, describing Cosgrave as a "ninny", who would be "egged on by the Church" against the anti-Treaty people[44].

In the Dail, the shootings were criticised by Tom Johnston, leader of the Labour Party and by Gavan Duffy in powerful speeches[45]. Cosgrave defended the summary executions, saying, "There is an elementary law in this case. The people who have challenged the very existence of society have put themselves outside the Constitution and only at the last moment, not thinking there was such infamy in this country, we safeguarded this Dail and the Government and the people of Ireland, from being at the mercy of these people...There is only one way to crush it and show them that terror will be struck into them". The Dail voted approval by 39 votes to 14. T.D Williams wrote that, "Cosgrave regretted, more perhaps, than some of them, the harsher aspects of the civil war, including for example the precipitate execution of Rory O'Connor and his comrades"[46]. The hierarchy were most critical of this reprisal. Archbishop Byrne had unsuccessfully intervened with Cosgrave to have the decision reconsidered. Tom Garvin writes, "WT Cosgrave, O'Higgins and Mulcahy were unusual in being unconditional democrats, and they killed people for the nascent Irish democracy that they saw as menaced by the anti-Treatyites"[46a].

On 20 December 1922, Kevin O'Higgins wrote to Archbishop Byrne telling him that on the morning of 10 December, a priest saying Mass at Mount Argus asked the congregation to "pray for the soul of Sean Hales T. D., whom the CID murdered, to give the government an excuse to murder the men who are fighting for the Republic". O'Higgins did not seek any intervention from the Archbishop, but wished him to know of the incident[46b]

Though several other reprisals, including murders, did occur to family members of the government, no further elected representatives were killed. However the country remained in a chaotic state, without law or order, despite the advent of the unarmed civic guard on 22 February 1922 under Michael Staines, a pro -Treaty T.D. It concentrated on civil matters feeling that the IRA activity was a matter for the national army. Groups of young IRA roamed the countryside, raiding banks, burning out their enemies. Cosgrave's own home at Templeogue, was burned on 13 January 1923. His uncle Patrick was murdered at the family home in James St. Churchill wrote to him saying, "It is indeed a hard service that is now exacted from those who are rebuilding the Irish State and Nation, and defending its authority and freedoms" [47]. O'Higgins' father was murdered. WT lived at Government buildings or at the Curragh Military Camp. Members of the Government felt that the army needed a freer hand to deal with the insurgents. Some were critical of the army for not being tough enough with more executions. This put pressure on Mulcahy from the 'civilians', particularly from O'Higgins and Hogan, who suspected that Mulcahy might still, after Collins, hope for a reconciliation with the Republicans. The government generally began to feel that if it did not destroy the opposition, the people would withdraw support and possibly favour the Irregulars.

COSGRAVE TALKS TOUGH

In late January, Cosgrave contacted Mulcahy with a document from the government law officer on the matter of 'Revolt Against the Constitutional Authority'[48]. Cosgrave told a neutral IRA group led by Donal Hannigan and MJ Burke on 27 Feb. "I am coming to the conclusion that if we are to exercise clemency at any time – it can only be of use to us when the irregulars crave it"[40]. He added, "I am not going to hesitate if the country is going to live, and if we have to exterminate ten thousand Republicans, the three million of our people is greater than this ten thousand"[50]. He was of the view, as was Mulcahy, that the civil war was provoked by deValera. He added that the civil war had meant that there was almost no hope that the North would come into the Free State. When the Free State came into official being on 6 December 1922, Cosgrave acknowledged the honourable manner in which the British had dealt with the Provisional Government, since the signing of the Treaty. He knew that the Northern Parliament was to meet soon. He invited it to opt into the Free State, as it had the right to do under the Treaty. He also added:

"On the other hand, should they decide to cut themselves off from all contact with us, we will regret very much such a decision. We will consider it both inopportune and unwise, believing, as we do, that it is bound to have disastrous reactions on the northern enterprise. Nevertheless, as they are perfectly entitled to take this course under the treaty, we are bound to respect such a decision in the event of it coming to pass". In speaking to the neutral IRA group, Cosgrave added; " You must know there is a fundamental difference between the vast majority of the Nation and those in armed hostility to the people. On behalf of the majority, we accept a free exercise of the ballot box. The people must be free to exercise judgement in elections, and armed resistance with the public will not be permitted. If there is to be peace on these terms, then the armed opposition to peace must be crushed and will shortly be entirely crushed. Irish democracy is too well founded to tolerate the imposition of a new political aristocracy. The people must be free to dispense with politicians who have rendered good service, but whose period of usefulness has for some time been eclipsed"[51].

Tom Garvin has estimated the cost of the eight-month civil war, caused by the Republicans, was the "sociological equivalent of £6,000 million in today's values"[52]. He adds that the Protestants suffered most proportionately.

Proportional Representation was introduced to ensure they would be represented in the Dail. It was this enormous debt, imposed by de Valera's supporters, which was used as a stick by them over the next ten years, with which to beat and ultimately to defeat the Cosgrave government[53]. Joe Lee writes that despite the debts, Ireland was a relatively modernised society. Ireland's standard of living was about average for Western Europe, though about 2/3 that of Britain. He says that this was based on large emigration and a late marriage rate, and rural inheritance modes.[54]. He comments " The manner in which the Cosgrave team performed, was quite remarkable. Apparently a fourth or fifth team, they played resolutely, as far as State building was concerned, as a First Team[55].

In February 1923 Joseph MacBride, a pro-Treaty T. D., leading IRB man in Mayo, and brother of Major MacBride, travelled from his home in Westport to Achill. The general area from Achill to Belmullet was still in the control of the 5th Brigade, 4th Western Division IRA. While crossing the bridge at Achill Sound onto the island, he was challenged by an armed IRA volunteer and arrested. When his identity was confirmed, he was taken further into the island, to Keem. There, word went round about his capture. A local priest, Fr. Prendergast got permission to take the prisoner to his house for dinner. A crowd gathered and a commotion arose. During this MacBride escaped[56]. As late as 1932 the IRA carried out an investigation as to who was responsible for the matter[57].

During that same month of February 1923, an incident occurred which was later revealed, by the lady involved, to have been part of a plan to kidnap President Cosgrave himself. The Irish Independent of 9 January 1923 carried an official report from the army GHQ, headed, "Arrests in County Dublin". It said that on Sunday, "troops proceeded to Loughlinstown and arrested four men found in charge of a motor car at the roadside. A fourth man and a woman named Miss Comerford, who comes from the city, and who were about to join the party were also taken into custody. Miss Comerford had a revolver in her possession. While being removed to Dublin, Miss Comerford made an unsuccessful attempt to escape by jumping out of the car". The man with Maire Comerford was Patrick McGrath. Their car had broken down and they tried to get a lift in a passing taxi. When they stopped the taxi, they saw that it had a passenger, Min Mulcahy. She recognised them and became suspicious, when they declined to join her. She reported her suspicions at the next police road-block, resulting in the army action[58].

The same days newspaper illustrates vividly the shocking state of disorder prevailing throughout the country. The same page that reports above arrests, also carried headers which read:

'Five Soldiers Charged with Acts of Treachery Executed', 'Items of Fighting from around the Country', 'Houses Burned', 'Outrages Repudiated', 'Troops Ambushed', 'Labour and the Executions', 'An Ambush in Offaly', 'Still Found after Sniping', 'Column Captures', 'Alarms in Middleton', 'Historic Mansion Burned', 'Raid on T.D's House',

MONSIGNOR LUZIO

In April of 1923 an unusual visitor to Ireland named Monsignor Salvatore Luzio, arrived. The purpose of his journey was to bring peace to the country. However his mission arose through a variety of Vatican and anti-Treaty Irish clergy in Rome. Monsignor Hagan, Rector of the Irish College there, and his deputy Fr. Cronin were very actively against the Treaty. Sean MacBride had worked as a secretary to deValera for a period in the 1920's. Together they visited Rome to meet with Monsignor Hagan at the Irish College. Hagan advised deValera to set up a political party and seek political power[59]. Hagan and others persuaded the Secretary of State, Cardinal Gaspari, to send a papal delegate to Ireland. The Vatican, which knew that the Free State was keen to establish an international status, was also interested in exploring the possibility of a permanent Vatican delegate in Ireland. Cardinal MacRory had also requested Gaspari to send a delegate.

Archbishop Byrne of Dublin, Cosgrave's close friend, did not favour the mission, believing that it might make the situation worse. When Luzio arrived, he went immediately to Armagh to see MacRory. He also met deValera, who was sympathetic, but felt that it was " a bad time for us". Luzio met a Dublin Sinn Fein peace group and let it be known that he was willing to intervene in the interests of peace. This angered the government. Cosgrave met him, but purely as a matter of courtesy and did not engage on any substantative talks. Luzio did not receive any assistance from the bishops, who resented his presence in the country. A *Freeman's Journal* editorial criticised him for not having produced any credentials. It then received a letter from MacRory, with a copy of Luzio's credentials signed by Cardinal Gaspari, dated 9 March 1923 The *Freeman's* criticised the fact that Luzio had been in the country one month and the government had to wait to see his credentials in the newspaper. At that point, the Government had called on the Vatican to withdraw Luzio. He then sought an interview with Cosgrave, who through Desmond Fitzgerald asked was it an official or unofficial meeting, he requested. When Luzio replied that it was an unofficial one, Cosgrave refused to meet him.

This was an embarrassing episode all round. As deValera had said at the outset, the mission was badly timed, as it was then clear to most people, that the civil war was in its last days. Cosgrave was very interested in the idea of establishing diplomatic relations with the Vatican. But he was acutely aware of the opposition of the bishops, and particularly Archbishop Byrne. Cosgrave would have to bide his time before he was able to move in that direction. Dermot Keogh says that Luzio reported that he had gone to Ireland to bring about peace, with the help of the bishops and found that he, "had to deal with twenty six Popes"[60].

Very gradually the army broke up and defeated the IRA, imprisoning thousands. On 1 July 1923 there were 11,000 prisoners. The IRA had held a meeting of their top commanders on 23 March, when Tom Barry proposed ending the war, but the motion was defeated by 6 votes to 5 by the vote of the Chairman, Liam Lynch, the IRA leader.

But in the course of an encirclement by National Army troops on 10 April, Lynch was killed. Ten days later the IRA commanders met again, and this time, agreed to end the fighting. Soundings were sent to the Government about a cessation. However only an unconditional surrender was acceptable.

SENATORS JAMESON & DOUGLAS

At that very time, on 23 April, deValera himself was putting out peace feelers to Cosgrave. Senator James Douglas received messages that a very important man wished to meet him. Movement around Dublin could be quite dangerous, as the army was vigorously seeking to apprehend all anti-Treatyites, including deValera. However Doughlas decided to allow himself to be taken to this meeting at an unspecified location.. He was not surprised to find deValera waiting to see him. deValera said that he and his colleagues thought that the civil war should be ended. He wanted to meet Cosgrave to that end. He was not prepared to meet O'Higgins. Douglas said that he would need somebody else to join him in the mission. deValera suggested Senator Andrew Jameson and this was agreed. However later in the conversation deValera appeared to change his mind and asked Douglas to forget all about their conversation and not to tell Cosgrave about it. However Douglas said it was his duty to inform Cosgrave. The latter was ill at home and Douglas did not see him for some days. In the meantime Douglas received another message that deValera wished to see him again. Doughlas then sought to get a most reluctant Senator Jameson, to join him. However Jameson assented, on condition that they sought Cosgrave's consent, and acted purely as intermediaries. Cosgrave told the Senators that he could not guarantee that they would not be followed or vouch for their safety or immunity to arrest.

On Monday 30 April 30 Senators Douglas and Jameson received letters marked 'confidential' from deValera. He asked them to meet him to discuss moves to an immediate end of the war. They replied that they could not discuss matters with him, but would act as intermediaries. deValera relied that that was his intention. When they had arrived next evening at the nominated address and were being welcomed by deValera, an army lorry pulled up outside. deValera went pale and said he realised that they were not responsible. While the three men waited apprehensively, a solider emerged from the lorry and went into the house next door. He came out within a few minutes and got into the lorry and it drove away. deValera requested a conference with government members, which he would attend alone or with other colleagues to discuss his proclamation published on 28 April. The Senators reported to Cosgrave on Wednesday 2 May. He said he would consult the Executive Council. On the Thursday Jameson met with Cosgrave and two other ministers. Jameson and Douglas were authorised to meet with deValera and tell him that personal negotiations were inadvisable. They were also to inform him that the government would not then negotiate on the Oath in the Constitution, with the British government. Jameson also received a document from Cosgrave for deValera, indicating the fundamental conditions for any agreement, which were:

All political action within the country should be based on a recognition by every party in the State of the following principles of order:—

(a) That all political issues whether now existing or in the future arising, shall be decided by the majority vote of the elected representatives of the people:

(b) As a corollary to (a) that the people are entitled to have all lethal weapons within the country, in the effective custody or control of the Executive Government, responsible to the people through their representatives.

The acceptance of these principles and practical compliance with (b) by the surrender of arms to be the preliminary condition for the release of prisoners, who shall be required to subscribe individually to (a) and (b).

Signed in acceptance of the foregoing principles this.................day of May, 1923.

....

Witness..............................

The Senators were instructed to tell de Valera that:

(1) Military action against him and his followers would cease when the arms held by them were delivered into the effectual custody of the Free State Executive authorities. The arrangements for the delivery of the arms and the place of their deposit would be made with as much consideration as possible for the feelings of those concerned.

(2) Prisoners to be released on the satisfactory fulfilment of (1) and the signature of each prisoner before release to the conditions of the document above mentioned.

(3) The Free State Government would keep a clear field for Mr. de Valera and his followers to enable them to canvass for the votes of the people at the next election, provided they undertook to adhere strictly to constitutional action.

The Government also wanted to know the names of the leaders for whom he could speak and what proportion of rank and file, and prisoners, would follow his instructions. The Senators saw de Valera again that same evening Thursday 3 May and conveyed their messages. He undertook to come back to them in a few days. Douglas met de Valera on the Saturday and he promised to have a written reply for the government on the Monday. They both met him on the Monday. The document he produced was a lengthy one and he undertook to redraft it and deliver it to the Bank of Ireland the next morning. This arrived, but remained a lengthy document, which is published in Dorothy McArdle's volume[61].

The government considered it and replied to Jameson on 8 May.

It found de Valera's document long and wordy, inviting debate where none was possible, as they were preparing for an early election. They insisted that they must control all arms and had made generous arrangements for their delivery. Once that was done prisoners would be released. They reiterated that their conditions, already specified, cannot and would not be departed from. No further communication with deValera would be entertained except for his acceptance of the terms stated. The letter was signed, LIAM MACCOSGAIR.

The Senators wrote immediately to deValera. He replied next day, 9 May, terminating matters, saying that, "Mr. Cosgrave's reply disappointed me not a little"[62].

Frank Aiken, chief of staff, ordered the IRA to dump arms, and on 24 May, and deValera issued his statement, "Soldiers of Liberty! Legion of the Rearguard. Your force of arms military victory must be allowed to rest for the moment with those who have destroyed the Republic can no longer defend the Republic successfully. Other means must be sought to safeguard the nation's right".

DeValera had conveyed to Cosgrave that the oath of allegiance would be their main difficulty in entering the political process fully. An informal message appears to have been sent to the IRA that the courts would not pursue them for acts of theft or murder committed between 6 December 1922 and 27 April 1923 [63].

The Public Safety Act, legalising internment, was in the process of being enacted and would pass all stages by 26 July.

W.T. Cosgrave between Eoin MacNeill and J.J.Walsh
at the funeral of Michael Collins.

Cosgrave continually received appeals from Archbishop Byrne on his concern about imprisonments, hunger strikers and executions. Cosgrave wrote to him on 28 May 1923 about the mass hunger strikes then taking place. The letter is again indicative that though he would always welcome the advice of his friend, Dr. Byrne, Cosgrave and his Government were their own men and would do as they felt best.

He wrote:

Saorstat Eireann.
Oifig an Uachtarain
(The President's Office),
Sraid Mhuirbhean Uach,
(Upper Merrion St),
Baile Atha Claith
(Dublin).
28.5.23.

Your Grace,

We had this matter of the hunger strikes under consideration during the week and definitely came to the conclusion that we could not give way on it.

This view is so firmly fixed in our minds that I believe each minister would prefer – in full conscience - to leave public life rather than yield.

There was some reason for releasing persons on hunger strike before the passing of the Public Safety Act – but these reasons do not now exist, as they are ruled by law.

I would like to be convinced that there had been a change of heart as well as label in this matter of armed men versus constitutional agitation. The documents we find disclose not opposition to the Government but what is a prime consideration - as to the Free State itself.

I would be sorry to see or hear of any deaths from a hunger strike. But as between deaths from hunger strikes and releases, I should say on my own account should a single man man be released the Government of this country will have an impossible task if the weapon of hunger strike is to be regarded as proof against the law of the State.

I shall be in the office tomorrow morning at 10.30 a.m. should your Grace wish further to communicate with me on this matter.

I am my Archbishop
Ever Your obedient Servant
Liam T. MacCosgair.

P.S. Our O.C's in the prisons and internment camps report today that in their view the end of the hunger strike is in prospect. I myself think there will be some casualties, which I think would have the contrary affect to that expressed by Your Grace.

L. T. MacC[63a].

On 26 July the Public Safety Act passed into law, legalising internment.

The violence used during the civil war was brutal, often more so by the national army than by the irregulars. However overall participation was confined to a small minority of the population. No social or economic revolution was involved. The British Land Acts had created a conservative proprietorial peasant class. Those who fought each other had far more in common than their divisions. Yet that short, sharp, civil war, has defined Irish political society into the 21st century.

Shortly before the August General Election, Cosgrave unveiled a forty-foot cross on Leinster Lawn, commemorating the first anniversary of the deaths of Griffith and Collins. This was to become an annual official event, though with ever decreasing government support, up to 1932. Thereafter the deteriorating structure became an object of political infighting until the 1950's.

GENERAL ELECTION AUGUST 1923

The anti-Treaty people were allowed to run in the election under the Sinn Fein mantle. Cosgrave expected that an early election, which did not have to be held until December 1923, would further demoralise the republicans. deValera made a statement that was designed to satisfy all his disparate supporters, including those who might consider taking the oath, saying: "It is not the intention of the republican Government or Army Executive to renew the war in the autumn or after the election - We intend to devote ourselves to social reform and education, and to develop the economic and material strength of the nation. If the present conditions of suppression continue, the elected republican members will all refuse to take any oath of allegiance to the King of England, will meet apart and act together as a separate body working along Sinn Fein lines, for the honour and welfare of our country"[64]. The Government did not lessen its action against republicans. At an election meeting in Ennis on 15 August deValera himself was arrested.

For the government, Cosgrave's emphasised his own interest in housing in the election manifesto. New judicial, educational and poor law reforms were promised. Dail bonds would be honoured and the Boundary Commission considered.

During this election WT became the first Irish politician to take to the air during a campaign. He was flown in an Air Corps plane, piloted by Col. Charles Russell, from Cork to Carlow and from Carlow to Dublin[65].

The election results came as a rude shock to Cosgrave and the pro-Treaty people. It was also a financial disaster for the party, which had great difficulty clearing its debts. The republicans understandably believed that their ultimate success was only a short time hence. The franchise had been extended to women over twenty-one since the 1918 vote. This increased the electorate from 1.37 million to 1.72 million. Cumann na nGaedheal increased its vote from 245,000 to 409,000 (39%): but Sinn Fein increased its vote from 135,00 to 290,00 (27.6%): Labour's vote dropped from its 1922 vote and it lost two T.D's. Independents vote increased from 115,00 to 220,000 (21%). Cosgrave had 63 T.D's, DeValera 44, in a 153 Parliament. The Government did not come under any Dail pressure, as Sinn Fein's 44 members did not take their seats.

The detailed results were:

Party	% of vote	Seats won
Cuman na nGaedheal	39	63
Sinn Fein	27	44
Labour	11	14
Farmers	12	15
Independents	11	17

When the Third Dail met on 19 September 1923, Cosgrave became President of the Dail, and announced his cabinet:

Vice-President, Minister for Home Affairs; Kevin O'Higgins.

Minister for Finance; Ernest Blythe.

Minister for Industry and Commerce; Joseph McGrath.

Minister for Education; John (Eoin) MacNeill.

Minister for External Affairs; Desmond Fitzgerald.

Minister for Defence; Richard Mulcahy.

Ministers not Members of the Executive Council.

Minister for Agriculture; Patrick Hogan.

Minister for Local Government; James A Burke.

Postmaster-General; James J. Walsh.

Minister for Fisheries; Finian Lynch

Cosgrave described the Third Dail as being a synthesis of the Dail tradition and the legacy of the Treaty, and deriving its legitimacy from both sources[66].

As he addressed the Dail, in a State of the Nation style, he reviewed the past year's events, giving his view of what had transpired since the treaty negotiations. He began by clarifying that the terms signed by the plenipotentiaries were not those, which had been earlier rejected by the cabinet, and which Griffith had pledged not to sign without first returning to the Dail Cabinet. He said that Griffith told him in London in June 1922, that deValera had said to him in November 1921, previous to the Cabinet considering the terms forwarded by the British, that it was a grave responsibility, to turn down that instrument without consulting the people.

Cosgrave added that Griffith kept his word, did not sign that agreement, returned with Collins to London. Negotiations were broken off, resumed and material concessions gained. Then they signed, what was a new instrument. Cosgrave claimed that deValera said there was a constitutional way of settling our difficulties, but when the constitutional decision went against him, " more elaborate designs were engineered against the Nation". He gave details of a convention of disaffected army personnel the previous March, which had planned to assume power.

Cosgrave outlined how the Dail regularised the Treaty, and took over administrative control from the departing British. Irish troops occupied Dublin Castle. He then outlined how in Collins' papers, it was stated how deValera had been invited to take part in the Interim Government, without prejudice to his right to oppose the Treaty at the election., so as to present a united front before the world. The Ard Fheis had agreed to postpone the election, yet when it was held, the anti-Treaty forces harassed those for the Treaty, including President Griffith, who risked his life at the time. He related how Collins, the most hunted man in Ireland by the British, during the late war, also encountered harassment, including armed opposition at meetings. Cosgrave said the protests by the anti Treaty party were few and feeble, lacking moral courage.

When a peaceful arrangement was agreed with Ulster, the Irregulars attacked the trains and organised the Belfast boycott.

He said that the Fours Courts had been handed over by the British and was used to administer funds of orphans, widows and the insane. Documents important to the life of the nation were stored there. The Record Office was of inestimable intrinsic value; the only Brehon Decree in existence was housed there. Though, those who occupied it were informed of same, they ignored it, despite the government continuing to offer a peaceful solution, provided that the Treaty was secured. It appeared that their opponents wanted a British re-occupation to occur. On 15 June Rory O'Connor and Ernie O'Malley sent a message to the Minister of Defence from the Four Courts, saying that they were ending all talks to reunite the army. They would maintain the Republic against British aggression. On 18 June the occupiers of the Four Courts seized munitions from the Curragh. On 18th June, Rory O'Connor, Ernest O'Malley, and Thomas Barry, with an armoured Lancia car, and a force of Irregulars from the Four Courts, dispossessed the armed Civic Guard at the Cross at Kildare, informing them, "that they had declared war on England, and they asked the Civic Guards "to come along with them". General Ginger O' Connell, was kidnapped and taken prisoner to the Four Courts. … An ultimatum was sent to the Four Courts, and military operations were begun against those who defied the authority. The Irregular forces could have withdrawn from the Four Courts, bowing to superior force, and still maintained, should it be so desired, an attitude of opposition on constitutional lines to the Government's policy, he declared.

Cosgrave continued, "If peace be made now it must be on well defined lines: it must be a constitutional peace. There must not, and will not, be an armed body in the community without the sanction of Parliament, and Parliament must have control of all arms, and an armed opposition to its will cannot be permitted. There must be no misunderstanding about that. We do not contemplate, and never said we would fire the last shot to consolidate the supremacy of Parliament. If those in arms think that the Government fears to assert the authority of Parliament, they are mistaken. Members of the Government may fall in that task which it is their duty to carry out, and others will take their place and accept the same responsibility".

He decried the destruction of so many houses, roads, piers, bridges, railways, signal boxes, water works, mansions, with such a consequent economic loss to the country. He said 'The Book of Lismore' and the 'Crozier of St Patrick', were saved by chance.

He declared that the truce with England held and that the armed minority would be defeated, saying that an Irishman's word of honour is dearer than his life. He demanded clear thinking on this subject of peace; they were the custodians of the rights of the people and would not hesitate to shoulder them. "We are willing to come to a peaceful understanding with those in arms, but it must be on a definite basis. We want peace with those in arms and with England, on the terms agreed to by the country.... The National Army is prepared to pay the price, and so are we"

He ended by saying that the previous December saw the country blossom in many aspects. However, the armed minority had caused chaos. He predicted further advances. "The Army and Police Force must be efficient; the Courts must command the confidence of the people. The Nation is still full of vigour and is conscious that a mere handful of violent persons is for the moment standing athwart its upward and onward march towards the achievement of its highest hopes"[67].

Problems continued to arise on almost every front. In the North many nationalists were imprisoned or interned, some on the ship Argenta moored in Larne harbour. Cosgrave was being pressed for economic assistance for them and their families, and being berated by republicans, Mary MacSweeney to the fore, for 'abandoning' them[68]. In October 1923 Cosgrave responded saying, " the only way out of this mess is to get a list of the men and a list of dependents. Some examination of the latter ought to be possible. If correctly vouched, we should make some grant out of the Special Fund and make representations to the British regarding the onerous conditions imposed on us"[69].

As Joe Lee has written, the civil war was really about majority right and divine right, as to whether the Irish people had the right to choose their own government or have a dictatorship foisted on them. He wrote, "The aspiring military dictators were crushed"[70]

Cosgrave later said that "the worst moments had been in February" when some Senators had " shown a tendency to buckle, and had come to tell him that he must make terms with deValera". He realised that the latter hoped to bring about negotiations, " which will enable him to make a dignified exit from his present position, but we are not going to help anybody in that way".[71]

Cosgrave set up a special committee in 1923, to find a permanent home for the Oireacthas. It considered the Bank of Ireland at College Green, Dublin Castle, the Royal Hospital at Kilmainham, which Cosgrave himself favoured. WB Yeats felt that it would be too far from the city centre. He felt that people coming to the capital would expect to find the Oireachtas situated there. In the end, the committee recommended that the Oireachtas remain at the premises of the Royal Dublin Society in Leinster House, which had been loaned to the government in 1922. This was agreed on the proviso, that the Royal Dublin Society could be accommodated elsewhere.

The Four Courts Dublin, burning under shellfire, June 1922.

CHAPTER TEN

ARMY MUTINY 1923 - 4

One inevitable problem occurred soon after hostilities abated. The size of the national army, which had been built up quickly to around 60,000 members, could not be sustained. Demobilisation had to occur, sooner rather than later. The old tensions between the militarists and the civilians came to the fore. Early on, the government had to divert the army into civilian duties, enforcing court rulings, collecting rates and making restitution. This politicised the army to some extent, though GHQ ordered the army to stay out of politics. The 'Old IRA' was set up in January 1923 by a group of officers who had been loyal to Collins. General Liam Tobin and Colonel CF D'Alton were leaders among them. These were shunned by GHQ and excluded from the vital Intelligence Unit, as well as the IRB. These blamed Mulcahy for this, believing him to be head of the IRB. Joe Lee wrote that Mulcahy, "increasingly succumbed to the temptation to use a revitalised IRB against the 'Old IRA"[1]. The latter took their dissatisfaction to the government, where O'Higgins in particular, listened to them. Mulcahy felt that the army could not tolerate this insubordination, and proceeded with the agreed policy of demobilization. The 'Old IRA' group wrote formally to Cosgrave and Mulcahy in June 1923, a sensitive time for the Government with the election pending. Cosgrave feared that this group might 'go political'. The Minister for Industry and Commerce, Joe McGrath, backed them in their demand for an inquiry on how the demobilization was being managed. Mulcahy, as Commander-in-Chief and Minister for Defence, was outraged that his cabinet colleagues would allow these officers a forum to utter such treachery in front of him and walked out of the meeting[2]. He was later inveigled to meet them again, as the election loomed. He emphasised to them that the army had to change, and all would be done fairly. He was anxious not to create a split in the army, which had held together against the IRA. After the election, several hundred officers were to be discharged, after due internal army process. The 'Old IRA' objected and asked for certain officers to be retained. Tension was raised particularly at the Curragh, where on 9 November 1923, seven officers refused to accept their demobilisation papers. The Government, to Mulcahy's great annoyance, set up a cabinet committee to hear complaints. In doing this they were politicising the matter of army organisation and discipline. An underlying notion was that the 'Old IRA' was loyal to the Republic only. Joe McGrath resigned from the government appointed committee, after some officers, whose case he wanted brought before the committee, were demobilized. Cosgrave tried to persuade McGrath to return to the cabinet committee, assuring him that the committee would have the power to do as he wished[3]. Army GHQ learned that the 'Old IRA' planned to seize arms and hold some barracks. Mulcahy informed Cosgrave and McGrath, and was reassured by them both, that demobilisation remained clear government policy. Maryann Gialaanella Valiulis writes that Mulcahy "erred in trusting Cosgrave and McGrath"[4] GHQ tried to rein in the officers concerned. On 6 March 1924 the 'Old IRA' issued an ultimatum to Cosgrave:

"Sir,

On behalf of the IRA organisation, we have been instructed to present the following ultimatum to the government of Saorstat Eireann.

The IRA only accepted the Treaty as a means of achieving its objects, namely to secure and maintain a Republican form of government in this country...It is our considered opinion that your government has not these objects in view and that their policy is not reconcilable with the Irish people's acceptance of the Treaty....We demand a conference with representatives of your government to discuss our interpretation of the treaty on the following conditions:

(a)   The Removal of the Army Council.

(b)   The immediate suspension of Army demobilisation and reorganisation.

Our organisation fully realises the seriousness of the action that we are compelled to take, but we can no longer be party to the treachery which threatens to destroy the aspirations of the nation[5].

In the Dail, on 7 March, Cosgrave described the letter as, "a challenge to the democratic foundation of the State, to the very basis of parliamentary representation and of responsible government. This government has never discussed the question of politics with army officers" McGrath sided with the 'Old IRA' and resigned from cabinet. Tobin and d'Alton were arrested[6]. The cabinet assigned Eoin O'Duffy, head of the Gardai, as General Officer Commanding in the army, much to Mulcahy's chagrin, though they had personal and ideological ties through the IRB. Over ninety officers resigned, with fourteen deserting

However, almost inexplicably, a total fudge was then to ensue, with the government accepting that the officers were simply angry with army authority. At a meeting of the Cumann na nGaedheal parliamentary party on 11 March, the matter was discussed at length, with most ministers present. McGrath convinced the meeting to allow him to induce the 'mutineers' to undo as far as they can, the mischief created by their actions'. There was little sympathy for the Army within the party and Mulcahy, strangely, did not attempt to make any major intervention during this meeting. McGrath's claim was that Mulcahy and the senior army staff had allowed the old IRB secret society element, to dominate the army officer corps, and that the 'mutineers' were reacting to that in organising their own group. The Government realised that if the matter was ventilated in the Dail, it could lose a vote on the matter and might have to resign.

Cabinet 1923 - 4,
L to R: R, Mulcahy, E. MacNeill, D. O'Hegarty, H. Kennedy, W.T. Cosgrave,
E. Blythe, D. Fitzgerald, K. O'Higgins.

The government bought into McGrath's explanation, and on 12 March, the day after the party meeting, Cosgrave ordered the army to cease searching for mutineers, and allow for their return to the army. He also agreed to McGrath's suggestion that an inquiry into the army be held. The 'mutineers' wrote to the government apologising for their earlier ultimatum. In the Dail, O'Higgins surprisingly accepted the 'mutineers' change of heart, declaring that, " It is all opportunism, if you wish, but in the handling of national affairs, and in the handling of very delicate situations, there must needs be opportunism"[7].

The *Irish Times* was not impressed, writing, "Mutiny is mutiny, and with all respect for Kevin O'Higgins, twenty four hours cannot change it into a merely frank expression of military discontent, not even twenty four hours of treatment in the secret alembic of the Cumann na nGaedheal"[8].

One of Cosgrave's strategic departures from the scene of government occurred at this juncture, as he took to his bed for a fortnight. This allowed O'Higgins to take control of the Executive. Mulcahy's wife, Min, later recalled that Mrs Cosgrave visited her in Rathmines during this episode and said, "O'Higgins is terrible…he wants Willie to resign"[9].

However on 18 March Cosgrave summoned O'Duffy and Mulcahy, to his bedside to instruct them to ensure an amicable resolution of the crisis[10].

When the army authorities discovered that an 'Old IRA' meeting was being held on 19 March in Devlin's public house in Dublin, they suspected that a coup d'etat was in train. Mulcahy and the Adjutant General, Gearoid O'Sullivan, acting on their own authority, organised the arrest of the eleven officers present and confiscated their weapons. With the information available to them, had Mulcahy and his staff ignored the meeting, they would have been derelict in their duties[11]. The Cabinet met the next morning and with Cosgrave, absent through illness or otherwise, Kevin O'Higgins acted as President. Mulcahy defended the action of the army against mutinous officers, but his colleagues saw the action as threatening the peace of the country, and unauthorised, if not treasonable. McGrath's defence of the mutinous officers swayed the Cabinet. Mulcahy made little attempt to defend his and the army's action and left the meeting[12].

The cabinet, subject to Cosgrave's approval, sought the resignation of the top army brass on the army council, and Mulcahy's removal from the Ministry of Defence. When O'Higgins conveyed the decision on the army council to Mulcahy, he resigned in protest, before O'Higgins was able to inform him that he was also to be removed from cabinet.

Despite Cosgrave's absence, Blythe and MacNeill were sent to his home to get him to agree with the demand for Mulcahy's resignation[13]. An army inquiry under Judge J. Creed Meredith, took place within a few weeks. When it reported on 24 June 1924, the military and political situation had calmed immeasurably. Mulcahy introduced a motion in the Dail claiming, "as contrary to the best interests of the State, the ill-considered action of the Executive Council". McGrath claimed the row was between the 'Old IRA' group and the IRB. Speaking in the Dail on the matter, Cosgrave said very pragmatically, "that particular incident which occurred three months ago is an incident which in my opinion, ought to be dead and buried and ought not to be resurrected, no matter what its influence was, either at that time or now"[14].

Though the loyal army officers, and Mulcahy, were treated harshly, the end result was that it was clear that civil government then held sway. Both Mulcahy and McGrath were out of cabinet. O'Higgins was glad to see Mulcahy depart as he always suspected that Mulcahy still hankered after a rapprochement with the IRA, after Collins, within the IRB ambit[15]. For Mulcahy as for Collins, the Treaty was to be a stepping-stone. O'Higgins was quite happy to be within the Commonwealth and had little sympathy with the older generation, which would have included the President, to a large extent. The mutinous army officers, who threatened mass resignations, were not allowed back into the army and Joe McGrath departed to form his own a ginger group. The brash new civilian pragmatists purged the old IRB nationalist element in the army and the Government, with WT Cosgrave still acting as Chairman to O'Higgin's increasing persona.

There is little doubt that O'Higgin's headlong and reckless pursuit of Mulcahy and the army council could have produced a disastrous outcome, were it not for the latter's democratic acceptance of the government's decisions. WT Cosgrave must share some responsibility in the matter. However, despite being kept fully informed by Mulcahy, he realised that O'Higgins had the majority cabinet support, particularly of Hogan and Blythe. O'Higgins had McGrath succeeded in cabinet by his close friend, Patrick McGilligan. Cosgrave, however, stymied O'Higgin's ambition to become Minister for Defence by taking on the role himself and holding it for eight months[16]. He succeeded in removing O'Duffy from the army within a short period. It would be 1927, before Cosgrave brought Mulcahy back into cabinet, and then his hand was forced to a certain extent by Mulcahy's strong position within Cumann na nGaedheal. When the new Minister for Defence, Peter Hughes, came to be appointed in November, he was described as a mere "green-grocer from Dundalk"[17]. His appointment was seen as a rebuff to the old guard and another victory for O'Higgins in cabinet.

Ferghal McGarry raises the possibility that O'Duffy secretly instigated the public house arrests to discredit the Army Council. McGarry argues that O'Duffy knew of, and authorised the arrests. He points out that shortly after the 'army mutiny', O'Duffy promoted the two arresting officers, Cronin and MacNeill, without asking Cosgrave's permission. He makes the point that both O'Higgins and O'Duffy were both highly ambitious men with a keen sense of their own capabilities. At that time they were working in tandem[18].

Discontent in Cumann na nGaedheal crystallised in a new group called the National Group, consisting of some T.D's, who were against the elite Treatyites in the government. The Standing Committee of the party was anxious to placate them, as well as McGrath's Old IRA group. Cosgrave as usual was placatory. He said: "it would be well if the actual work done by the government were known in detail by members of the Organisation. Disagreements in a political party, representative of all sections, were inevitable and they ought to be faced and thrashed out. A Government, like a family, will have its differences, but the Government was not the slave of the Civil Servants. He had never known a case where civil servants dominated policy"[19.] There was grave disappointment with the appointments procedures for the civil service among party activists. The Standing Committee set up a policy committee on economics, which irked Blythe. The Standing Committee also made overtures to McGrath. John Regan questions Cosgrave's probity when, later, in October, he manoeuvred with representatives of both groups. He writes that, " Cosgrave's role in the proceedings is intriguing, and his volte face between 29 September and 2 October remains unexplained"[20.] Regan sees Cosgrave possibly considering reinstating the mutineers but more importantly, he sees Cosgrave as bargaining for the unity of his party against the independence of the newly appointed Civil Service Commission. Cosgrave feared a political split, which could make Sinn Fein into the majority. Regan also has Cosgrave's manoeuvring in an attempt to force O'Higgin's resignation and the formation of a more nationalist party at the forthcoming national convention. This did not materialise and O'Higgins won out with majority cabinet support, against any negotiating with the National Group or McGrath, or any interference with the Civil Service. The civil service and the army, but especially O'Higgins, once more, were all the stronger for it. With the departure of Mulcahy and McGrath, no other ex-Sinn Fein members were ever again to attain high office in the government. Joe Lee deems Cosgrave, after Mulcahy and McGrath, the main loser in this struggle, where only Attorney General Hugh Kennedy supported him[22.]

Cosgrave's political fears were well grounded for as the National Executive policy became a mere statement of government policy, McGrath and eight of the National Group resigned their seats in the Dail on 31 Oct. Cumann na n Gaedheal lost two by-elections in November and the party faced a crisis with the nine outstanding contests to be held in March 1925. However, disaster was averted when, after much-detailed organisation and planning, the party won seven of the seats, with the Farmer's Party winning one and Sinn Fein one. However the anti-Treaty side continued to make electoral progress in percentage terms, and deValera began to think of what would happen if their abstentionist policy could be discarded.

CHAPTER ELEVEN

CUMANN nGAEDHEAL

WT Cosgrave saw his position as President of the Executive Council of the Irish Free State, as the leader of the nation first, and as a party politician second. He wanted the Dail to be a forum for all kinds of community groups and not necessarily comprised of purely rival political parties. However, in the run-up to the August 1923 general election, a General and Election Committee of his supporters was appointed to prepare for the election. It decided that a countrywide organisation was necessary. Some few deputies, along with Ernest Blythe attended and articulated the government's elitist position, as propounded by Cosgrave. However a sub-committee was given the task to draw up the objects of the new national party. A provisional convention of the new party was scheduled for 7 December at Oliver Gogarty's house at 5 Parnell Square. Thirty-eight deputies, including members of the cabinet and Cosgrave, attended this. Fifty-eight invited delegates represented the country. A suggestion to attempt to recapture the old Sinn Fein organisation was defeated. The name for the new party proved contentious. The elite wanted An Cumann Naisiunta or the National Party. But the majority favoured Cumann na nGaedheal. This linked the new party clearly with Arthur Griffith's earlier grouping of nationalist organisations, of the same name. John Regan writes that this was " to be a rare victory" for the party members[1].

Griffith had founded Cumann na nGaedheal in 1900 after his return from South Africa, to advance the cause of Ireland's national independence. It was a loose broadly based organisation; an umbrella organisation for political, cultural and social organisations. It incorporated the Celtic Literature Society, Inghinidhe na hEireann. It had no clear political policy, as Griffith disliked political organisations, believing that they "developed into tyrannies". He later developed a policy that Irish M.P.'s should withdraw from Westminster and meet in Dublin. It favoured a local courts system and a boycott of British administration. Griffith developed these ideas in his *Resurrection of Hungary* and his series of articles on the Sinn Fein Policy in the *United Irishman* during 1904.

However on 7 December 1922 at lunch-time, as two T.D's , Sean Hales and Padraig Ó'Maille were going to lunch in the Ormond hotel from the Cuman na nGaedheal meeting, they were ambushed and Hales shot dead and his companion wounded. The delegates were naturally horrified and a decision was taken not to publicise the convention. This proved very wise, when in the next morning's aftermath, four prisoners were executed in Mountjoy. A Standing Committee, with Fred Allen as Chairman, got the task of organising the new party countrywide. The elite remained almost completely aloof from this exercise. They were written to, asking what their relationship with the party was

The Standing Committee decided to hold the first public convention of Cumann na nGaedheal on 27 April 1923, at the Mansion House. It requested from Cosgrave that government ministers attend and outline their legislative programme. This was greatly resented. Meetings then took place between the Standing Committee and Cosgrave, Blythe and Mulcahy. The latter two were best disposed towards the party, with O'Higgins almost hostile. This meeting occurred only two days before the first public convention, when the constitution of the party went for ratification. The Committee asked Cosgrave for a statement of policy. He responded in a vague way:

"that the principal thing that would have to be attended to would be the Financial Adjustment and the Boundary Commission, and that he would like to ask any group that would like to come along, to take on the settlement of these two questions. That it was very important that there would be a political party, as distinct from a Farmer's or a Labour party. That only a political party could hope to get two other such parties to work in agreement and to overcome laziness and irresponsibilities, and a tendency from both employers and employees to grab too much for themselves"[2].

Addressing the 150 delegates in the Mansion House, Cosgrave was equally vague, saying that he hoped for a group, "to attract the best elements of the nation and bring home to everyone the need for a sound national organisation, which knew neither creed nor class but worked for the best interests of the people and the nation". Eoin MacNeill became party President.

When Mulcahy was co-opted to the Standing Committee, he went to Cosgrave to discuss relations between the Executive and the party. He outlined the concerns the Standing Committee had with the distance the Executive was keeping from the party. The most Cosgrave was prepared to do, to reassure the Standing Committee, was to assure Mulcahy that " all the present Ministers were standing with the Political Party"[3]. This was a telling example that the elite in government felt far removed from the operation of a political party and may not have understood its relevance. In 2005, Dr.Garret Fitzgerald commented to me that it was not until the 1960's that the party's successor, Fine Gael, took party organising seriously. It had been a major contributing factor in the continued success of Fianna Fail in the interim[4].

The objects of the party were:

1. To carry on the National Traditions.

2. To utilize the powers of Government in the hands of the Irish people as well as other forms of public activity for the fullest development of the Nation's heritage- political, cultural, and economic.

The Programme of the Party included a United Ireland, restoration of the language, development of natural resources, fostering of industry, a national housing scheme, reafforestation, roads and waterways, work schemes, land purchase and national security.

Initially, Cosgrave had assured the General and Election Committee, that election funds would be forthcoming, without identifying the source. James Burke, Minister for Local Government in 1923, has written that at a cabinet meeting[5], "When the question of finding funds to finance our campaign arose, Cosgrave announced that Mr. Andrew Jameson and certain other ex-unionists had assured him that, on condition that certain ministers would be retained, they would undertake that there would be sufficient funds available for the election. Nobody raised any objection".

The party later put out an appeal for election funds, minus WT. Cosgrave's signature, as he refused it. Little money was forthcoming and election expenses for organisers and election candidates fees were paid centrally, resulting in a large deficit for the party. It was also an early symptom of a hands-off approach by the members, where on the other side, Sinn Fein had numerous voluntary workers. Cosgrave's attitude that the Government was somehow apart and distant from the party, founded to fight elections, was common to the elite in the party. It was the reason why Cumann na nGaedheal did not become a mass party, with any popular enthusiasm among its members. It was a top - down party, without any firm foundation, or policies, except those, which appeared from the Government on an ad hoc basis. The Ministers were still understandably mired in the business of keeping the State afloat, financially and constitutionally.

After the 1923 general election, the party was badly in debt and struggled to clear it. One member of the Standing Committee identified the problem with the party thus, "Cumann na nGaedheal was a shell, not an organisation, and out of touch with what was going on. The main inducement to people for joining should be the opportunity for influencing legislation"[6]. The National Executive then sought to pull against being a mere semi-detached adjunct to the party for the convenience of the elite, and promote policy itself. It decided to call on the Government to act on the Boundary Commission, as a means of reviving the old nationalist sentiment in the party.

A good summary of Cumann na nGaedheal says it was " a classic cadre party, which first formed as a parliamentary group, around a group of local notables. Founded while in office and without winning any election, and lacking an effective opposition in the Dail until 1927, the party adopted a complacent attitude to electoral politics. Ministers such as JJ Walsh and Kevin O'Higgins shared a contempt for grass roots organisation; while party leaders such as WT Cosgrave rarely took part in canvassing. The result was that they never developed strong local organisations, instead relying on the personalities of their notables to accrue votes"[7].

In October 1923 WT suffered a major crisis when his brother, Phillip Cosgrave T.D. died shortly after attending a meeting at College Green with him. Phillip had been governor of Mountjoy prison.

Winston Churchill

David Lloyd George

CHAPTER TWELVE

BOUNDARY COMMISSION FIASCO

Article 12 of the Treaty had made provision for, "a Commission of three persons, one to be appointed by the Government of the Irish Free State, one to be appointed by the Government of Northern Ireland, and one who shall be Chairman, to be appointed by the British Government, shall determine, in accordance with the wishes of the inhabitants, so far as may be compatible with economic and geographic conditions, the boundaries between Northern Ireland and the rest of Ireland". Initially on 21 January 1922, James Craig agreed to appoint a Commissioner, in the belief that only small changes were envisaged. On hearing that the southerners were expecting large transfers to them, he dropped the idea. Frank Pakenham wrote " Collins had said to Lloyd George, apparently without contradiction, that under the Boundary Commission, the Free State would gain two counties and parts of three others. Collins had gone on to plead, not for a change in the Ulster clause, but for a definite answer from Craig"[1]. It subsequently became clear that Lloyd George had said different things to Collins and to Craig about this Article, without which, as Cosgrave later said, " there would not have been Irish signatories to the Treaty"[2].

As Joe Lee has written, "deValera, like Griffith and Collins, assumed that the Boundary Commission would so emasculate Northern Ireland that the rump would be forced into a united Ireland for economic self-preservation. All nationalists, whatever their position on the treaty, insisted on mis-interpreting the Ulster situation. They would predictably complain in due course when nobody came to rescue them for the consequences of their own proclivity for self-deception"[2a]

Ernest Blythe was deemed a suitable commissioner for the South. Kevin O'Shiel, who later succeeded him, kept a watching brief as Director of the Free State North Eastern Boundary Bureau. He prepared a detailed case on the matter[3]. It envisaged the transfer of all of Fermanagh, much of Tyrone, one third of Armagh and Derry and one quarter of Down. This would still have left 266,000 Catholics within the unionist orbit. Catholics in Belfast argued for as many of their religion to remain within the north, to bolster their overall position. O'Shiel claimed that the transfers he envisaged would be in line with the wishes of the inhabitants. O'Shiel was not optimistic about the actual commission itself and counselled caution on proceeding until the civil war was over. The accession of Bonar Law, a firm unionist supporter, as Prime Minister in July 1922 did not augur well for early movement. O'Shiel reported that, " If we are certain that impartial justice will be done, we should press the Boundary Commission for all we are worth; but if we are certain that the result will be against us, then we should work for an adjournment". On 21 April 1923 he gave the latter advice[4]. Cosgrave had been questioned about the matter in the Dail in 1922, and was very cautious in reply, saying:

"I am not in a position at present to make any announcement upon that matter. It has been the subject of consideration by the Executive Council on many occasions and also by the late Provisional Government... Even in the case of suitable persons being on a panel for selection for this position, one must have regard to the opinions of those affected in the area, and I think anybody who has any experience of meeting representatives or other persons from the six counties, will quite appreciate the advisability of considering their views upon a matter of this sort. I do not think it would be advisable to make any further statement upon that matter, until the Dáil meets again on the 3rd January".

However the pressure remained constant and finally, the government felt that it should make some movement on the matter, as public opinion and the anti-Treaty elements demanded the return of the " lost lands". On 19 July 1923 it requested the British government to move on the Commission. Cosgrave believed that his Commissioner should be a minister, a northerner and a Catholic. On 23 July, only Eoin MacNeill fitted that bill. Cosgrave met a northern delegation to hear their views. There had been 500 murders between the summers of 1920 and 1921, mainly in Belfast. Of these 80 were Crown forces, 170 Protestants and 300 Catholics. Internment and flogging became common, as Cosgrave protested to the Northern authotities[5].

The Northern authorities refused to appoint a representative to the Commission and the matter rested until August 1924, when WT Cosgrave and Ramsay MacDonald agreed that the British government would make that appointment, nominating an Orangeman JR Fisher.[5a] Thus the Boundary Commission, with MacNeill as the Free State Commissioner and Judge Feetham, an Oxford educated South African, in the chair. The Commission sat for a year and took detailed written and oral submissions. MacNeill took the terms of appointment seriously and did not communicate with Cosgrave on the process during the year, unlike JR Fisher,[5a] who kept Craig fully briefed. Judge Feetham ruled that the wishes of the inhabitants would have to be subservient to 'economic and geographical conditions'.

The Conservative Morning Post of 7 November 1925, carried details of the Commission's proposals. The minimal changes involved South Armagh going to the south and East Donegal to the north. It is probably true that Cosgrave did not envisage much gain from the Commission, tilted as it was to British control, but he had not prepared his followers for such an outcome. They were outraged and began to question the Treaty itself. Cosgrave's government came under immediate pressure in the Dail and Senate. Cosgrave summoned MacNeill to meet him on 16 November, and on 19 November MacNeill attended a meeting of the Commission in London and resigned. He had received a letter from Cosgrave, on matters, which had transpired since their meeting.

Cosgrave wrote, "I should also say that the others agree with me now without any qualification, that the best thing to do, is to retire and leave nothing undone to bring about no report" Cosgrave spoke in Emyvale Co. Monaghan, the next day and attacked the Commission, saying, "I am forced to the conclusion that they allowed themselves to be swayed in the discharge of their judicial duty, by threats and political influences which have been brought to bear on them"[6].

On 24 November Cosgrave contacted Baldwin directly, asking for an immediate meeting with Craig and Baldwin. Britain still remained fearful of a republican take-over in the south. A Conference took place at Chequers over several days, with O'Higgins speaking bitterly. Diarmaid Ferritear, quoting, from Bew, Gibson, Patterson, wrote rather prominently, that at one stage,"Cosgrave burst into tears" over the debacle[7]. This may be accurate, but it does not ring true and the source for it, is problematical. It came from Wilfred Spender, the most senior civil servant in Northern Ireland. Spender had commanded the Ulster Volunteer Force and was an Ulster supremist. In 1943 Sir William Spender admitted to John Andrews, that in relation to the employment of Catholics in the Civil Service, "he would find it a source of embarrassment if he produced any statistics or defended himself in this matter"[8]. It is worthy of note that Clare O'Halloran in dealing with this point, writes, "The incident recorded, and no doubt exaggerated, by the head of the Northern Ireland civil service, Sir William Spender"[9].

Publication of the Report would make it legally binding, so Cosgrave argued for it to be shelved. He was then in the position of trying to salvage something from the debacle. He hit on a financial measure, which would be very beneficial to the Free State, if he could convince the British to agree. The atmosphere at Chequers that weekend was very tense, with Mrs Baldwin trying to be friendly with all sides, and getting the Irish to sign the Visitor's Book. Occasionally she got signals from her husband that all was going well, but with difficulty[10].

Cosgrave's decision to accept the status quo on the border and seek financial improvements, sent the delegations back to London on the Monday to negotiate on a financial package. All the Irish travelled together and their car got a punctured tyre. As they waited by the roadside they engaged in friendly banter. Craig told his fellow passengers that now the Commission Report was buried, he would "help you get all I can to get as much as you can out of these fellows". Churchill who was recently returned to government, as Chancellor of the Exchequer, was nominated by Baldwin to preside over the protracted negotiations in London. Three days of negotiations on Article 5 of the Treaty ensued, with Churchill joined by Birkenhead and Lord Salisbury. Article 5 was concerned exclusively with finance. It said that Ireland should assume liability for the service of its public debt and payment of war pensions "in such proportions as may be fair and equitable". Cosgrave had wanted this liability waived.

Birkenhead wrote about the bi-partisanship of both Irish governments on the matter, "They both developed a friendly and competitive enthusiasm in the task of plundering us". As I stated in my study of Winston Churchill, "It was fortuitous that it was

Churchill who was leading these negotiations, for he above all British politicians, knew that financial measures could not be allowed wreck what had been achieved in Ireland". Eventually, Cosgrave agreed to accept about £5 million debt for war reparations, and the British waived annuities valued at £155 million. Craig, who was interested in getting a secure border with the South, told Churchill, "You have done the right thing in a big way"[11].

Cosgrave told the Dail that the agreement would lead to the cabinets of North and South meeting together "to remove prejudices and allay anxieties and promote better understanding". He was confident that such meetings would result "in a favourable manner upon the position of the Nationalists of the Six Counties by becoming a connecting link, instead of a wall of partition between Dublin and Belfast". The Council of Ireland element in the Treaty was dropped. Cosgrave said, "In abandoning the Council of Ireland, the Free State will lose nothing. It will gain goodwill"[12]. He told the Belfast Telegraph "I firmly believe that we have found the only solution in a very difficult situation, to which the representatives of all the governments could have subscribed. I believe the result is a constructive one, and that it will tend to foster cordial relations, a better understanding, and a greater measure of mutual respect and good will. It will remove obstacles, which have ever been a source of bitter conflict between the peoples of Northern Ireland and the Irish Free State. I want to put on the record my belief, that this solution will tend more surely and more speedily towards bringing about the ultimate political unity of the two sections of the country, than any other course that could have been adopted in the circumstances, with which we were confronted"[13]. However despite Cosgrave's hopes as expressed in the Dail, Craig and he, never met again, nor did their cabinets.

The handling of the Boundary Commission has many unanswered questions. Despite Kevin O'Shiel's optimistic advice in April 1923, that the time to move was opportune, the composition of the Commission was always going to be totally one-sided. However, some Irish government would have had to move on it. The choice of Eoin MacNeill, as commissioner, was disastrous. He was a man of integrity, who played by the rules, looking upon his role as quasi-judicial, regarding his loyalty to his fellow commissioners, rather than to his political colleagues. Geoffrey Hand writes "the evidence of correspondence during the operation of the commission is overwhelming on these points"[14]. MacNeill even stonewalled Cosgrave's firm statements, saying-

"If I use any advice of this kind, I shall of course have to communicate it to both of my colleagues. I must in the last resort act on my own judgement"[15]. He accepted the Chairman's interpretation of the relevant Article on territorial integrity and viability, when these were fundamentally flawed against him. Article 12 was political fudge from the beginning and MacNeill did not have the guile to negotiate in a necessarily effective way. Nor did he even keep his constituency briefed on what was afoot. This, in a way, may have suited Cosgrave and O'Higgins, as MacNeill became the sacrificial scapegoat to the disappointed and frustrated nation. There is evidence that MacNeill had foreseen this development, when there was a possibility that Paddy McGilligan could have become an alternate commissioner in March of 1924, on his accession to cabinet. McGilligan believed that MacNeill had decided to remain as commissioner, and become the scapegoat, rather than allow his younger friend and former election agent, to do so[16]. Another inbuilt weakness in the nationalist position, lay in the fact that northern nationalists were split on the matter. The beleaguered Catholics of Belfast were very glad that the nationalists within the Six counties, would continue to form a substantial section of the body politic. They would have regarded a four county state, as a total disaster for them

When nationalists from the North requested permission to address the Dail on the Boundary Commission, Cosgrave was reluctant even to have the request debated, least it set a precedent. He said, " An occasion may arise in the future in which some of our own citizens for whom we have a direct responsibility, may have a case if precedent has been set in respect of those for whom we only act as trustees"[17]. The Dail accepted this view almost without demur, even from those who had opposed the Boundary Agreement. Thus, as Clare O'Halloran writes, partition was by and large, ignored in the Free State press, and journals and featured mainly in political speeches at election times, as part of the official rhetoric of a Gaelic, Catholic and United Ireland. Unhappily for northern nationalists, they were left to the tender mercies of a unionist-dominated statelet. As Ronan Fanning wrote, "The achievement of sovereignty took precedence over the aspiration of unity in the minds of those who controlled the destiny of independent Ireland"[18]. Northern Ireland came more and more to be regarded as unattractive, a British colonial enclave, ruled by a bigoted people, with an apathetic minority, dependent on the south[19].

When Fianna Fail arrived in the Dail in 1927, Frank Aiken sought compensation for his neighbours in South Armagh for damage done to property between 1919-23, which had been refused by the North. Cosgrave rejected this saying that the State could not be expected to pay for property outside its jurisdiction. Aiken renewed the matter in 1929 and Cosgrave made a similar reply. He added significantly that his government repudiated any responsibility for continued armed action by the IRA in the North, "activity such as that was not much different from activity against the State here"[20]. Fianna Fail governments later adhered to this general policy.

Tom Jones wrote that Cosgrave said, "MacNeill's conduct was deplorable; he was a philosopher and had been out of touch with the feeling on the border"[21]. MacNeill himself wrote, "Personally I was glad to escape from politics and get back to my own congenial work"[22].

deValera vilified the government for having sold out to the British and he became all the more determined to enter the Dail and take control of government. The outcome of the Boundary Commission bolstered his policy, against his doubters, for taking their T.D's into the Dail, as soon as possible.

In the Dail Cosgrave lost a T. D. as Professor Magennis formed his own party, Clann Eireann. Captain Willie Redmond, a son of John Redmond, formed a party called the National League in September 1926.

Cumann na nGaedheal Poster

CHAPTER THIRTEEN

A HEALING SENATE

An attempt to gain international recognition for the Dail, led to WT Cosgrave raising a strange notion for a second chamber in March 1921. He was also thinking of course of pleasing Catholic Church authorities, but he may not have realised that the local hierarchy was adamant in keeping the Vatican as far away from their own diocesan independence, as possible. He wrote:

"The suggestion is that there should be a sort of 'Upper House' to the Dail, consisting of a Theological Board, which would decide whether any enactments of the Dail were contrary to Faith and Morals or not. There is also a suggestion that a guarantee be given to the Holy Father that the Dail will not make laws contrary to the teachings of the church, in return for which the Holy Father will be asked to recognise the Dail as a body entitled to legislate for Ireland" deValera read the 'theological proposal' and ordered the idea to be shelved[1].

However, in real life, when Cosgrave emerged as leader, the main idea behind having a second chamber was that it would be a vehicle to ensure that southern unionists could be guaranteed representation in a constituent House of the legislature, after consultation with representative persons and bodies. An agreement with these, set the number of members of the Senate at sixty. It would be composed of citizens, who had done honour to the nation through useful public service, or that they possessed special qualification or attainments, representing important aspects of the Nation's life. The first Senate was to have 30 of its members nominated by Cosgrave, with special regard for groups or parties not adequately represented in the Dail. The Dail, under proportional representation, which was introduced to guarantee Protestant representation in the Oireachtas, would elect another 30. One quarter of the Senate would be renewable every three years.

However, the powers of the Senate were restricted. It could only consider Financial Bills for 21 days, and the Dail was not bound by their views. With other Bills, the Senate could make amendments and delay Bills for nine months. Then the Bills could be sent to the Governor General for his signification of the King's assent. The Senate was given the power to force a referendum, which it never used. Senators could not become members of the cabinet.

Cosgrave named the representative bodies to be consulted in the Dail on 25 October 1922. They were, Chamber of Commerce, Royal College of Physicians, Royal College of Surgeons, Benches of Kings Inns, Law Society, Councils of the County Boroughs.

Cosgrave listed his thirty nominations in the Dail on the day the Constitution came into force, 6 December 1922. They were:

Mr. John Bagwell, H. G. Burgess; Dowager Countess of Desart, Lord Dunraven; Mr. J.C. Dowdall, Sir Thomas Grattan Esmonde; Sir Nugent Everard; Edmund W. Eyre; Mr. Martin Fitzgerald; Dr. Oliver St. John Gogarty; Mr. James Perry Goodbody, Mr. Henry Guinness, Lord Granard; Lord Glenavy; Capt. Grear, Mr. Benjamin Haughton, the Marquis of Headfort; Mr. Andrew Jameson, Mr. Arthur Jackson, Sir John Keane, Lord Kerry, Sir Bryan Mahon; Lord Mayo; Mr. James Moran. Sir Hutchinson Poë, Mrs. Wyse-Power; Sir Horace Plunkett; Dr. Sigerson; Earl of Wicklow; Mr. W. B. Yeats[2]

Cosgrave's personal imprint was clear on several of the names. Gogarty was a long-time friend. Eyre had been an official of the Dublin Corporation, who had done great service to Cosgrave in his role as a Sinn Fein Councillor and Minister for Local Government. Jameson and Guinness had provided vital bank credit to Cosgrave for Dublin Corporation and the fledgling State. As Cosgrave later wrote, " Guinness and Jameson gave the accommodation so urgently required for the Corporation. It was for this reason that when President of the Executive Council at a later stage, I nominated these two gentlemen as Senators"[2a]. Sir Bryan Mahon had assisted Cosgrave in paving the way for a dignified funeral for Thomas Ashe and as Cosgrave later wrote, "It was as a token of appreciation for this that I subsequently nominated him as a Senator"[2b]. Each name represented important areas of public life, which would be vital for the orderly progression of society. Sixteen names were connected with the southern unionists; the others were leaders in industrial and commercial life. Mrs Wyse Power was a direct link with Arthur Griffith and John MacBride.

The thirty members elected by the Dail also contained fine people. They were:

(1) Mrs Alice Stopford Green	(16) Linehan, Thomas.
(2) Griffith, John Purser.	(17) O'Farrell, John Thomas.
(3) Douglas, James.	(18) Butler, Richard A.
(4) O'Rourke, Bernard.	(19) Bennett, Thomas Westropp.
(5) Moore, Maurice.	(20) Barniville, Henry.
(6) Molloy, William John.	(21) de Loughrey, Peter.
(7) McKean, James.	(22) Irwin, Cornelius Joseph.
(8) Costelloe, Ellen.	(23) Mansfield, Eamónn.
(9) O'Sullivan, William.	(24) MacLysaght, Edward.
(10) McLoughlin, John.	(25) McEvoy, Edward.
(11) Kenny, Patk. Williams.	(26) Nesbitt, George.
(12) Barrington, William.	(27) Love, Clayton, Joseph.
(13) Duffy, Michael.	(28) Parkinson, James J.
(14) McPartlin, Thomas.	(29) Counihan, John C.
(15) Farren, Thomás.	(30) O'Dea, Michael[3].

Twenty-four of the 60 Senators lived in or around Dublin, with the rest scattered around the country. Two lived primarily in England Only five of the 26 counties were not represented. Thirty-six were Catholics, one a Jew.

It was a dangerous time in Ireland to become a Senator, as those on Cosgrave's list, were among fourteen categories of persons who were to be shot on sight, by orders of the Chief of Staff of the IRA, Liam Lynch. deValera on 13 November, had agreed that both their names should appear on official documents, issuing from their notional, Department of Defence. T.D's had already become targets for shooting and bombing.

On 7 December Sean Hales was shot dead, with Padraigh Ó'Maille wounded.

On 10 December Sean McGarry TD's house was fired. His son later died of burns

On 28 December McCullagh's music warehouse was demolished.

On 13 January WT Cosgrave's house was burned.

On 11 February Kevin O'Higgins' father was murdered.

On 10 December Mrs Wyse Power's business was attacked.

Hutcheson Poe was ambushed and had his car burned.

On 9 January 1923 John Bagwell's valuable house and library were burned.

On 12 January Gogarty was kidnapped but escaped in a fusillade of gunfire.

On 29 January Lord Mayo's home was burned.

On 29 January Plunkett's home was burned.

On 29 January, John Bagwell was kidnapped but later escaped.

On 1 February Maurice Moore's home overlooking Lough Cara in Mayo was burned.

On 1 February Lenihan's house was burned.

On 3 February, an attempt was made to burn Mrs Wyse Power's Henry St restaurant..

On 4 February Dr. O'Sullivan's house in Kerry was burned.

On 5 February Dr. Sigerson, 84, was intimidated to resign. Cosgrave dissuaded him.

On 16 February Sir Bryan Mahon's house at Ballymore Eustace was burned.

On 19 February Sir John Keane's house in Cappoquin was burned.

On 22 February Desart Court in Kilkenny was burned.

On 23 February Gogarty's home at Renvvyle in Connemara was burned.

On 26 February Lord Granard's home, Castleforbes, Co.Longford was destroyed.

On 9 March Esmonde's house in Wexford was destroyed.

On 24 March Guinness' house, Burton Hall at Stillorgan was destroyed.[4]

Despite condemnation by the Catholic Church's hierarchy, deValera stood behind the carnage, saying, "In so far as we are concerned, we are in arms against and resisting now, exactly what the whole nation resisted in the period 1919-21. The only difference is that in the earlier period, England was maintaining her claim directly; now she is maintaining them indirectly through Irishmen. This is a continuance of the former war"[5].

When the Senate met, it elected Lord Glenavy, the former James Campbell, associate of Carson, and Attorney General who had denied the 1916 men defence counsel. Only Mrs Wyse Power and Maurice Moore dissented. Mrs Wyse Power said;

"... I do believe that the appointment of Lord Glenavy will not bring the North to us. There is only one thing that will bring the North, and that is the economic condition. I do not think that electing Lord Glenavy as the mouthpiece of this the most important body in Ireland, perhaps, except the Dáil, will stand for the regeneration of Ireland in the traditional way we have been brought up to believe, and that we are all working for. I cannot vote for Lord Glenavy, and I am sorry that I cannot".

Maurice Moore clearly was not willing to forget Glenavy's recent past as Edward Carson's right hand man. He said, "I regret very much that I feel bound to oppose the election of Lord Glenavy I cannot regard the present state of the country without looking back to the past. I cannot hide from myself that the present state is due to causes that happened some years ago, beginning principally in 1912 and 1913. I have been asked not to rake up questions. The state of affairs now is because of a certain rebellion raised in Ulster. Everybody knows that. It was on account of that the Irish Volunteers were raised in the South to prevent a rebellion. The result of that was that two armed forces were raised up, one against the other. Arms were forced into the hands of people who were unwilling to fight, and who did not wish to raise bloodshed in this country. The greater part of the people of this country who wished to settle these matters constitutionally, and who had been working and acting for forty years or more on constitutional lines have been pushed on unwillingly. We are not yet complete in our freedom. But this Treaty may be limited. ...I will not consent, to a person whose political future I cannot to a certain extent foresee, being placed in that position"[6].

The Dail, and WT Cosgrave, expected the Senate would be a compliant body, subservient to it. However, they soon learned differently. One of the first Bills sent by the Dail concerned indemnifying British military on acts done in the Black and Tan period. The Senate refused to back it, on the grounds that there was no reciprocity for Irish soldiers in the British army who had mutinied out of sympathy with Irish nationalism. Senator WB Yeats repudiated Cosgrave's suggestion that such an objection would come better from the Dail. Yeats said, " I think it is very important to the Senate, because of the very nature of its constitution, that we should show ourselves as interested as the Dail is, in every person in this country. We do not represent constituencies; we are drawn together to represent certain forms of special knowledge, certain special interests, but we are just as much passionately concerned in these great questions, as the Dail"[7].

In June 1923 Yeats wrote to Cosgrave on the matter of art. He felt that the State was giving official sanction to artwork, which did not do "justice to the real intellect and force of the Irish government". He sought an interview with Cosgrave to put a proposal before him on the formation of an unpaid committee, which could advise the government. He said that he and Sir John Lavery felt that, "other artists of eminence would be ready to act"[8].

WB Yeats owed his nomination to Gogarty, who also proposed AE Russell, but who after considering the offer, declined it.

Yeats was a welcome addition to the Senate, as he was a very well known figure in Ireland and abroad. He had a firm background in nationalist activity for many years, and only ceased such involvement in 1903, when his muse Maud Gonne married John MacBride. He dubbed 1916 as the 'poet's rising', and wrote several canonical poems, which served to immortalise the Rising and the executed leaders. While living in England he famously spoke at the Oxford Union, castigating the Black and Tans and defending the Irish claim to independence. At the instigation of his wife, he moved to live in Ireland and give his backing to the new State. He became an international figure in 1923 when he was awarded the Nobel Prize for literature. He became friendly with WT Cosgrave and socialised with him on several occasions. Yeats took membership of the Senate very seriously. He was an assiduous speaker in all sorts of debate. He chaired the Irish Coinage Committee. His most remembered speech in the Senate occurred in 1925, when he again demonstrated his independence from the government, on the divorce issue[9]. However that speech was a highly sectarian one, and was an embarrassment to many. At one point, Lord Glenavy, asked him could he not leave the dead alone[10].

Yeats declined the request.

During 1922 Gogarty and Collins had begun a routine of visiting Cosgrave's home in Templeogue for afternoon tea. It was an opportunity to let off steam in those difficult times. Cosgrave recalled, with a twinkle in his eye, "I often thought that that pair of rascals took more delight in shocking me, than in talking serious business when they came out to tea". Cosgrave believed that Collins was the greatest Irishman who ever lived, being only on the threshold of his career. "He died with so much of his greatness in him, we will never know what he could have achieved. He had courage, you see; so had Gogarty" Cosgrave told Ulick O'Connor[11].

Cosgrave and Yeats joined Gogarty and a select group of his friends, on a famous occasion, on 24 March 1924. They first dined at the Shelbourne Hotel. Then they travelled to Dublin Zoo to collect a pair of swans, which Gogarty had promised to place on the Liffey, in thanksgiving for his deliverance from kidnapping the IRA[12].

Gogarty, the Buck Mulligan of James Joyce's *Ulysses*, and the conservative Catholic Cosgrave, had a unique relationship, where Gogarty was free to act and speak wittily, disparagingly and sometimes with vulgarity. Ulick O'Connor has put it thus; "Mr Cosgrave, was another friend of pius instinct, who was nevertheless susceptible to the wit inherent in Gogarty's irreverence's". On the occasion of Gogarty accompanying Cosgrave on an audience with the Pope, Gogarty mistakenly received the Papal medal intended for Cosgrave. When challenged, Gogarty mocked Cosgrave, questioning whether any mistake was possible, given his devout belief in the infallibility of the Pope. Gogarty later commented that the Pope was embarrassed by Cosgrave's piousness[13].

Sean MacBride was an implacable enemy of the Treaty, though his mother, because of her long-time association with Arthur Griffith, had initially supported it. She then became a well-known activist against the Provisional government and WT Cosgrave in particular. Sean MacBride had been in the Four Courts and shared a cell with Rory O'Connor. Maud Gonne began protesting against his internment and the harsh laws against the IRA. She castigated WB Yeats for becoming a Senator and threatened to terminate their long friendship.

Cosgrave realised that among the most virulent and intransigent critics of the treaty and his government were republican women. He ventured the exasperated opinion that it "was not possible to regard these women as females" as they were "the mainstay of the trouble" and regarded any negotiation as a sign of weakness[14.]

Despite their strained relationship, Maud did not hesitate to contact Yeats, when on 24 August 1927 her son was arrested, on suspicion of the murder of O'Higgins. Yeats contacted Cosgrave, but without success. He wrote to Maud saying, "I am very sorry I have had no more success. I dare say you are right about Shawn's reputation, but one thing I am sure. The heads of the Free State do not want to be unjust to the son of John MacBride. He is a hero to these men. Cosgrave was in the next cell to him in 1916, and was to have been next executed"[15].

Maud was not impressed. She wrote to Yeats saying, "Cosgrave repeats ad nauseum at election meetings, where he thinks it might suit, that he was in the cell next to John MacBride in 1916. The Mayo papers answered his cheap heroics well by asking, Is this the reason he is now persecuting his son? Luckily Sean MacBride was able to produce no less a person than Senator Bryan Cooper as an alibi. Nevertheless he was not released but charged under the Public Safety Act and interned in Mountjoy[16]. Maud again wrote in harsh terms to Yeats saying, "Though my son is at present the solitary victim of the public safety act I ought to rejoice for what has brought Cosgrave's government down and what has turned the country against it are just these flogging bills, Treason Bills and public safety bills. The Irish People will not forgive them"[17].

One of the best female public representatives during the early years of the State was Jenny Wyse Power. Unlike some others, she spoke up for women's rights when as so often, successive Irish governments trampled them on. In 1925 women were denied to sit examinations for the civil service. In 1932 the ban on married female teachers was extended to all civil servants, forcing their retirement. Mrs Wyse Power opposed the 1927 Juries Bill saying that "During the last 50 years the men who led the political movements, utilised women in order to achieve their object… If this Bill becomes law, the civic spirit that is awakening in women will be arrested. In fact the suggestion that there shall be only male jurors in the future, cuts at the very root of this development in the awakening of the civic spirit"[18].

FIANNA FAIL AND THE SENATE

When the Senate was due for the second Triennial election in 1928, it sought a joint committee with the Dail to discuss the powers and methods of election to the Senate. deValera opposed the matter and declared that he wanted the Senate abolished, as it was too costly and did not serve any useful function[19]. Sean Lemass said clearly that they regarded it as a sop to the unionists and a bulwark to imperialism[20]. However, in the restricted election to the Senate, the two main parties in the Dail had the upper hand. Fianna Fail won six of the nineteen seats available. Three of those had been T.D's, including Mrs Kathleen Clarke. Four of Cosgrave's party won seats, with three of them being former T.D's and the other Oliver Gogarty. Tom Johnson of Labour won the sole Labour Party seat. Independents won eight seats. These included four outgoing senators, with Sir Bryan Mahon and Alfie Byrne among the four new senators. Lord Glenavy was among the senators whose term was up and had to retire. He died on 22 March 1931. WB Yeats left the Senate and politics in 1928. He became disillusioned with the conservativism of the State.

HAZEL LAVERY & THE LANE PICTURES

Hugh Lane was a critic and art collector from county Cork. He mounted an exhibition of paintings at the Royal Hibernian Academy in 1904. He offered thirty-four of them to Dublin Corporation, if it would build a gallery to house them and raise funds to purchase the rest of the collection. The paintings on offer were very valuable. The Corporation declined the offer and Lane willed the paintings to the National Gallery in London. In 1914 Lane was appointed Director of the National Gallery in Dublin. In 1915 he added a codicil to his will, leaving his collection to Dublin. He was drowned in the Lusitania that same year. The codicil to his will had not been witnessed and had no legal validity. A very long drawn out struggle between Ireland and England began over the paintings, with very many people becoming involved over the decades. During the Treaty negotiations in London, Michael Collins had become very friendly with Hazel Lavery, wife of the painter Sir John Lavery. She was an American, and already a good friend of Oliver Gogarty. She made a career of facilitating important people engage in pursuits of common interest. During 1923, both WT Cosgrave and Kevin O'Higgins had their portraits painted by John Lavery. During these sittings, both had got to know Hazel[21].

In 1923 John Lavery was commissioned by the Irish Government to paint a portrait of his wife. It appeared on Irish banknotes for many years. In his autobiography John Lavery attributes the idea of using his wife as a model for the Irish currency notes, to WT Cosgrave. He quoted Cosgrave as saying, " Every Irishman, not to mention the foreigner who visits Ireland, will carry her portrait (on the banknotes) next to his heart"[22].

The controversy over Hugh Lane's paintings continued over many decades, with the British refusing to part with the paintings. At various times it appeared that the paintings might be sent to Ireland and at other times, the opposite appeared to be the case. Hazel Lavery became involved and in 1929, when it appeared that the Prime Minster, Ramsay MacDonald was about to deny all hope of Ireland getting the paintings, Hazel intervened and met with Malcolm MacDonald, the Prime Minister's son, and persuaded him to intervene with his father[23]. Lady Gregory described her as an angel. Hazel did not hesitate to write directly to Cosgrave on the matter. She wrote in an surprisingly personal manner: "I know I ought not to write to you, but I want to so much and I am indulging myself and giving myself a sort of Christmas present, it being the festive season and all. Of course you will realise by now that I've a favour to ask! It is this. Please have a little talk with Mr. Thomas Bodkin[23a] about the Lane pictures and the future procedure in connection with making "representations to the British Government...you know how many enemies we still have in England and worse still, very half-hearted friends and I am sorry to say that many people who were splendid supporters, have been alienated by various unlucky events that really (I quite appreciate) were unavoidable, but have given an unhappy and false impression over here"[24].

Cosgrave in conversation with General Séan MacEoin.

CHAPTER FOURTEEN

CONSERVATISM REIGNS

"THE LAWYERS HAVE SAT IN COUNSEL"

Another issue from the past, which the government had to deal with, arose from the local parish courts system, organised in the era of the Volunteers and Sinn Fein. These were organised as a parallel system to the British courts system, for the dispensing of justice. The first court under the direct authority of Dail Eireann sat at Ballinrobe, Co. Mayo on 17 May 1920. Aptly enough, it concerned land agitation and boycott. Kevin O'Shiel from the North and a local solicitor, Conor Maguire from Claremorris, were the legal representatives. When the case went against the local agitators, Tom Maguire, the local IRA commander, enforced the courts' decision[1]. In June 1920 the Dail authorised Austin Stack, minister of Home Affairs to initiate under its own authority a system of civil and criminal courts to replace the British system. Stack was advised by a committee of lawyers and in September 1920 published the Constitution of new Republican Courts, revised in January 1921. The British government was well aware of their significance and acted against them. They were well used around the country and after the Truce in July 1921, flourished particularly well. They continued to function after the Treaty. However, during the civil war, and after the Collins-deValera Pact election of June 1922, the anti-Treatyites sought to use the Dail Courts for their own 'political' purposes.

Count Plunkett sought to have his son, George Oliver, released from Mountjoy Jail, where he had been since the surrender of the Four Courts. He applied to the courts on 18 July and Judge Crowley, an ardent follower of deValera, ordered that the prisoner be produced in court on 26 July. When this was not complied with, Crowley ordered the arrest of Richard Mulcahy, Minister for Defence and Phil Cosgrave T. D., Governor of Mountjoy. The judge had received a letter from the Minister for Home Affairs on the previous day 25 July rescinding the decree establishing the Dail Courts, save for the Parish and District Courts outside Dublin.

A meeting of the Second Dail had been scheduled for 30 June. Due to uncertain security and political situation, this was prorogued to 15 July. On 13 July it was further prorogued under the signatures of Griffith, Blythe, Cosgrave, Gavan Duffy, Duggan, Fitzgerald, Hayes, Hogan, Collins, Lynch, Mulcahy, McGrath, MacNeill, O'Higgins and JJ Walsh. The sittings of the Supreme Court were also suspended that same day. Eoin MacNeill was Speaker of the Dail with responsibility for summoning the Dail. When he did not act, Mrs Thomas Clarke, an elected Deputy, applied on 4 August, to the Republican Supreme Court for a declaration Mandamus ordering MacNeill to summon the Dail[1a]. Judge Crowley granted a Conditional Order directing MacNeill to show cause as to why he had not done so. This was served on MacNeill but was ignored. The order was then made absolute, but could not be enforced by the anti-Treatyites[2]. Gavan Duffy, a solicitor, foreign minister and signatory of the Treaty, resigned in protest at this period[3]. At that time Cosgrave was acting Chairman of the Provisional Government, as Collins had become Commandant in Chief of the Army. Cosgrave responded to a 'People's Rights Association', which had written to Collins, saying that the Second Dail should be allowed to reassemble, "to decide on the necessity or policy of a bitter and prolonged civil war". He wrote, "The function of the Second Dail came to an end on June 30th. The meeting, which was to have taken place on that date, would have been purely formal for the purpose of bringing its business to a conclusion. The Sovereign Assembly of Ireland is now the Parliament elected in June last, whose authority the irregulars have flouted"[4]. Judge Crowley himself was arrested and imprisoned briefly[5].

Mary Kotsonouris writes that when Gavan Duffy raised the matter in the Dail, he admitted that Judge Crowley could be a cantankerous and difficult person, but that it was wrong to imprison him and other people without a trial. At that point Crowley had just been released. Kotsonouris writes that "Cosgrave was unsympathetic and he treated it with a pronounced skittishness"[6]. When asked why Crowley had been let out, he replied, "Because he was an old cod. And I think that Deputy Gavan Duffy himself informed me one time that that was his real title of distinction"[7].

. A Decree published on 17 October completed the abolition of District and Parish Courts outside Dublin. The dissolution and merging of the old courts with the new High Court, was announced in the Supreme Court. Twenty-two District Justices were appointed in November 1922.

A Judiciary Committee, to guide the Government on a new Courts of Justice Bill, with Lord Glenavy in the chair, was appointed in early 1923. Cosgrave, addressed it saying:

"In the long struggle for the right to rule in our country, there has been no sphere of the administration lately ended, which impressed itself on the minds of our people as a standing monument of an alien government more than the system, the machinery and the administration of law and justice which supplanted in comparatively modern times, the laws and institutions till then a part of the living national organism. The body of laws and the system of judicature so imposed upon the Nation was English (not even British) in their seed, English in their growth, English in their vitality... The manner of their administration prevented them from striking root in the fertile soil of this Nation. Thus, it comes, that there is nothing more prized among our newly won liberties, than the liberty to constitute a system of judiciary and an administration of law and justice, according to the dictates of our own needs and after a pattern of our own designing. This liberty is established and the headline is set in the Constitution drawn up and passed by the elected representatives of our people"[8].

The leading features of the measure were provision for expeditious and economical disposal of legal business, with the advantage of local hearings for the ordinary run of litigation of the country.

Tom Johnston , leader of the Labour Party doubted whether the Bill could be passed within three days, as Cosgrave wished. This proved to be the case and the Bill lapsed due to the forthcoming general election.

When he reintroduced the Bill in the Dail on 20 September, Cosgrave had changed dramatically from his earlier attitude and said, "the Bench in Ireland had the most distinguished and able jurists and conscientious lawgivers, so the Bill endeavoured to regulate the necessary alterations with as little disturbance and as free as possible under the circumstances".

He made a point that would not have proved popular to those opposed to the Bill, saying: "The law is going to be made somewhat cheaper for the ordinary citizen in the country. Naturally, if a particular commodity that was very expensive, is going to be made cheaper, somebody must suffer, and, consequently, there will be dissatisfaction among the sufferers". He sought to answer some of the criticisms and made great play that the Bill adhered to the recommendations of the Judiciary Committee. The Bill provided that each court would have a Rule-making Authority to settle the detailed scheme of administration of the courts. The Rules would come to the Oireachtas for examination to see that they were administratively satisfactory and really enable the new courts to fulfil the high hopes entertained for a more efficient, expeditious, and less costly judicial system.

It was in the Senate that extensive detailed opposition to the Bill surfaced. The legal people there opposed the Bill vehemently. Lord Glenavy, who had drawn up the Report on which the Bill was supposed to be based, vacated his Chair, to gave his view on the Bill. In the presence of Cosgrave, he first praised aspects of the Bill but then launched into fundamental criticisms, saying that the judiciary could not be subservient to the Legislature. He rejected any interference in judges making their own Rules of Court. He said that the government wanted the Minister to formulate the Rules of Court and then see if the judges would concur in them. He deemed this "as a badge of humiliation which the Government would have the judges and the Bar wear. I think this Section is a distinct violation of the Constitution. I also think it is a very grave mistake to run the risk of having the Government implicated in disputes with the judges over these matters. The Bar, as I have said, derive no advantage from the Government or from the public purse at all. I am very proud and very jealous of the traditions and honour of the Irish Bench and Bar. I believe that they have fulfilled and played an honourable part for many centuries in the history of our people, though I know it sometimes has been said that members of the Bench in this country, have made themselves the tools or the creatures of the Government of the day. Although such a charge as that is almost inevitable in any country where promotion to the Bench is made by the Government of the day or by the Crown, on the recommendation of the Government of the day. The Bar are not in any sense officials of the Government. They are as free and independent to wear any costume they like as any member of the public. Will it not be an extraordinary state of affairs if we find the Government in a short time in collision with the Bar of Ireland on the question of whether they are to wear trousers or kilts? There it is in black and white".

Cosgrave replied:

"This Bill simply creates the judicial framework, and further legislation will be necessary to set up the staffs and the establishment. Formerly it was the Lord Lieutenant who made the rules. The Minister for Home Affairs will not make rules without the concurrence of the majority of the Committee. Power is reserved to alter or annul these rules, only with the concurrence of a majority of this Committee. I do not know that there is any more democratic method that can be suggested.

I do think, with all respect to the Bench and the Bar, that some regard must be had to the necessary economies, which must be made in this State.

We must take into consideration the balancing of our Budget. We must consider every single service that we have got in relation to the fundamental principle that we have to cut our cloth according to the measure.

Under the Bill there is a huge number of judges—three Judges of the Supreme Court, six Judges of the High Court, eight Judges of the Circuit Court, and thirty District Justices. Really it is a pretty considerable number of appointments. I do not know that any profession has got such security behind it for an ultimate satisfactory mode of income as this particular profession. We have got to consider all the needs of the country in this case

Those Courts will not appear to the people in the same light as the Four Courts did in the past. Of the Four Courts it was said: "When you go in you will never come out, and whatever you have in your pocket it will not be worth very much after you are finished with the Courts. Here there is going to be law well within the purse limits of the citizen, and there will be absolute and implicit confidence in every institution".

It was a very difficult period for Cosgrave, as O'Higgins, the relevant Minister absented himself from piloting the Bill through Parliament. Cosgrave was very frustrated in the debates as he saw the Executive's plan thwarted. At one point, he threatened to withdraw the Bill from the Senate and have it put to a referendum. He said, "I have been obsessed from reading in the Press for some time past an extraordinary disposition to belittle, to reduce, the status of the Executive Council of the State and its officers in every possible way"[10]. Judge Mary Kotsonouris wrote that the Executive wanted "to retain the power to bring recalcitrant judges to heel"[11]. She castigates Cosgrave's performance as "particularly inept...by the nonchalant attitude that the strongly felt concerns voiced by members of both Houses of the Oireachtas could be met by cajolery or a slippery refusal to face the issue of judicial independence over months of discussion"[12]. She does admit that the lawyer-legislators dominated the debate and that they openly read from briefs prepared by the Bar Council and the Incorporated Law Society.

The Senate made forty-four amendments to the Bill and returned it to the Dail. It came back to the Senate on 3 April 1923, with all amendments accepted, save two. The Senate accepted this and the Bill became law.

Cosgrave's attempts to exert some control on the operation of the legal system, was thwarted by vested interests, and as Joe Lee comments, "Recourse to law remained limited to those who could afford to go to law in the first instance"[12a].

ECONOMIC CONSERVATISM

Cosgrave's government was at pains to demonstrate to the people that it was capable of good and responsible government. They meant by this a very conservative policy in all matters, particularly fiscal. They had inherited a civil service model of public service from the British, which had been time proven as efficient and uncorrupted. Yet there had to be some re-organisation. Cosgrave induced a good friend of his, CJ Gregg, to move on a temporary basis from the Board of Inland Revenue in London, to reorganise the civil service in Dublin. He, "more than any other single man, was responsible for the reorganisation of the new civil service"[13]. Gregg headed the Committee on Government Reorganisation, which recommended the details of the crucial Ministers and Secretaries Act of 1924. This Act enshrined that Ministers were responsible for the work of their departments. His attitude to Blythe, the sole minister on the committee, reminds one of the famous TV programme, Yes Minister[14]. The civil service was to continue in the path of the departed administration. Even the traditional mode of dress by Ministers, formal morning suits, wing collars and top hats also reinforced the image that the government was continuing with British tradition. However the conservative policy was most evident and politically damaging, when in September 1924, the Minister for Finance Ernest Blythe reduced the old age pension by one shilling and reduced salaries if teachers and other public servants by ten per cent. Blythe gradually reduced government expenditure from £42 million in 1923-4 to £32 million in 1924-5 and £24 million in 1926-7. Income tax was reduced from 5 shillings in 1924 to three shillings in 1926. However fiscal rectitude did not create economic policy. Much expectation that agriculture would deliver prosperity was not well founded. The government felt that industrialisation could not be 'forced', and did little to assist development[15]. Cumann na nGaedheal was made up largely of people who were fairly comfortable within the current situation. The poor, the aged, and the unemployed all had to endure the inertia of the middle class. Even in housing, where Cosgrave had long experience, only saw 14,000 houses built with public subsidy between 1922 and 1929. McGilligan made an outrageous statement in the Dail, "

People may have to die in this country and may have to die from starvation…If it is said that a the government has failed to adopt effective means to find useful work for willing workers, I can only answer that it is no function of government to provide work for anybody"[16].

It was however natural that state centralism would he the hallmark of the government as Local Authorities, many of them still with an an-Treaty majority of representatives, were forced to become subservient to State bodies. The Local Appointments Commission and the Civil Service Commission were the two most outstanding examples of the State seeking to bring order and equity to areas where they were badly needed.

RELIGIOUS CONSERVATIVISM

Cosgrave was a conservative Catholic, a friend of the clergy and a frequent visitor to Rome. On a visit there in 1924 as President of the Executive, Oliver Gogarty accompanied him[17]. He was made a Papal Knight of the Grand Cross First Class of the Order of Pope Pius IX in 1925, after he led the National Pilgrimage to Rome. The papers concerning this trip indicate that Mrs Cosgrave was, like her husband, a devout Catholic. Her purchases included six crosses, three medals, five pairs of rosary beads, five dozen medals and nine blessings, for which she paid 698 lira, out of her own pocket. In 1927 the Government imposed a 33% tax on imported rosary beads, to last for five years. A letter issued to the Italian consul in London thanked various people for their assistance during the visit. The letter reads in part, "In particular the President desires that His Excellency Signor Mussolini should be made aware of the lasting impression which his signal sets of favour and kindness made upon the President"[18]. It was around this same time that Mussolini was granted a British Knighthood.

WT's close friend, Archbishop Byrne, got special Vatican approval for him to erect an altar in his home for the celebration of private Mass. Cosgrave wrote to the Archbishop on 12 February 1925 thanking him " for the cherished privilege of maintaining a private oratory at my house at Beechpark. I can only inadequately express the feelings of gratitude of Mrs Cosgrave and myself for the great favour shown to us and for all the trouble Your Grace has taken in preferring my request"[18a].

The Church had been of great assistance to the government during the civil war. When the matter arose of retaining the right to petition for divorce through a private Bill in the Dail, it became necessary to establish standing orders for same. This was a procedural matter. Cosgrave's first inclination was to continue to allow for the possibility to those who wanted this facility, mainly Protestants. He was keen not to do anything which would negative the position of Protestants in the State. His Attorney General Hugh Kennedy thought likewise. When the fundamentalist *Catholic Bulletin* of March 1923 mischievously raised the matter of the introduction of divorce, the procedural matter became a religious and political issue. Cosgrave felt he had to consult his friend, Archbishop Byrne, who insisted that divorce was contrary to the

Natural Law and should be banned. Byrne sent. Cosgrave a Memorandum titled 'Catholic Teaching on Marriage'. Cosgrave replied on 4 March 1924:

"I hope to be able to show it to some members of the Committee in time for the meeting.

I do not anticipate any difficulty whatsoever in the matter of a correct interpretation and action by Catholic members of the Oireacthas. The crux of the whole business is how the Committee can best decide to put the matter before the Houses. It is on this that we are all experiencing the real difficulty"[18b]

In the event the government did not introduce the standing order and technically divorce by a Private Bill remained possible.

When an attempt was made to introduce Divorce legislation by a Private Bill in 1925, Cosgrave opposed it. He told the Dail, "I consider that the whole fabric of our social organisation is based upon the sanctity of the marriage bond, and that anything that tends to weaken the efficacy of that bond, to that extent, strikes at the root of our social life". This would have been in accord with the vast majority view, including many Protestants. Cosgrave has been criticised for facilitating a certain Catholic triumphalism in the Free State. Ronan Fanning has written, "Those who too readily deride that triumphalism should recall that just such anti-Catholic prejudice and discrimination, in a particularly virulent form, remained a distinguishing feature of that part of Ireland still within the United Kingdon"[19].

John Whyte has noted that Cumann na nGaedheal and Fianna Fail were at one in social values. He wrote, "Mr Cosgrave refused to legalise divorce. Mr deValera made it unconstitutional. Mr. Cosgrave regulated films and books. Mr. deValera regulated dancehalls. Mr. Cosgrave's government forbade propaganda for the use of contraceptives. Mr. deValera banned their sale or import. In all this, they had the support of the third party in Irish politics, the Labour party"[20]. On 5 March 1939, the Minister for Justice received an extensive Memorandum on Film Censorship from the Bishops of Ardagh and Kilmore, on behalf of a Committee appointed by the Irish hierarchy[20a].

However, not all the bishops offered their support to Cosgrave and his government. Bishop John Dignam made it very clear that he was a firm supporter of DeValera[21]. Cosgrave was later to introduce another piece of reactionary legislation in the Censorship of Publications Act, 1929.

The celebrations of the centenary of Catholic Emancipation were held countrywide over one week during June 1929. A series of events and lectures took place in Dublin. These were notable for the involvement of people from the North, who emphasised that their freedom of religion could not be taken for granted. The climax of the celebrations was a mass in the Phoenix Park with over 300,000 people attending. An enclosure in front of the altar contained the dignitaries. These included Cosgrave, Blythe, Governor General MacNeill and their wives. It also contained the Chancellor of the National University Eamon deValera and the Presidents of the constituent Colleges. After the mass there was a procession to Watling St Bridge for Benediction. Cardinal MacRory carried the Host. Four people carried the canopy in relays. First to carry it were Cosgrave, Marcus O'Sullivan, Dr. Hayes, Speaker of the Dail, Mr. Westropp, Chair of the Senate. Next up, were the four university people led by deValera. He was happy to have the opportunity to demonstrate, that he and his Fianna Fail Party, were no less ardent Catholics than members of the government.

The *Irish Times* spoke of and for the Protestant community, editorialising, " In the breath and sincerity of their aspirations for Ireland they yield nothing to the most patriotic of their Roman Catholic fellow citizens. ..They glory in the Free State's proud position as a Dominion of the British Commonwealth. They pray for the time when Ireland will be a united country. They are thankful for every act of either Irish government that promises her peace, her welfare or her fame. Irish Protestants hope that the present celebrations will not only mark a fulfilment, but a beginning, - the beginning of a great reconciliation, the birth of a new fellowship"[22].

When Paschal Robinson, a Dubliner, became Papal Nuncio in 1930, he and Cosgrave became close friends. Cosgrave called to see Robinson at least once a week and on occasional Sundays, while Cosgrave was at the local races, he would deposit his two sons at the nunciature residence. Robinson also visited Cosgrave at home and said mass there for the family[23]. Ulick O'Connor quotes Desmond Gorges a nephew of WT's wife talking "a lot about his Aunt Louie swinging her rosary and the fact that his Uncle Willie went to three masses every day to make up for polishing off a number of his best friends during the civil war. Des maintains that he was often shanghaied from his bed at 7.00 to serve first mass in the Cosgrave private chapel. As he knelt at the foot of the altar he would see... Meehawl (who should have been serving mass), slipping upstairs after a night on the town"[24]. Cosgrave may have helped Robinson to become accepted by the bishops, who were initially suspicious of his presence in the country.

When John Charles McQuaid became President of Blackrock College in 1930, he became friendly with Cosgrave, who agreed to speak at the College prize day. Mrs Cosgrave presented the prizes at the revived College sports-day[25].

In 1930 too, an issue of the clergy and income tax was raised in the Dail and the suggestion was made that the Revenue Commissioner, William O'Brien, was being unduly harsh in the circumstances. Cosgrave addressed the matter privately and advised Archbishop Byrne to ensure that the clergy made realistic returns. A precedent was reached, whereby all would give a figure around £300, from which they would become liable for tax. Hitherto, as Blythe made clear in the Senate, the clergy were returning ridiculously low figure of £25, from which expenses had been paid[26].

When the Vocational Education system was being introduced in 1930, Cosgrave had the minister, John Marcus O'Sullivan, assure the bishops that it would not challenge their diocesan secondary school system. The thinking of the bishops heavily influenced the Committee on Criminal Law Amendments Acts, which reported in 1931.

Planning for the Eucharistic Congress, to celebrate the arrival of Christianity in Ireland fifteen hundred years previously, was ongoing for several years. A collection at all masses was held on 30 November 1930 to cover costs, which for the church authorities came to £75,000. The State assisted the celebrations and a Eucharistic Congress (Miscellaneous Provisions) Bill passed through the Dail. Half a million Catholics attended the mass in the Phoenix Park, where the chief steward was Eoin O'Duffy. As with the earlier Catholic Emancipation celebrations, the Eucharistic Congress did give the impression that Ireland was a confessional state.

Declan Kiberd has argued that the early governments not only had to secure the state against internal attack but also demonstrate to the British, and others, that they could govern successfully. This led to an extreme conservatism. Kevin O'Higgins declared that he and his colleagues were probably the most conservative revolutionaries in history. Kiberd wrote, "War and civil war appeared to have drained all energy and imagination away: there was precious little left with which to reimagine the national condition"[27].

A Shrine erected in Dublin's Liberties in 1929,
in celebration of Catholic Emancipation.

Grave of Arthur Griffith at Glasnevin, Dublin.

CHAPTER FIFTEEN

TREATY STEPPING STONES CROSSED

INTERNATIONAL RELATIONS

The Dail had bitter memory of the failure of the post-war Peace Conference to give it a hearing. It also knew that the League of Nations gave no support to Sinn Fein's claims for international recognition for Ireland as an independent entity. The fact that successive governments had a portfolio of External Affairs indicated how important they viewed the matter of international relations. The British were ready to support Ireland's membership of the League, once a new constitution was agreed, Lloyd George had told Arthur Griffith on 13 December 1921. The Constitution came into effect on 6 December 1922. The Government again made overtures for membership during 1922. Alfred Cope, the assistant Irish secretary, had told WT Cosgrave during 1921 that any application to the League would be referred to the British Government for adjudication, on the State's status as defined under Article 1 of the Covenant of the League. Cope had later reiterated Lloyd George's position to Cosgrave, when Ireland would become a fully self-governing Dominion"[1]

In early 1923, Cosgrave told Desmond Fitzgerald Minister for External Affairs that,"this question of our entry to the League of Nations ought to be definitely decided. Unless the state of war interferes or prejudices our application, we ought to apply in my opinion"[2]. As usual, Cosgrave then delegated the matter to his Minister. The Irish Free State joined the League and set up a permanent presence in Geneva. It was the first Dominion country to do so, though Canada followed in 1924. In general, Ireland and Canada were keen to establish their international freedom of movement, independent from Great Britain. Cosgrave led the eight men Irish delegation to its first meeting of the League in September 1923. He addressed the assembly, first in Irish, to inform his audience that Ireland had its own language. He spoke at length about Ireland's heritage and her historical links as a European country. He concluded by saying, " ...Ireland comes amongst you as an independent Nation, and as a co-equal member of the Community of Nations known as the British Commonwealth, resolved to play her part in making much of this great institution for peace as complete and efficient as possible". Ireland gave a new impetus to the League as in 1923, the Dominions were an unknown factor in international law[3]. Cumann na nGaedheal organised a celebratory banquet at the Metropole to mark both the 13th centenary celebrations of St Columbanus at Bobbio, which Cosgrave had attended and the triumph at Geneva for 14 September 1923[4]. The Irish Independent of 15 September reported Cosgrave saying at the elaborate ceremonies, which welcomed him home, " Ireland has formally taken her place in the League of Nations. Her sister States received her with cordial and enthusiastic welcome. We come back from Geneva more than ever proud of our country: more than ever determined to work for the well-being of her people and we hope that the whole Irish people will see to it that the high esteem in which our country is held shall be justified". The Irish Times of the same day said in an editorial: "In the interval between the election of 1922 and that of this year, President Cosgrave and his colleagues had, under difficulties such as rarely confronted any new government, to face the task of establishing peace and order and ensuring security for life and property. They not only succeeded in accomplishing that work but they also carried through many legislative reforms. The crowning achievement was the admission of the Free State as a member of the League of Nations. This is a demonstration to the other nations of the world of the independent status which the Free State enjoys under the Anglo-Irish Treaty".

Lionel Curtis has written that Cosgrave was most keen to return to Dublin, as the results of the August general election were coming through and placed a great strain on him, as his health was poor. Curtis thought Cosgrave "might crack at any moment, a change of leadership at this moment would be most disconcerting"[5].

Ireland appointed a High Commissioner in London in 1923, and in 1924 one to the United States. Gradually, appointments were made to Tokyo, Paris Geneva, Ottawa, Berlin, and the Vatican. Ireland attended its first Imperial Conference in 1923, as a newcomer and observer. On 11 July 1924 it registered the Anglo-Irish treaty with the League's of Nations Treaty Bureau. This led to an objection from the British, who regarded the Treaty as an inter Commonwealth agreement, and not allowed to be so registered, under Article 18 of the League. For Ireland, the precedent of registration would imply sovereignty from Britain, on the basis of an international treaty and copper fasten the legitimacy of the Irish Free State at home and abroad. During sensitive negotiations Cosgrave was asked, on 3 October, an embarrassing parliamentary question on the matter. He replied that, " the subject of the question is one which must obviously receive its consideration in due course and proper time"[6]. On June 1924 Cosgrave received a letter from Alfred O'Rahilly in Geneva, urging the immediate registration of the Treaty. Michael Kennedy writes, "Cosgrave took centre stage and took the decision on his own initiative, surprisingly, when Fitzgerald was in London. Cosgrave also consulted Attorney General Hugh Kennedy. Monday 23 June was the key date for registration. Cosgrave took the decision to go ahead., Kennedy cautiously agreed; and finally Joe Walshe gave his perspective….Never before in Irish League policy, had decisions been taken at such speed. Cosgrave's desire to implement the registration policy on his own initiative and with Fitzgerald out of the country, are two actions not in line with the accepted view of Cosgrave's character"[7].

The registration of the Treaty was a major accomplishment of the Government.

Over the next two years Ireland joined Canada and South Africa in developing the Commonwealth into an association of equals.

The Imperial Conference of 1926 laid down principles, in the Balfour Declaration, which allowed the development to remove all restriction remaining on the absolute co-equality of the member states of the British Commonwealth with Great Britain[8].

At the League of Nations Council in March 1927, Austen Chamberlain sought to claw back some British prestige by implying that only Britain could represent the Dominions on the Council. Ireland played a major role in organising the election of Canada to the Council in September.

Cosgrave signed the Renunciation of War Pact on 27 August 1928[9]. He introduced it to the Dail, as an "international instrument of very considerable importance". Fianna Fail argued and voted against the measure, despite the fact that it was such a breakthrough, being the first time a Dominion State had signed an international agreement independently of Britain[10]. Indeed Britain had refused to sign it and no Commonwealth country had yet signed it. Paddy McGilligan summed up the Pact as acknowledging:

...that the time has come when a frank renunciation of war as an instrument of national policy should be made, to the end that the peaceful and friendly relations now existing between their peoples may be perpetuated; convinced that all changes in their relations with one another should be sought only by pacific means and be the result of a peaceful and orderly process".

Fianna Fail deemed it a pact for the 'haves' against the 'have-nots'.

The matter was passed by 84 votes to 60.

FOR:	FOR: cont.
Aird, William P.	Coburn, James.
Alton, Ernest Henry.	Cole, John James.
Anthony, Richard.	Collins-O'Driscoll, Mrs. Margt.
Beckett, James Walter.	Colohan, Hugh.
Bennett, George Cecil.	Conlon, Martin.
Blythe, Ernest.	Connolly, Michael P.
Bourke, Séamus A.	Cooper, Bryan Ricco.
Broderick, Henry.	Corish, Richard.
Broderick, Seán.	Cosgrave, William T.
Byrne, John Joseph.	Crowley, James.
Carey, Edmund.	Daly, John.
Cassidy, Archie J.	Davis, Michael.
Clancy, Patrick.	Doherty, Eugene.

FOR: cont.
Dolan, James N.
Doyle, Edward.
Doyle, Peadar Seán.
Duggan, Edmund John.
Dwyer, James.
Egan, Barry M.
Esmonde, Osmond Thos. Grattan.
Everett, James.
Fitzgerald, Desmond.
Fitzgerald-Kenney, James.
Good, John.
Gorey, Denis J.
Haslett, Alexander.
Hassett, John J.
Heffernan, Michael R.
Hennessy, Michael Joseph.
Hennessy, Thomas.
Henry, Mark.
Hogan, Patrick (Clare).
Hogan, Patrick (Galway).
Holohan, Richard.
Jordan, Michael.
Kelly, Patrick Michael.
Keogh, Myles.
Law, Hugh Alexander.
Leonard, Patrick.
Lynch, Finian.
Mathews, Arthur Patrick.
McDonogh, Martin.

FOR: cont.
McFadden, Michael Og.
McGilligan, Patrick.
Mongan, Joseph W.
Morrissey, Daniel.
Mulcahy, Richard.
Murphy, James E.
Myles, James Sproule.
Nally, Martin Michael.
Nolan, John Thomas.
O'Connell, Richard.
O'Connell, Thomas J.
O'Connor, Bartholomew.
O'Donovan, Timothy Joseph.
O'Hanlon, John F.
O'Leary Daniel.
O'Mahony, Dermot Gun.
O'Sullivan, Gearoid.
O'Sullivan, John Marcus.
Reynolds, Patrick.
Rice, Vincent.
Roddy, Martin.
Shaw, Patrick W.
Sheehy, Timothy (West Cork).
Thrift, William Edward.
Tierney, Michael.
White, Vincent Joseph.
Wolfe, George.
Wolfe, Jasper Travers

AGAINST:
Allen, Denis.
Blaney, Neal.
Boland, Gerald.
Boland, Patrick.
Bourke, Daniel.
Brady, Seán.
Briscoe, Robert.
Buckley, Daniel.
Carney, Frank.
Carty, Frank.

AGAINST: cont.
Clery, Michael.
Colbert, James.
Cooney, Eamon.
Corkery, Dan.
Corry, Martin John.
Crowley, Fred. Hugh.
Crowley, Tadhg.
Derrig, Thomas.
Fahy, Frank.
Flinn, Hugo.

AGAINST:cont.
Fogarty, Andrew.
Gorry, Patrick J.
Goulding, John.
Hayes, Seán.
Holt, Samuel.
Houlihan, Patrick.
Jordan, Stephen.
Kennedy, Michael Joseph.
Kent, William R.
Kerlin, Frank.
Killane, James Joseph.
Killilea, Mark.
Kilroy, Michael.
Lemass, Seán F.
Little, Patrick John.

AGAINST:cont.
Maguire, Ben.
McEllistrim, Thomas.
MacEntee, Seán.
Moore, Séamus.
Mullins, Thomas.
O'Dowd, Patrick Joseph.
O'Leary, William.
O'Reilly, Matthew.
O'Reilly, Thomas.
Ruttledge, Patrick J.
Sexton, Martin.
Sheehy, Timothy (Tipp.).
Smith, Patrick.
Walsh, Richard.
Ward, Francis C.

In 1929 the Free State became a signatory to submitting disputes to the Permanent Court of International Justice at Geneva. In September 1930 the State was elected to a non-permanent seat on the Council of the League of Nations. in succession to Canada, and through the good offices of Australia[1].

STATUTE OF WESTMINSTER

The biggest breakthrough diplomatically, which lent credence to the Treaty being a stepping to greater independence from Britain, came in 1930-1, when Ireland was to the fore in having the Statute of Westminster enacted. This laid down that no law passed by the Parliament in Great Britain could apply to any of the Dominions, without their requesting and agreeing. The Colonial Laws Validity Act of 1856 was repealed in its application to the Dominions. The key passage of the Act provided that:

"No Act of Parliament of the United Kingdom passed after the commencement of this Act, shall extend or be deemed to extend, to a Dominion as part of the law of that Dominion, unless it is expressly declared in that Act, that Dominion has requested, and consented to the enactment thereof….No law and no provision of any law made after the commencement of this Act by the Parliament of a Dominion, shall be void or inoperative on the ground that it is repugnant to the law of England, or to the provisions of any existing or future Act of Parliament of the United Kingdom, or to any order, rule, or regulation made under any such Act, and the powers of the Parliament of a Dominion shall include the power to repeal or amend any such Act, rule or regulation in so far as the same is part of the law of the Dominion".

The Cosgrave government could possibly have made more of this major political advance, were it not for the fact that it did not wish to unduly upset its unionist citizens. The reality then was that the Irish Free State emerged, in constitutional theory, as well as in actual practice, as a completely autonomous nation; and the sole link between it and Great Britain was the King. But the King was to function entirely, so far as Irish affairs were concerned, at the will of the Irish Government[12]. However, once more Fianna Fail opposed the measure in the Dail[13].

The fundamental nature of this Act in relation to Ireland was highlighted, when on 20 November 1931 Winston Churchill opposed it on the Second Reading debate in the Commons, where it referred to Ireland. He had resigned from Baldwin's Shadow Cabinet earlier, on the issue of giving Dominion Status to India. In 1931 Baldwin and Ramsey MacDonald had combined to form a national government, in which there was no office for Churchill. He sought in 1931 to have the Irish Free State omitted from the Statute, " as this Bill confers upon the Irish Free State, full legal power to abolish the Irish Treaty…It would be open to the Dail…to repudiate the Oath of allegiance…they could repudiate the right of the Imperial Government to utilize for instance, the harbour facilities at Berehaven and Queenstown". He sought to introduce an amendment to the Bill saying " nothing in this Act shall be deemed to authorise the Legislature of the Irish Free State to repeal, or alter the Irish Free State Agreement Act 1922, or so much of the Government of Ireland Act 1920, as continues to be in force in Northern Ireland". Mr. Amery, who had been first Lord of the Admiralty and Secretary of State for the Dominions, said that he had extended to his colleagues from the Irish Free State the same complete confidence, loyalty, and whole-hearted welcome that he had extended to any other statesmen of any other Dominion. He added, "If you give, you must give generously, and without looking back"[14].

After the debate, Chamberlain understood Churchill had been reassured that Cosgrave would give a declaration about future action However two days later Churchill wrote to Austen Chamberlain saying that he did not think that an assurance by Cosgrave, would be any substitute for the amendment he proposed. He continued, "It is at best even money, that deValera will have control of the Irish government very soon, and the mere fact that Cosgrave made this declaration, would only spur him on all the more to stultify it. Pray, therefore, do not assume me placable by any such assurances"[15].

Cosgrave wrote to Stanley Baldwin after the Second Reading. Baldwin read the letter to the Commons. It said, "I need scarcely impress upon you that the maintenance of the happy relations which now exist between our two countries is absolutely dependent upon the continued acceptance by each of us of the good faith of the other. The situation has been constantly present to our minds, and we have reiterated time and again, that the Treaty is an agreement, which can only be altered by consent. I maintain this particularly, because there seems to be a mistaken view in some quarters, that the solemnity of this instrument in our eyes. could derive any additional strength from a parliamentary law. So far from this being the case, any attempt to erect a Statute of the

British Parliament into a safeguard of the Treaty, would have quite the opposite effect here, and would rather tend to give rise in the minds of our people to a doubt, as to the sanctity of this instrument"[16]. Cosgrave added that the Statute was an agreement between all the Governments of the Commonwealth, which had been considered at great length by the Irish representatives at the Imperial Conference and endorsed, as it stood, by Dail and Senate. He declared that any amendment of the nature then suggested, would be a departure from the terms of the Imperial Conference Report and would be wholly unacceptable to them. The interests of the peoples of the Commonwealth as a whole must be put before the prejudices of the small reactionary elements in these islands", he said.

Baldwin rejected Churchill's attempt, saying, "any restrictive clause would offend not only the Irish Free State, not only Irishmen all over the world, but other Dominions as well. The Statute of Westminster has to be an act of faith, or it was nothing". The Act became law on 11 December 1931. It included the governments of the United Kingdom, Canada, Australia, New Zealand, South Africa, Irish Free State and Newfoundland. Each was to be completely self governing, but united by allegiances to the monarchy, the succession to which, each Dominion would have a say". The Bill was passed by the Commons by 360 votes to 50.

Churchill later acknowledged that the whole case of the freedom of manoeuvre for the Irish Free State rested on solid legal ground in the Statute of Westminster[17].

This latter measure was to prove of the utmost import to Ireland, as ironically, it was to be used by deValera, during the abdication crisis of King Edward VIII in 1937, to remove all monarchical language from the Constitution of the Free State. Another Dominion, which would also later become a republic, South Africa, had its Parliament formally "approve" of the King's decision.

Desmond Fitzgerald wrote, "Knowing the history of these last few years, as I do, I am amazed at the way we have changed the situation… By accepting the Treaty we certainly are getting all that the most fervid supporters were claiming for it – and more"[18]. Michael Collins' prophetic words on the Treaty as providing stepping stones, were realised first by the Cosgrave government, then by the deValera government, and later by the First Inter-Party Government. In the latter case, the State was declared a Republic, with a son of Major John MacBride, the Minister for External Affairs, and a son of WT Cosgrave, Parliamentary Secretary, Chief Whip and Secretary to the Government. As Frank Pakenham said in Peace by Ordeal, "from the Statute onwards, it would be hard to name a single respect in which qua Dominion she was prevented from enjoying full practical autonomy".

Eamon deValera himself recognised the diplomatic advances made by the State, when speaking in the Senate in June 1932, on the motion of abolish the oath of allegiance, he acknowledged to Senator Milroy:

"I thought for one, at any rate, that the Twenty-six Counties here, as a result of the 1926 and 1930 conferences, had practically got into the position—with the sole exception that instead of being a Republic it was a monarchy—that I was aiming at in 1921 for the whole of Ireland.

I am quite willing to give to Senator Milroy or anybody else, any credit that can be got for the policy they aimed at, and I am prepared to confess that there have been advances made, that I did not believe would be made at the time. I am quite willing to confess it"[19]. .

John Regan in writing about the civil war and its aftermath, uses the phrase, "Great hates grew over small divisions"[20]. This, sadly, appears very accurate. deValera was essentially a constitutionalist, well realising the real politique, that imperial Britain, was not going to be defeated in the neighbouring island. The British Government had its limits, especially with a hostile opposition in the House of Commons. It had brilliant leaders. deValera, of all the Irish leaders, realised this at the earliest stage. Yet for whatever reasons, he took the course he did, until in time and circumstances, he accepted the validity of the Treaty.

Eamon deValera

CHAPTER SIXTEEN

CHURCH STATE CONFLICT

DUNBAR-HARRISON

The appointment of a librarian in Castlebar county Mayo became a cause celebre during the last period of Cumann na nGaedheal government. It also developed into a major constitutional joust between Church and State, with WT Cosgrave, despite his natural disposition to propitiate the Church at all times, being forced to lay down some fundamental markers.

The Mayo County Mayo library service was established in 1925, three years after the first County Library scheme was introduced in Donegal. The library service was funded initially by a three-year grant, provided by the Carnegie Library Endowment Fund.

Miss Letitia Dunbar-Harrison was an honours languages graduate of Trinity College. She was a successful candidate for the position of librarian in Castlebar. Local agitation arose, and local councillors voted against the appointment ostensibly on the basis that her knowledge of Irish was not sufficient for the post, but as became apparent quickly, because she was a Protestant.

The local paper, *The Connacht Telegraph*. gave the matter extensive coverage and in January 1931 provided a summary of the state of proceedings. It may be due to the fact that *The Shaughran* was in rehearsal in Castlebar at the time, that the newspaper reported proceedings as a drama. It read:

THE DRAMA SO FAR

ACT ONE The Appointments Commissioners select four librarians for four posts.

ACT TWO: Mayo Library committee objects to Miss Dunbar's appointment, on the grounds of her meagre knowledge of the Irish language, and her being a Protestant, unsuitable to cater for the needs of a 69% Catholic community.

ACT THREE: Mayo county council approve the action of the Library Committee and refuse to sanction the Ministerial appointment

ACT FOUR: The Minister for Local government orders a sworn inquiry.

ACT FIVE: At the Inquiry, Mr. MJ Egan, county Secretary vindicates the efficiency of Mayo County Council, with the exception of their refusal to appoint Miss Dunbar. The Inquiry lasts fifteen minutes.

ACT SIX: The Minister authorises the calling of a special meeting for Saturday last, to adopt or repudiate the selection of the Appointment Commissioners.

ACT SEVEN: At the Special meeting of the Council, after a few hours deliberation, and by a majority of fifteen votes, the Council refuses to appoint Miss Dunbar.

CURTAIN

At the meeting Mr. JJ Duffy seconding the motion to appoint, said, "the government of the country had established the Appointments Commissioners, and since that body had started to function, they had recommended more than one thousand candidates to fill vacancies and their recommendations had been carried out so far, except in this case. It was not a matter for them if the appointment was not carried out, for Miss Dunbar was appointed under an Act of Parliament and the appointment rested with the Commissioners, who in the usual way, called the applicants to Dublin".

Mr. JT Morahan, made it quite clear, what the real issue was, saying, "Trinity culture is not the culture of the Gael, rather is it poison gas to the kindly Celtic people. At the command of the bigoted and Freemason press, Catholic rights are ignored. We are the connecting link between the past generations and of our great Catholic dead and the generations yet unborn "[1].

The Chairman of the county council was outraged that anyone could suggest that they wished to see a local candidate appointed. The matter was so politically sensitive that Cumann na nGaedheal T.D.'s felt obliged to vote against the appointment. Indeed later in the year, the Cumann na nGaedheal Chairman of the Council, criticised the government for its action. In the September election of 1927, both Cumann na nGaedheal and Fianna Fail held four seats in Mayo, with Labour holding one.

The local Catholic clergy became very vocal on the matter, outdoing their lay brethren in their language. Dr. Hegarty of Killala said, "if the people of Mayo cannot have a library without a Protestant librarian, being made Director of the literature distributed to their children, then they will do without a library. They have made bigger sacrifices in the past."[2]. That same day *The Standard*, describing itself as 'An Organ of Irish Catholic Opinion' headlined, " Will the Catholics of Mayo be Overruled ? Will Mayo Co. Council be Dissolved ? An Extraordinary Rumour of Compulsory Secularism". *The Catholic Bulletin* headlined, "WELL DONE MAYO! A SOUPER LIBRARY NEAR CLAREMORRIS. PACKING BACK ALL THE BOOKS ALL OVER MAYO". Dean d'Alton, the future Cardinal d'Alton, suggested that Miss Burke, an unsuccessful candidate, had been discriminated against and he published her version of events in a letter she had written to him from Bank House in Longford. He said that the appointment was not that of a, "washerwoman or a mechanic, but an educated girl who ought to know what books to put into the hands of the Catholic boys and girls of this county, which was at least 99% Catholic"[3].

d'Alton introduced a wider issue by referring to a recent Lambeth Conference, which considered birth control. While condemning the use of contraceptives for motives of selfishness, luxury or mere convenience, it stated: "Nevertheless in those cases where there is such a clearly felt moral obligation to limit or to avoid parenthood, and where there is a morally sound reason for avoiding complete abstinence, the Conference agrees that other methods may be used, provided that this is done in the light of the same Christian principles". D'Alton asked what would the librarian do with books attacking the Catholic position? He asked was it safe to entrust a girl who was not a Catholic, and not in sympathy with Catholic views, with such books?

Cosgrave asked for the file on the matter, and after legal advice, received it. It showed that a losing candidate, Miss Ellen Burke, had been before two separate Boards and had faired poorly on both occasions. She had not passed the Irish test. She scored 250 marks out of 700 on the first occasion and 230 out of 700 second time around.

The matter was raised in the Dail on 11 December 1930 and Cosgrave explained the appointments procedure in some detail. It transpired that Miss Dunbar had chosen the post in Mayo herself. He said that the qualifications prescribed as essential for the post of county librarian were a good general education and training in, or experience of, library work. A diploma in library training and practical experience in office organisation were stated to be desirable, but not essential. A substantial preference was to be given to qualified candidates with a competent knowledge of Irish. He said that there were five posts to be filled. The Selection Board, having interviewed all the candidates, reported that only five were fully qualified, according to the terms of the advertisement. Two of these had a competent knowledge of Irish; the remaining three had some slight knowledge of the language. Preference having been given, as prescribed, to the two candidates who had a competent knowledge of Irish, the five candidates were placed in order of merit and a choice of the five posts was given to the candidates according to their place in this order of merit. The recommendation of Miss Dunbar for the appointment in Mayo resulted from these arrangements. Miss Dunbar had attended a course of library training in the National University and her library experience, was obtained during a training of $1^{1/4}$ years in the libraries of County Dublin and of Rathmines.

Cosgrave said that in the ordinary way, neither he nor any Minister would know the names of the persons who had acted on the Selection Board. But he called for that information in the case, and was in a position to state that the Board consisted of a University Professor and three librarians of much experience. As a Board for the purpose of the appointment in question, he was satisfied that this was a thoroughly competent one.

deValera decided to become involved and made a lengthy speech on the issue at Irishtown in Mayo in early January 1931. His speech was an excellent example of the political astuteness of the man, in the run-up to a general election, where Mayo was marginal, politically. He covered all angles in such a way that all sides could take support from his words. He appealed to local pride by questioning the notion of having a Local Appointments Commission in Dublin deciding on local matters. He acknowledged that Mayo was a Gaeltacht area and Irish was very important. He felt that as it was reasonable for majority religious areas to be concerned about their own ethos, then the same would have to hold for minorities, and they would also be entitled to have similar facilities provided out of public funds. He alluded to the Six Counties, where the rights of minorities were not being catered for.

Cosgrave was annoyed by de Valera's intervention and said of him: " That man is a type of mental arrested development – or perhaps a new type of administrator – who is prepared to spend public money to meet every contingency that may arise – republican police, republican Attorney General, republican judge to try republicans- Labour ditto for Labour prisoners and so on"[4].

The Local Appointments Commission had made the appointment. This body had been set up by Cosgrave to avoid the notorious prevalence of jobbery around the country. It was most unpopular with local dignitaries, clerical and secular, who had been used to having major influence in appointments, great and small. The government reacted to the council's position by dissolution and replacing it with a Commissioner, a Mr. Bartley, who then appointed the lady to the post. This immediately heightened the local political temperature. The displaced Fianna Fail councillors, held a meeting at a local hostelry, and refused to accept the Commissioner and considered setting up a 'provisional' council in Castlebar.

The Archbishop of Tuam, Dr. Gilmartin, became involved in the matter. Cosgrave decided that he would send an emissary, Sir Joseph Glynn, to Tuam with a government memorandum on the matter. Glynn did not meet Gilmartin, but delivered his message to the Vicar General of the diocese. He also passed on a message from Cosgrave suggesting that if the appointment of librarians were on the same plane as that of teachers, that "might create an entirely new situation", which Cosgrave would debate "sympathically with the government". Whether Cosgrave realised it or not, he was skating on thin ice with such a suggestion, as it would potentially cede carte blanche to the hierarchy on the appointment of librarians, something he would never get through cabinet. Nor was the hierarchy keen on allowing the Mayo issue to became a national issue for them. They wanted it settled locally with Gilmartin, who to Cosgrave's horror, mentioning the matter in his Lenten Pastoral.

Cosgrave was aware that the librarian issue was just a symptom of a wider problem, which arose with the question of appointing dispensary doctors. There, the hierarchy were united on the validity of their opposition to appointing Protestants to such sensitive posts. The bishops were taking their guidance from the Maynooth Statutes but Cosgrave had to take his guide from the Constitution. Cosgrave and Marcus O'Sullivan, the Minister of Education met Gilmartin on 25 February, when they discussed the conflict between the two sides. While agreement on the librarian issue appeared to be possible, the wider issue proved very difficult. Cosgrave wrote to

Gilmartin on 2 March, acknowledging that, "we are faced with a problem arising from an apparent conflict between the discipline of the Catholic Church and the constitutional position of the State". He recognised that they hoped "to prevent a situation arising in which the good relations happily existing between the church and the government may be endangered". Gilmartin replied on 4 March that the issue of the librarian could be solved by;

1. The Mayo County Council to be elected next June allowed function.

2. The recognition by the government that a librarianship is an educational position and that a place is found elsewhere for Miss Dunbar-Harrison.

3. Until Miss Dunbar-Harrison leaves, the people cannot use the library, in principle.

Cosgrave himself had put somewhat similar suggestions earlier and was hoist to his own petard. But since then, he realised that his cabinet colleagues disagreed fundamentally. In a note in the departmental file, described by Dr. Keogh as a 'fragment' there is clear indication that during conflict at cabinet, Cosgrave threatened resignation on the matter of the librarianship becoming educational posts. He wrote,

"If the bishops claim that the office of Librarian should be filled in the same manner as that of a teacher in a national school, I am not prepared to oppose this claim in public and in consequence, I am prepared to retire from public life".

It is shocking to contemplate that Cosgrave could have agreed to make the appointment of librarians into such a sectarian mode. Whether he was serious about his threat of resignation is unclear, though quite probable. He could have been using it as a bargaining chip with the bishops, who realised that he was very much on their side, where at all possible, or pressuring his cabinet colleagues, or both. His colleagues would have certainly have been more disposed to welcome his departure, prior to the election, than the bishops would.

In any event, Cosgrave's dealings with the bishops altered radically, when on 11 March, he wrote to Gilmartin, repudiating his three-point solution. He told him that to discriminate against a person on the grounds of his/her religion "would be to repudiate some of the fundamental principles on which this State is founded"[5].

Cosgrave wrote to Cardinal MacRory on 28 March, stating some fundamental principles on church-State relations. He was at pains to reiterate how smoothly both worked together and hoped that when problems arose, the Church would approach the government directly on the matter, rather than first going public. He felt confident that the bishops, "appreciate the effective limits to the powers of the government which exist in relation to certain matters, if some of the most fundamental principles on which this State is founded are not to be repudiated. Such repudiation, direct or indirect, by an Irish government would, we are convinced, entail consequences very detrimental to the country's welfare". He also mentioned how Catholic newspapers were attacking the government and without any intervention by the bishops, most Catholics believed that they act with the backing of the bishops.

On 15 April Cosgrave and Marcus O'Sullivan met with Gilmartin, who was much more pliable. There remained a clear understanding however that Miss Dunbar-Harrison would be found a suitable position in due course.[6].

The Irish Press reported later, that Miss Dunbar-Harrison was very happy to remain in Castlebar. She told the paper that, " I like the work; I love the people who have shown me every kindness, and I am not likely to resign my position because some people think I should go elsewhere". The paper however knew better, writing correctly that she would be transferred 'within a certain time' and that the newly elected county council would be allowed to function". It foresaw this happening "on the eve of a general election, which might sway opinion in favour of the Cumann na nGaedheal party, there being clear indications that only a few of the Mayo priests will on this occasion support the government nominees"[7]. On 4 January *The Irish Independent* reported that Miss Harrison was to resign. Two days later it confirmed the report, stating that she had resigned and would take up an important librarian post in the Department of Defence in Dublin.

Cosgrave has received much criticism for apparently being so willing to capitulate to Catholic pressure. Yet the question must be asked why did he hold out for so long and against such odds, if all he was interested in was securing the Catholic vote? The dissolution of Mayo County Council was a major political move fraught with negative political consequences. Cosgrave decried Fianna Fail's pleasure at the closing of the Library saying: " the sad spectacle of Deputies Ruttledge and Walsh gloating over the demise of a Library – one may be pardoned the thought about the contribution made to the debate by County Mayo members that few counties want greater educational facilities – less talk and more action and deeper reading…"[8].

Hubert Butler, a Protestant commentator, has raised another issue, challenging the Protestant community itself, on its role in the matter. He criticised them for allowing their cultural influence diminish in the provinces. Their lack of attendance at meetings of Carnegie Libraries, led to them losing such reserved places. Butler writes that though the government supported the Protestant candidate, it received only lukewarm support from the Protestant community. Ultimately the government did capitulate, though this did not help them electorally, as Fianna Fail won five seats in Mayo at the 1932 election[9].

The advent of *The Irish Press* on 5 September 1931, proved of enormous assistance to Fianna Fail, though it was always more of a deValera newspaper than a Fianna Fail one. After a shaky start, it became a vibrant popular paper under its first editor, Frank Gallagher. It left the Cumann na nGaedheal paper, *The Star* in the shade. As *The Irish Press* flourished, *The Star* reduced in sales and went from a weekly to a monthly in September 1930, to closure after the 1932 election.

CHAPTER
SEVENTEEN

FIANNA FAIL FOUNDED - 1927 ELECTIONS

O'HIGGINS MURDER

deValera decided that the aftermath of the debacle of the Boundary Commission provided the opportune time for him to make a decisive political move. He realised that de facto, the State existed and was proceeding well on many fronts. The longer he remained outside real political life, the more dangerous was it that he could become obsolete. That was never on his political or personal agenda. In a Dail of 153 T.D's, 103 accepted the Treaty, taken the oath and their seats. deValera's forty-four T.D's refused to take the oath and thus could not take their seats. Their loyalty was to a notional republic, which had been rejected by the people on two occasions; the army of that republic had been defeated and finally had repudiated deValera himself. The latter saw clearly what he had to do; that was get into the Dail and take political power from Cosgrave. He set out with the plan of bringing as many republicans with him as possible. He raised the question of political action at a General Council of Sinn Fein in January 1926, but received little support. Another meeting was called on 9 March to discuss the matter. The motion was to enter the Dail if the Oath could be negatived. This was a major departure for deValera from his previous stances. However, an amendment reading, " that it is incompatible with the fundamental principles of Sinn Fein to send representatives into any usurping legislature set up by English law in Ireland", was put and passed by 223 votes to 218. When this was put as a full motion, it was carried by 179 votes to 177, with 85 abstentions. DeValera resigned from Sinn Fein the next day as he, " was compelled to regard the vote as against his policy"[1]. He and his senior colleagues met in the house of Colonel Maurice Moore in Sandymount and took the fateful decision to launch the new party[2].

deValera was in a hurry and his new party Fianna Fail was launched on 16 May in the Scala Theatre in Dublin.. He attended "as President of nothing; he came there simply as a private and a Republican". Tom Garvin writes, "In a strange and ironic sense the true founder of Fianna Fail was WT Cosgrave, because he clearly offered deValera a 'middle way' between outright acceptance of the 1922 settlement and armed insurrection against it. He deliberately made possible a separation between deValera nd the extremists of the IRA. Possibly on the advice of the Catholic bishops, he had apparently begun to hope that deValera was not politically irredeemable"[2a].

Around this time the Women's International League for Peace and Freedom held its congress in Dublin. WT Cosgrave and deValera attended with their entourages. It was the first occasion the two men had occupied the same room since the Treaty debates. It was noted that "The two rival groups in front of the platform, stiffened and glared at each other"[3].

THE GOVERNMENT VIEW OF SECURITY

The government had been forced to remain continually on a state of high alert against the IRA. It brought in a Treasonable Offences Bill in April 1924, but could only attract 30 votes in the Dail. Had the anti-Treaty T.D's been there, it could have defeated it. Sean MacBride, Seam Lemass and Frank Aiken were arrested in the spring of 1925. In October the IRA staged a mass breakout from Mountjoy Prison. On 14 November 1926 the IRA attacked twelve police barracks simultaneously, resulting in two Gardai being shot dead. Immediate police arrests of leading members of the IRA followed.

As the scheduled 1927 general election approached, the IRA was anxious that some understanding should be made between Sinn Fein and Fianna Fail. In January 1927 Dan Breen T. D. shocked many republicans by taking his seat in the Dail, after taking the oath. On 6 April in his maiden speech he sought to introduce a motion to abolish the oath. Breen said, "My principal reason for introducing this Bill is that I am convinced that you will have no prospect of unity amongst national forces until such time as that Article which debars a large number of elected representatives from entering this house is removed". Cosgrave opposed the move saying that it sought to remove a fundamental provision of the Treaty. He added, "That Treaty has been approved by the Dail and endorsed by the people at two General Elections as well as 17 out of 21 by-elections" The Bill was refused a First Reading by 47 votes to 17. Labour (11) Clann Eireann (1), Farmers (2), National League (1) and Independent Labour (1) voted for, with Cumann na nGaedheal (34), Farmers (6), Independents (7) voting against.

A general election was scheduled for 9 June 1927. The IRA, caught between Fianna Fail and Sinn Fein, sought to broker an agreement, whereby the two parties would run a joint panel of candidates. This foundered on the question of not taking the oath, as this was a *sine qua non* for Sinn Fein.

deValera made an early visit to America in March 1927 to seek to get hold of some of the $3 million, he had collected for the Irish cause in 1920. He had agreed with Collins at the time that that money 'should not be used for party purposes'[4]. The right to this money had been contested between Cosgrave and deValera for some years. Eventually the American courts ruled that it should revert to the subscribers. However deValera remained in America until 1 May, fundraising successfully in Irish-American circles. This enable Fianna Fail to run 87 candidates compared to Sinn Fein's 15 in the June election. The latter was as usual a tough exercise, with Coogan writing that in certain parts of the country, "Fianna Fail Cumainn by day, drilled as IRA columns by night"[5].

Fianna Fail campaigned clearly on the notion that they were going into the Dail, oath or no oath.

The June election result was a triumph for Fianna Fail, as they nearly matched the government party for seats. The result was;

Party	% of vote	Seats Won
Cumann na nGaedheal	27	46
Fianna Fail	26	44
Labour	13	22
Farmers	9	11
National League	7	8
Sinn Fein	4	5
Independent Republicans	1	2
Independents	7	14

On 23 June after attending mass at Westland Row church, deValera made an ostentatious entry to the Dail precincts, where a huge crowd had assembled. The Captain of the Guard, Colonel Brennan, the Dail Clerk, Colm Ó'Murchadha, and his assistant met him. They escorted the Fianna Fail T.D's to a committee room, having already taken the precaution of locking the doors of the Dail chamber.

Despite this both deValera and Sean T. O'Kelly tried forcibly to proceed in the direction of the chamber, but were prevented from doing so. Back in the committee room a discussion began on the matter of the oath. Ó'Murchadha would not budge from the necessity of the Fianna Fail T.D.'s taking the oath, before they could be allowed entry to the chamber. The Irish Independent of 24 June reported that tense excitement permeated the city streets with a series of demonstrations, as the Fianna Fail T.D.'s returned to their party rooms in Lower Abbey St.

Fianna Fail, early masters of publicity, saw two further options, recourse to the courts, but more realistically, recourse to Article 48 of the Constitution, where 75,000 signatures could force a referendum on the issue. The party began collecting signatures on 1 July 1927.

On being nominated for President of the Executive Council, Cosgrave said that he did not seek the office and would accept, only if the opposition were unable to elect a candidate. He said that the oath could only be removed by agreement with Britain. He did not seek any such a mandate from the people, and the party that did, "did not obtain it". He said that Fianna Fail promised the people an end to emigration and partition, no land annuities, bread and work and smaller taxes. They wanted some other party to get them off the hook of the oath. He said, " We have no intention of imperilling our good relations with Great Britain, to secure a dishonest saving of faces, or to acquiesce in a national deception"[6].

MURDER OF O'HIGGINS

Kevin O'Higgins had been in Geneva, and when he returned on 9 July, his wife told him of a rumour that Cosgrave was going to be assassinated. He discounted the idea. On the following morning, as he walked alone to Mass on Booterstown Ave, he was shot by three men and fatally wounded. Eoin MacNeill was first on the scene. O'Higgins lived for a few hours and was able to cradle his baby daughter and forgive his killers before he died. The government presumed that it was the work of the IRA, and arrested all the leaders it could find. Speaking in the Dail on 12 July,- Cosgrave said:

"Kevin O'Higgins had in the dawn and morning of his manhood, brought to his motherland such great and generous offerings of labour, of ability, above all of character, that his life in full maturity revealed a softness, a charm, and a kindness that have been among the greatest devoted to her service. The hands that struck him down, struck at our common country.

Private individuals have not committed this crime against Kevin O'Higgins. It is the political assassination of a pillar of the State. It is the fruit of the steady, persistent attack against the State and its fundamental institutions. On the heads of those who have devoted their energies to the direction of that attack, lies the bloodguilt.

What shall I say of the crime against the home, the wife, the infant children, the mother and brothers and sisters of our murdered colleague? There are some things too sacred for debate in a public assembly, and I dare not intrude upon that sorrow and drag it into the public view. Indeed, it is not within the compass of ordinary speech. I can only, Sir, pray that you will convey from this Dáil, a humble and reverent message of our heartfelt, deep sympathy in an overwhelming grief".

The Labour Party's Tom Johnson met Cosgrave on 18 July and offered an all-party coalition. But Cosgrave told him of the impending new legislation. He said that he proposed an election to fill the fifty-one seats of the abstentionists and offered a deal to split them with Labour. Johnson refused the offer and conveyed the information to deValera. This information only increased the urgency on him to enter the Dail, and quickly. Cosgrave was so used to having Labour as the opposition party, that he never appeared to make a concerted effort to meet their political needs and gain their support[7].

It was at this point that Sean Lemass tried to contact Archbishop Byrne on the matter of the Oath of Allegiance. He wrote to Archbishop's house from Rokeby, Terenure, on 19 July 1927 indicating that though he wished to contact the Archbishop. "I did not consult any political colleagues on my intention to ask his advice with reference to the Oath of Allegiance[7a]"

The government then introduced a Public Safety Bill, which allowed the Executive to declare unlawful an association, which had its aim the overthrow of the Government, or pursued similar treasonable or seditious activities. The possession of related documents was treasonable; the Bill allowed powers of search. Special Courts composed of army officers, save one, with legal experience, were to be established, with powers to bring in sentences of death or life terms of imprisonment. The measure went through the Oireacthas quickly, becoming law on 11 August 1927.

An Electoral Amendment Bill, introduced on 11 August, would make it obligatory for all candidates in Dail and Senate elections to swear that they would, if elected, take the oath of allegiance. Failure to do so would make their election void.

The Government also stymied Fianna Fail's attempt to call a referendum on the oath, proposing to restrict it to those T.D's, who had taken the oath, and withdrawing it entirely from the general population. The Dail only passed this measure on 28 June 1928, after a scene of disorder in the House

FIANNA FAIL ENTER DAIL

As the government was forcing the issue of entering the Dail on Fianna Fail, pressure again materialised from their own ranks On 26 July Patrick Belton, a Fianna Fail TD had taken the oath and entered the Dail. As government proposals were in the process of being considered and becoming law, Fianna Fail TD's met over two days. On 12 August, deValera led his TD's to the Dail escorted by a large crowd of supporters. He announced that he would not take the oath, but nevertheless signed the book as directed by the Clerk of the Dail, which was the process for 'taking the oath'. deValera said, "I am not prepared to take the oath. I am not going to take the oath. I am prepared to put my name down in this book in order to get permission to go into the Dail, but it has no other significance"[8]. J.Bowyer Bell put the matter this way, " The 11 August legislation was calculated to force the first swallow of legitimate parliamentary opposition down its throat. If deValera would not drink, there were many who would, which was nearly as good"[9].

Gerry Boland could not understand why Cosgrave had not abolished the oath earlier and facilitated the entry of abstentionist T.D's, which was Cosgrave's aim. Cosgrave was not enamoured of the oath himself. Deputies had originally taken it in the Dail chamber, but Cosgrave soon assigned it to a private room.

The Fianna Fail deputies were:

Aiken Frank, Blaney Neil, Boland Gerry, Boland Patrick, Buckley Daniel, Carney Frank, Clarke Mrs Kathleen, Colbert James, Corkery Daniel, Corry Martin, Crowley Timothy, Derrig Thomas, deValera Eamon, Fahy Frank , Fogarty Andrew, French Sean, Hayes Sean, Holt Samuel, Houlihan Patrick, Kennedy Michael Joseph, Killelea Mark, Kilroy Michael, Lemass F. Sean, Little Patrick John, McCarvill Patrick, McEllistrim Thomas, MacEntee Sean, Moore Seamus, Mullen Eugene, Mullins Tom, O'Dowd Patrick Joseph, O'Kelly Sean T, O'Leary William, O'Reilly Matthew, O'Reilly Thomas, Powell Thomes P, Ruttledge Patrick J, Ryan James, Smith Patrick, Tubridy, Tynan Thomas, Victory James.

This immediately created the very real possibility that the government would be voted out of office, but it was willing to take that risk. Cosgrave felt reassured that in the eventuality, the army was professional enough to accept the matter, without recourse to any action. He also felt that a new government would not last long. Negotiations took place between Fianna Fail and Labour, and the National League. Agreement was reached to vote out the government. On 16 August, Tom Johnson, leader of the Labour Party said, " There has been a change by the entry into the Dail of 43 Deputies …There is the alternative of a combination of parties on my right and on the Government's left. He then put forward the motion, " That the Executive Council has ceased to retain the support of a majority in Dail Eireann".

Cosgrave responded in a very calm and measured way, quite content to accept the verdict of the Dail. He outlined the economic and security policies of his government. It was clearly evident that he was very happy, if not proud, that his policy of having all 152 seats in the chamber occupied, fulfilled. He recalled the death of the "ablest Minister in the Executive", and asked would his assassins feel easier by the passage of today's motion? He said:

"…Well, after five years of office, and they were fairly strenuous years, I am sleeping well. I wish I had more of it... The eyes of the people of this country are on this Parliament to-day, looking for that constructive effort, looking for some appreciation of the responsibility which is on us, and we are not offered a solution by the motion that is before the House The policy of this Government has been explained on many platforms. We stand for a balanced Budget, for easing the burden of taxation on all the citizens, for developing the country's resources in every possible way, for improving and increasing the efficiency of every service we have got, for one Army, one armed force in this country, under this Parliament, no other, no matter what sacrifices may be entailed by nailing that on our mast. The policy of this Government during the last few weeks had nothing else in mind. We have not talked about sacrifice. We told this Parliament within the last two or three weeks, that we wanted 152 seats filled in this Dáil. Within the past week I have seen the vindication of that policy, and I am glad of it. Do not think for a moment that we are upset by any change that may take place on these benches.

I was wondering during the past few hours just exactly what was in the minds of those who deprived us of the ablest Minister in the Executive Council. For two months they have been feeling uneasy, with nothing but condemnation from every citizen of this State. I put to this House one question: Will they feel easier if this motion passes"?

The opposition of Labour, the National League and Fianna Fail had a majority of one, on paper. After Captain Redmond, leader of the National League Party, announced that his seven members had unanimously decided to support the opposition, everyone was prepared to see the motion carried. However when the division took place, one of the National League deputies, John Jinks, an ex-Mayor of Sligo, did not vote. Desmond Fitzgerald had gone against medical advice to attend and vote. This resulted in a tie of

71 for each side. in the Dail. The Ceann Comhairle then intervened to say, " It devolves on me in pursuance of Article 22 of the Constitution and Standing Order 68 to give a casting vote...I vote against the motion". The Irish Times of 17 August reported, " It was a crestfallen party that Mr. DeValera led from the chamber at a few minutes past eight tonight, when the House adjourned".

John Jinks arrived back in Sligo that night by train where a crowd of about 150 met him with cries of 'Here's the missing Deputy'. On his return to Dublin the next day, Mr Jinks asserted to the *Irish Times*, that he had not been inveigled out of the Dail in any way. "There is no truth in that; I acted purely on my own initiative...I felt that I could never have anything to do with Mr deValera...I have been and remain a constitutional nationalist". However the accepted version is that Jinks was plied with drink and put on the train to Sligo by RM Smylie of the *Irish Times*..

Cosgrave was always interested in horses and at his suggestion a horse was called after Jinks. It won the Two Thousand Guineas in England in 1929.

There were two bye-elections pending and Cosgrave undertook to recall the Dail, if the government did not win both. It won both, and on 25 August, he called another general election for 15 September 1927.

A short bitter campaign followed, with deValera seeking to appeal to enlist support from moderates, by emphasising that his party would act as a responsible constitutional government, acknowledging that all power comes from the sovereign people, who were entitled to be taken into the fullest consultation[10]. There was little money available for the campaign and as a result, only 261 candidates stood, as against 383 in June.

In his autobiography, Patrick Lindsay writes,

"It was the final rally in Ballina prior to the September 1927 General Election and the principal speaker on the platform was WT Cosgrave. Somehow or other I felt, while listening to this frail little man with a quiff in his hair, speaking of affairs of the country which I, of course, did not understand, that there was a sadness, a sad prophetic tone in his voice as to what might ultimately happen in this country"[10a]

The results of the 15 September 1927 General election were:

Party	% Vote	Seats Won
Cumann na nGaedhael	39	61
Fianna Fail	35	57
Labour	9	13
Farmers	6	6
National League	2	2
Communists	1	1
Independents	8	12

The smaller parties did poorly, with the Labour Party doing particularly so, and losing its leader Tom Johnson. Cosgrave's party formed a government on 11 October 1927, with the assistance of the Farmers Party and Independents.

As Cosgrave had been elected for both Cork and Carlow-Kilkenny constituencies, he told a meeting of Cumann na nGaedheal on 10 October that it was with some regret he decided to sit as T.D. for Cork.

Eamon deValera's first speech in the Dail, was in Irish, on the election of the Ceann Comhairle. He presented a frugal face to the electorate, who were experiencing such hard times. He said Fianna Fail would call for a reduction from over a thousand pounds per annum, for the Ceann Comhairle, Ministers and other officers of the Oireachtas, by £700.

On the nomination of WT Cosgrave as President on 11 Oct 1927, his erstwhile Sinn Fein colleague from Dublin Corporation, Sean T. O'Kelly, opposed the nomination. He acknowledged that Cosgrave "had preached the gospel of Ireland independent, Ireland free, Ireland united, Ireland one nation, and that free and Gaelic — the gospel of Pearse, the gospel of independence as preached by Tone". However, he added, "the political history of the last five years made the Deputy unfitted for the office". O'Kelly referred to the sorrows that the policy pursued by Cosgrave brought on Ireland, and of the anguish of mind that he and his policy brought into so many homes. He said that he did not want to evoke these things, saying, "I do not want to start on a bitter note, though God knows I could, and God knows I would have justification, in thinking of those who lie in cold graves — 77 of my comrades who lie in cold graves to-day — and the fathers and mothers, and the sons and daughters of these people expect us and look to us to vindicate them in some way. The gentleman who has been nominated came into public life pledged to work for and to devote his life to achieve an Ireland free and independent. That is my recollection of the political gospel he preached when I used to stand on platforms with him — thanks be to God, I do not now. Deputy Cosgrave brought partition into full and complete operation for the first time in the history of our country".

After the vote in his favour, by 76 votes to 70, Cosgrave acknowledged the very great honour conferred on him by the Dail. Referring to some of the speeches made against his nomination, he said that from the strict point of view of Irish nationality he yielded to no man, in the House or outside it. "That is a thing I would advise Deputy O'Kelly not to laugh at. Irish nationality is much more sacred than perhaps even he or his friends think".

MR. O'KELLY: You know a lot about it.

THE PRESIDENT: Whatever action I may have taken at any time during the last five years, I have taken it with the authority of the people of this country, with the authority of this Dáil.

MR. O'KELLY: You have not.

THE PRESIDENT: The Deputy's seat was vacant for five years. If he had a case to make against my administration, this Dáil was the place to make it in, the first institution in this country.

MR. O'KELLY: The seats of many are vacant. We know where their graves are.

THE PRESIDENT;   And so do I.

A DEPUTY: Kevin O'Higgins.

On 19 October 1927, Cosgrave announced to the Dail that, the Deputies to be Ministers and members of the Executive Council:—

Deputy Ernest Blythe, Vice-President, (Finance and the Department of Posts and Telegraphs). Deputy Desmond Fitzgerald, (Defence). Deputy J.M. O'Sullivan, (Education). Deputy Patrick McGilligan, (External Affairs and Industry and Commerce). Deputy Patrick Hogan (Galway), Lands and Agriculture. Deputy Finian Lynch, (Fisheries). Deputy Richard Mulcahy, (Local Government and Public Health). Deputy James Fitzgerald-Kenney, (Justice).

Sean Lemass would later admit that, " perhaps it was good for us we had not succeeded in getting any responsibility for government at that time"[11]. Gerry Boland expressed thanks, saying, " I was glad we were beaten in that effort against the government. At that time we knew nothing about parliamentary procedure or the science of government". He appreciated the five years apprenticeship that followed[12].

That year of 1927 saw the government, in an attempt at populism, exempt the GAA from paying income tax. It was the sole sports organisation so allowed in the Ernest Blythe's Finance Act[13].

Seán Lemass, Eamon deValera, Seán T. O'Kelly, P.J. Ruttledge withdraw from Dáil in June 1927, after refusing to take the Oath of Allegiance to the King of England.

W.T. with his son Liam on left, at a Phoenix Park Horse Race event, in 1959.

CHAPTER EIGHTEEN

AMERICAN VISIT: LEGITIMACY STILL DENIED

ECONOMICS - THE RED SCARE

1928-1932

In January 1928, Cosgrave and Desmond Fitzgerald travelled on a semi-official visit to the United States of America and Canada. The visit was of enormous diplomatic and symbolic significance for the country, as both states had an intimate relationship with Ireland. Their leaders made the point that more Irish people probably lived in their countries, than in Ireland itself. Cosgrave sailed on the *Homeric* from Cherbourg accompanied by Desmond Fitzgerald, D. O'Hegarty, secretary to the Executive Council, and JJ Walsh, secretary at External Affairs. All participated in the usual social niceties of the ship's voyage. According to fellow passengers, Cosgrave clocked up at least ten miles every day on his walks around the ship. In mid Atlantic, they encountered severe weather and arrived two days behind time. This put continual pressure on their schedule. They docked in New York at the Battery on the foot of Broadway, where a 19-gun salute and the anthems of both countries greeted them. Sixty reporters came aboard to interview Cosgrave. He met Mayor Walker and Cardinal Hayes in the afternoon. At City Hall he said, "I thank God I have lived to see this day and that Providence has been good enough in our times, to grant our people that recognition which they have so long sought and to the realisation of which, New York has so magnificently testified today". A small group of protesters waved Union Jacks and called out, "Welcome to the Prince of Wales" and "Up deValera".[1]

Cosgrave left for Chicago that same day, as he was guest at Mayor William Hale Thompson's mayoral banquet that night. Five thousand people attended and over five million listened to his speech, which was carried on radio. His next stop was Washington, where he spent three days, staying at the Mayflower hotel. There, he was met with the normal welcome of a head of government. He met President Coolidge at the White House, where he announced that he was merely returning the visit paid in 1771 by Benjamin Franklin to the Irish Parliament in Dublin. He was received at both Houses of Congress, where business was suspended in his honour. He told the Congressmen, "I come to thank the American people for the part they have played in the achievement of our liberty". He received a Doctorate of Laws from Archbishop

Curley, at the Catholic University of Washington. He was also to receive an honorary LLD, from the National University of Ireland in 1929. He laid a wreath at the Tomb of the Unknown Soldier, and also at the graves of Thomas Addis Emmet and Dr. William MacNevin. He visited Washington's tomb at Mount Vernon and had lunch at the National Press Club. There he was asked the loaded question of what he thought of Prohibition. He replied that he had been so busy with his work in Ireland that he was unable to keep up to date with events in other countries. When asked, which Americans he admired most, he replied coyly; " One does not institute comparisons with saints". His main theme during all his speeches was the sovereign status of the Free State. He attended a lavish banquet hosted by the British Ambassador, Sir Esme Howard. Cosgrave summed up his Washington visit, " The greatest compliment paid to Ireland in modern times. It overwhelmed me with pride and gratitude".[2]

The Irish party next paid a short visit to Philadelphia, but to their great regret had to cancel a planned visit to that most Irish of cities, Boston. From Philadelphia they travelled to Montreal by train. There, they were assigned a special carriage on a train for Ottawa. However not far from Ottawa, at Limoges, the train ran off the tracks while travelling at sixty miles an hour. The train driver was killed and four carriages overturned. Luckily the carriage carrying the Irish party remained on the tracks. First reports spoke of possible sabotage. Desmond Fitzgerald among the Irish party, fared worst in the melee, but a large brandy soon revived him. As the driver was laid out, in a white shroud, Cosgrave recited the *De Profoundis* over his body. An inquiry into the crash later found that it was caused by the neglect to close the points, after an earlier train had passed the way.

The arrival in Ottawa was delayed, and the visiting party went direct to lunch at Government House and in the afternoon attended a session of the Dominion Parliament. During the twenty-four hour stay in Ottawa, Cosgrave emphasised the corresponding constitutional status of Canada and the Irish Free State. Then it was back to New York for more engagements.

deValera was also in New York at that time, on one of his regular visits in connection with his mission to collect funds for the establishment of his newspaper the *Irish Press*. When asked at a press conference, whether he might call to see deValera, Cosgrave replied, "I see no reason why the head of the government should call on one of his citizens". DeValera had earlier told the same paper that his own party, would adhere to constitutional methods for as long as possible[3]. Cosgrave met John Devoy and Judge Cohalan, two important leading Irish-Americans, and long-time admirers of his. He said that the Free State Government was willing to fully pay the holders of Irish Republican Bonds, provided that the money was deposited to the Irish Republican account in America and turned over to the Free State[4]. The *Olympic* delayed its departure from New York for Southampton, to allow Cosgrave attend the annual Emerald Ball of the St Patrick's Society. It is likely that deValera travelled home on the same voyage[5].

One can only surmise how this man of whom it was said, that he was "the enemy of all pomposity, which wakened in him, a spirit of mischievous humour and that he was an expert at puncturing it with a whimsical comment or a seemingly innocent query; a modest man, who never showed the slightest ambition to be at the head of affairs or to claim, much more less to monopolise the limelight", found these exciting North American experiences. However he did tell *The New York Times*, that it would be a good thing for Ireland, if there was a change of government. It was about time that the opposition took over and had an opportunity of running the country. He said that it was not good for the same government to rule for too long[6].

On arrival at Dunlaoire, a nineteen-gun salute, fireworks and the entire cabinet, and hundreds of dignitaries met Cosgrave. He proceeded into the city where a huge crowd had gathered to welcome him home outside the Gresham hotel in O'Connell St. His concluding remarks were, " God bless the people of America, the United States and Canada and God bless Ireland"[7].

LEGITIMACY DENIED

The advent of Fianna Fail to the Dail might have been expected to lead to a normalising of politics in the Chamber and the State. But this did not happen. Though they had aspired to an immediate ascent to form a government, Fianna Fail was far from ready to form an administration, even in a technical role. During their early months in the Dail, it became clear, not unnaturally, that they were not *au fait* with a vast array of procedures of government. In a real way, Fianna Fail was fortunate that it did not gain power in 1927, and was afforded an apprenticeship of five years, during which the Cosgrave administration, had established an international political platform, from which it could safely pursue its constitutional programme. But even within the narrow local politics of the Dail and country, Fianna Fail did not act as a normal political party. It claimed, proudly, that it was "a slightly constitutional party", in Sean Lemass's words. Speaking in the Dail on 21 March 1928, he declared that Fianna Fail only adopted political agitation in a pragmatic manner. He said that if politics did not work, then they "may recoup our strength sufficiently to go on the offensive", as they did five years earlier. Fianna Fail refused, in the Dail on 28 March 1928, to give any assurance that its members would cooperate with the Gardai in apprehending the murderers of O'Higgins. Sean T. O'Kelly referred to the Minister for Defence as "the so-called Minister for Defence" on 27 February 1929, in the Dail.

deValera himself, gave his views in an extraordinary statement in the Dail, on 14 March 1929. He regarded the Dail as illegitimate and did not necessarily feel bound by majority rule. He was prepared to return to force again, if necessary. He recognised the legitimate continuity of Sinn Fein and by inference of the IRA, as the legitimate army. He accused the Executive of using force. He said: " I still hold that your right to be regarded as the legitimate government of this country is faulty, that this House itself is faulty. You have secured a de facto position…you brought off a coup d'etat in the summer of 1922...there is a moral handicap in your case...we had to come in here, if there was to be a majority at all of the people's representatives in any one assembly...As a practical rule, and not because there is anything sacred in it, I am prepared to accept majority rule, as settling matters of national policy".

SHANNON HYDRO-ELECTRICAL SCHEME

On 2 April 1925 the Minister for Industry and Commerce, Paddy McGilligan, introduced a motion in the Dail for the first stage in the exploitation of the river Shannon, to bring electricity to all towns and villages of above five hundred in population.

In July 1929, President Cosgrave pressed the button and raised the gates of the intake weir, at O'Brien's Bridge, to allow the first of many millions of tons of water from the dammed-up river Shannon, to trickle down the dusty rock bed of the canal, to the closed sluice gates at the big penstocks at Ardnacrusha. In the twelve months that followed, the canal slowly filled up to a majestic volume. On 29 October 1929, the great turbines in the power station set the generators in motion. The electricity created travelled all over the country. A great economic and social revolution ensued. The scheme had cost a total of five and a half million pounds. The first sugar beet factory set up at Carlow also proved of major economic significance[8]. It was noticeable and understandable that these enormous technological advances were made through the use of German expertise.

Another important initiative assisted by Cosgrave, was the establishment in 1926 of the Irish Army Equitation School. The barrister who assisted Cosgrave at his court-martial in 1916, Wylie, was then a leading figure in the Royal Dublin Society, where Cosgrave was also a member. The RDS was the centre of animal husbandry in the country and the location of the world famous Dublin Horse Show. Wylie together with Col. Hogan of the army, met with Cosgrave to explore the idea of the school. Cosgrave was enthusiastic always being interested in horses. So much so, indeed, that funding was made available to have Ireland field jumping teams for international events. The intention was to advertise the new State and to promote the Irish horse. Cosgrave was a keen follower of the Ward and Hillside Hunts.

The Free State governments were not overly enthusiastic about industrial development, and employment in manufacturing may have fallen during their period in office. Though Cosgrave often described himself as a businessman, in July 1926, he referred disparagingly, to Irish businessmen as, 'antique furniture'[9].

ECONOMIC DIFFICULTIES

The great economic slump that had begun with the Wall St stock marker crash of 1929, helped to create added difficulties to the already poor economic situation in Ireland. The natural inclination of the Cosgrave governments was, in line with conventional wisdom, to, at all cost, balance the budgets. This naturally alienated the Labour Party, which decided to offer support to Fianna Fail, as a possible way of changing the economic prospects of the country. The economic policy of the government naturally caused great social unrest among workers and the unemployed and disaffected. Cumann na nGael was clearly the party of the property owning classes, farmers and professional people. Their economic well being, was dependant on high emigration and late marriage, if not permanent celibacy for many. They were not overly concerned about the underclasses. Many believed that that was the natural order of things. The Catholic Church also supported this 'controlled' view of society, and was more than willing to encourage a closed and inward looking State, which outlawed materials, which might lower the morals of the people. Indecency and sexual immorality were regarded as the great evils. It was not helpful that a majority of the less well off in Ireland were republicans, who believed that they were being discriminated against, by the State apparatus.

Revolution remained in the air for republicans, if only it could be tapped. Both the army and the Garda were in the vanguard of the state apparatus in seeking to defeat the republicans. They sometimes felt that the government and the judiciary were too soft on the republicans, and the forces of law and order had often to 'take matters into their own hands'. This became somewhat institutionalised when in August 1929 army officers formed the National Defence League, ostensibly for educational purposes, which Eoin O'Duffy and other senior Gardai also joined.

This quickly became a forum for discontent on pay and conditions and the resolve to defeat terrorism. It soon came into conflict with the Minister for Defence, Desmond Fitzgerald. On 16 October 1930 the Council of Defence requested all serving army officers and reservists resign from the NDA. Its executive committee protested in great detail to Cosgrave, with definite connotations of the earlier army mutiny period in the air. O'Duffy was a leading member and he used his role as a tool to pressurise the government. He did this clearly, in the furore over Saor Eire and the resulting bishop's pastoral letter. He also made representations on behalf of his members, who were outraged to find a third reduction in their wages being mooted at the end of 1931. Gardai wages had been reduced by 14% in 1924 and 3% in 1929. In a meeting in late 1931,with Blythe, who was deputising for Fitzgerald, O'Duffy made it clear that most Gardai were supporters of Cumann na nGaedheal and acted on behalf of the party at election time.

He said that Gardai felt let down by the government and it would not be "readily forgiven or forgotten"[10]. By 1931, the government had decided to sack O'Duffy, if returned to power in the forthcoming election. Cosgrave, in particular, had always been suspicious of his reactionary tendencies.

In November 1931 the government felt obliged to bring in a supplementary budget, which added four pence to a gallon of petrol, increased income tax by six pence in the pound and cut wages of teachers and Gardai. Fianna Fail repeated its success of June 1930 in wining another bye-election.

THE RED SCARE

When Fianna Fail entered the Dail, the IRA felt that it had to protect its flank from losing out to the politicians. A political wing became a constant topic for debate, as Sinn Fein became almost moribund. However many within the IRA were hostile to any tendency towards politics. Gradually though this idea got support and in 1931, Sean MacBride officially launched a new organisation, called Saor Eire. It had a distinctly communistic flavour. Its subtitle was "An Organisation of Workers and Working Farmers". Its objects were:

1. To break the connection with England.

2. To vest all political power within the Republic...

3. To abolish, without compensation, landlordism in land, fisheries and minerals

4. To develop the Agricultural Industry, the Fishing Industry, the mineral Resources, by State credits through Industrial and Workers' Cooperatives.

5. To establish a State monopoly in Banking and Credits...

6. To establish a State monopoly in Export and Import services...

7. To have all forms of Public Inland transport taken over by the State..

8. To make provision of Housing for citizens a State matter.

9. To guarantee a minimum standard of living for each citizen.

10. To establish a Social Insurance Scheme for old age, widows, orphans and for the maintenance of the physically and mentally incapacitated.

11. To end the payment of every form of Imperial Tribute.

12. To restore and foster the Gaelic Culture, Language and pastimes.

13. To bring about the closest cooperation between workers in agricultural and in rural districts, and those in towns and cities; to bring them to realise that their interests are mutual; that, therefore, they should be allies, as they are all victims of the same exploiting agencies[11].

Cosgrave condemned Saor Eire in the Dail in September 1929, as a new patriotism based on Muscovite teachings with a sugar coating of Irish extremism, completely alien to Irish tradition. He said that the right to private property was a fundamental principle of Christian civilisation, and the first citadel attacked by the Russian Communists[12].

The Government was so concerned with Saor Eire, that it set out to seek its condemnation from the church. Cosgrave briefed Cardinal MacRory, telling him that he had delayed as long as possible in adding to the Cardinal's many anxieties. But the facts made it imperative that the head of the church in the country should be given the fullest information, about a situation which threatened the whole fabric of both church and state. Cosgrave told the Cardinal that he did not want any meeting between them to give rise to any conjecture, but "every exit of mine from Dublin is duly chronicled". He suggested that the Cardinal might come to his house for a secret meeting. Cosgrave told MacRory that the situation was desperate. He said; " We are confronted with a completely new situation. Doctrines are being taught and practised which were never before countenanced amongst us and I feel that the influence of the church alone will be able to prevail in the struggle against them. Only through the powerful influence of the Church will innocent youths be prevented from being led into a criminal conspiracy, escape from which is impossible because it involves the certainty of vengeance and the grave danger of death. The Church alone, in my view, can affect the conscience of parents and others in regards to the dangers, to which our young people are exposed. The Church moreover can bring powerful influence to bear on those, who through inadvertence or otherwise have in the past, by unreasonable or uninformed criticism of State institutions and State servants, as apart from political leaders, parties or programmes, contributed in some degree towards preparing the ground for the spread of doctrines mentioned"[13].

On 17 September 1931 Cosgrave circulated an extensive Memorandum on the subversion involved to all the bishops. He wrote to Archbishop Byrne:

My Lord Archbishop,

         My colleagues and I have been watching for some time with grave anxiety the rapid growth in this country of subversive teachings and activities. A situation without parallel as a threat to the foundations of all authority has arisen, and we have come to the conclusion after very serious consideration that it was our duty to put before the Cardinal, the Archbishops and the Bishops of Ireland, a statement of the facts so that they might be enabled to judge the extent and gravity of the issues involved.

I have the honour to send Your Grace herewith a memorandum on the situation together with copies of certain documents referred to therein.

I have the honour to be

Your Grace's most obedient humble servant,

Liam T. MacCosgair[13a]

Not to be outflanked, deValera, who was shown the Cosgrave memoranda to the bishops, sought a meeting with the Cardinal. This took place in Maynooth. It was a cordial discussion. However on that same day, deValera saw the danger of his party being associated by the Communistic mantle, when one of his chief lieutenants, Frank Aiken, called in the Dail, on 16 October, for all-party talks with Saor Eire[14]. A few days later, just after the publication of the bishops pastoral letter, Aiken wrote directly to the Cardinal, saying that, "the excommunication of members of the IRA creates such a danger to the future of the church and to the people, that I am compelled, as an

Irishman who wants to see the church stand as a bulwark to the faith and rights and liberties of the people, to appeal to you not to be content with condemnation of the results of evil, but to take active and fatherly steps to deal with the root cause"[15].

A massive public welcome marked the arrival in January 1930 of the Papal Nuncio, Paschal Robinson. Cosgrave felt that Robinson, a Dubliner and a very experienced Vatican diplomatic, would give a fillip to his attempts to enlist the support of the hierarchy against the IRA and Saor Eire.

Activities outside the Dail were to mirror the above sentiments, with law and order a moveable feast for republicans. Murders continued and juries came under pressure. The Government were forced to introduce a Juries Protection Bill on 1 May 1929, which envisaged the secret empanelling of juries, majority verdicts of nine out of twelve, penalties for the intimidation of jurors and imprisonment for refusal to recognise the courts. But the shootings continued. During 1931, two members of the IRA were executed for giving information to the police. A garda was shot dead in Tipperary. One hundred men were found drilling in Laois. An arms dump was discovered at the Hell Fire club in the Dublin mountains. Prison warders were attacked. Frank Ryan, an IRA leader, stated in an interview in *An Phoblacht* in August 1931 that shootings, drilling, intimidation were all IRA policy and that they would be escalated. The Government banned that summer's march to Wolfe Tone's grave at Bodenstown. But the IRA went ahead and was joined by Fianna Fail, led by deValera.[16]. As trial by jury proved impossible to secure, the government on 14 October 1931 inserted a new Article 2A into the Constitution which established military courts, to deal with political crime, from which there was no appeal.

In the Dail, Cosgrave named the IRA as the foremost avowedly militaristic organisation, challenging the State, with Cumann na mBan and other women's organisations close collaborators in terrorisation and the breakdown of the judicial system. He named a variety of Communistic groups, such as "The Friend's of Soviet Russia", "The Irish Communist Party", "The Irish Working Farmer's Committee", "The Workers' Revolutionary Party in Ireland", "The Irish National Unemployed Movement", "The Worker's Defence Corps", and "The Irish Labour Defence League".

He said that murder, attempted murders, intimidation, arms dumps, drilling were commonplace. He gave detailed examples of such happenings from around the country; the murder of informers, of a Garda Superintendent, intimidations, destruction of public facilities, jury intimidation, expulsions. He declared the attacks upon the Courts as "a complete success". Cosgrave said that due to the absence of serious political crime for a considerable period in 1928, and due to political pressure in the Dail, the Government in December 1928, had agreed to repeal special legislation on anti-State activities. No sooner was this done than the whole situation deteriorated drastically. He declared that no self-respecting nation and no government could allow itself to become enslaved by the terrorist activities of a small minority. The IRA, he said, had recently accepted Saor Eire as its ally. Its aim is to set up a State on the lines of the Russian Soviet Republic.[17]

deValera decried Cosgrave's long list, describing them as 'incidents', and of creating unnecessary "excitement" in the Dail and country. He accused him of creating Black and Tan tactics. He claimed that the "ordinary law" quite capable of dealing with the matter. He said that they should deal with the causes of the unrest, referring to the occasion when Mulcahy was demoted for activities in a secret society. There were political and economic problems, but there was no catastrophic situation imminent, as Cosgrave said. deValera declared that Fianna Fail was against crime and said that "If there is no authority in this House to rule, then there is no authority in any part of the Twenty Six Counties to rule". He then moved to distance himself from an earlier speech, which he claimed was misinterpreted by others, as suggesting that he did not subscribe to majority rule. Despite the fact that he was rowing back furiously, he could not resist again referring to the, "situation created by the Treaty and the coup d'etat by the gentlemen on the opposite benches", as he announced that he did accept majority rule.

Cosgrave accused deValera of posing as a pacificator, a great man with great ideals who, when he used one sentence, followed it with another, which made it impossible for anybody to understand what he meant. He accused deValera of pretending to show him respect, but who in reality, "dislikes me more and has greater hatred for me, than any other man in this country has for another". The new Bill became law on 17 October, resulting in leading IRA men leaving the country[18]. The vote in the Dail on 14 October was 82 for and 64 against. Three days later, the IRA, Saor Eire and ten other organisations were banned.

BISHOPS' PASTORAL

On 18 October the Catholic hierarchy issued a pastoral letter, saying that no Catholic could belong to the IRA or Saor Eire[19]. It said in part;

"Dearly beloved in Christ,

Assembled in Maynooth for our October meeting and deeply conscious of our responsibility for the Faith and morals of our people, we cannot remain silent in the face of the growing evidence of a campaign of Revolution and Communism, which if allowed to run its course unchecked, must end in the ruin of Ireland, both body and soul". It went on to condemn Saor Eire by name.

The government was disappointed that the pastoral was not stronger, but the bishops knew that their area was pastoral and not political. They remained strictly neutral between the government and the opposition and refused an endorsement to the Public Safety Act. Like everyone else they knew that an election was imminent and the outcome uncertain. Sean T. O'Kelly kept up a strenuous effort to let the bishops know that Fianna Fail was made up of Catholics too. The government, through the secretary of the Department of External Affairs, Joseph Walshe, tried foolishly to have the Papal Nuncio intervene with the bishops. When the Irish envoy to the Vatican, Charles Bewley sought to take soundings with the nuncio, he was rebuffed with the information, "Sean MacBride was here with me yesterday. A nice fellow". Bewley asked in surprise, "Your Excellency did not find him a dangerous communist". "No, I didn't notice it", the nuncio replied"[20]. The gardai did not quite see it that way, as Sean MacBride had become public enemy number one, for the state security forces. The Gardai raided the MacBride family home at Roebuck House in Clonskeagh on a regular basis.

IRISH NATIONAL WAR MEMORIAL

The Royal British Legion had instituted an all Ireland project in 1919 to create and develop an Irish National War Memorial to ex-servicemen in Dublin. A National War Memorial committee was established for that purpose. Though WT Cosgrave had declined to attend a Remembrance Day Service at the Cenotaph in London, Kevin O'Higgins had no such inhibitions. O'Higgins said, " Commemoration of the dead is a pious and proper thing, and we should always try to distinguish very clearly between commemoration of the dead and glorification of the living…Unless we are careful the 11th of November commemoration that was intended to be a very solemn act of reverence will degenerate into simply an opportunit for one tradition to go out with symbols and emblems that must be offensive to people of another tradition"[20a]. In the early morning of 11 November 1928 attempts were made to destroy an equestrian statue of King William III at College Green, that of King George II at St. Stephen's Green and the Memorial Fountain at Herbert Park to King Edward VII. In a follow up search the Gardai located an arms cache at Inchicore containing, 3 machine guns, 6 rifles, 30 revolvers, with thousands of rounds of ammunition; 300 detonators, 3 dozen Mills bombs along with military equipment and documentation[20b].

The Memorial Committee considered various sites around Dublin until, in July 1929, on advice from WT Cosgrave to Senator Jameson, it settled on the site at Islandbridge.Cosgrave wrote to Jameson, "There are many schools of thought now, but this is in the main, a big question of Remembrance and Honour to the dead. The war memorial is really not a concern of mine, nor is it a concern of my office esxcept that it must be always be a matter of interest to the Head of the Government to see that a project which is dear to a big section of the citizens, should be a success"[20c].

Sir Edwin Lutyens was retained to design what turned out to be an enormous project. Cosgrave's action attracted virulent republican criticism, such as "The old English garrison, pampered and nursed by the present Free State Government, have votes; and it is through them Mr. Cosgrave hopes to secure another five years in office. The secret circular from the Unionists to their fellow-Masons soliciting funds to return Mr Cosgrave at the next election and Mr. Cosgrave's grant of £50,000 out of Irish people's money for their English Memorial Park, throws off the mask of Irish Nationality"[20d]. When the War Memorial was eventually completed in the mid 1930's, the Committee sought agreement from President deValera for its official opening. He prevaricated until in May 1939, he postponed it indefinitely due to the "triumphal presentation proposed by the British Legion and on the grounds of the developing political situation in Europe" Eventually the Islandbridge Memorial was officially opened in 1980.[20e]

As an election loomed, Cosgrave endeavoured to put the record of the government before the public and praise those who had assisted them in the Dail. He and Richard Mulcahy attended a meeting in Kilkenny in February 1931. Cosgrave listed the government record.

1.   World reputation for national solvency.

2.   Improved essential services.

3.   Reduction in national taxation.

4.   Shannon scheme progress beyond wildest expectations.

5.   Further work to augment electricity.

6.   Praised agricultural output.

7.   A new Land Act would lessen annuities and eventually dispense with them.

8.   Praised the patriotism of the Farmers Party and Independents for Dail support.

9.   Praised Labour Party for playing constructive role in Dail.

Fianna Fail was a menace to the country, meriting no commendation, he said. However he went on the say that the people had a perfect right to hand over to the tender mercies of the Government opponents, the work which they had accomplished, and to elect a government which would destroy the institutions under which this work was possible. He added that every day proved more conclusively the wisdom of President Griffith's exhortation, "Let the people stand firm for the Free State; it is their national need and salvation"[21].

The adjournment debate at the end of December 1931 was on unemployment. Fianna Fail decried the attempts by the government to improve economic life in the country. However, as was usual, bitter party politics always came to the fore. Fianna Fail wanted to raise the treatment of political prisoners, which they termed, anybody sentenced by the Military Tribunal. Dr. Ryan deemed the President as a man who "has a reputation of being a very pious man and having a conscience". When Sean Lemass offered to tell Cosgrave of his own personal experiences as a political prisoner, the latter retorted, "You cam tell them on the hustings".

Cosgrave, in closing the debate ranged over many of the measures that the government had taken to improve the economy of the country. He said that peace and good order were essentials. He said the main industry in the country was agriculture. He instanced various Acts which were passed to improve matters; Live Stock Breeding, Butter, Eggs, Dead Meat, Sugar Beet Industry, Drainage, Afforestation, Electrification, using the River Shannon. He noted that Sean T O'Kelly had practically charged him with responsibility for housing conditions in Dublin. He reminded O'Kelly that he had not been a member of the Corporation since May 1922, though O'Kelly was a current member. He said that over 6,000 houses were built in Dublin with the assistance of the government. The health of Dubliners was improving. The death rate had dropped from 35.0 in 1890, 26.0 in 1900, 27.5 in 1910, 19.9 in 1920, 18.1 in 1 and in 1930, 15.0 per thousand.

To this information Frank Aiken interjected, "Reduce the cost of government". Cosgrave then informed the House that the cost of government in 1922 was £25 million, of which £1 million went to local authorities. The cost of government in 1931 was £21.7 million of which £3.7 million went to local authorities. At the end of Cosgrave's speech, Sean Lemass replied, "If that is the President's election speech, he can bow himself out now". Cosgrave replied, "If the Deputy likes to think so, he is welcome".

Tom Garvin has written that there was a deep sense of admiration in Sean Lemass for WT Cosgrave as a fellow inner city Dubliner. John Horgan writes that when some years earlier Lemass was being criticised for his mode of public speaking, He adopted Cosgrave's style, clipped and direct without long rambling sentences[21a]. This was certainly reciprocated, as Cosgrave reckoned that Lemass would have been a better successor as President of the Executive Council than DeValera. Their common sense of humour, is I think captured by Padraic Colum, writing in 1922 of Cosgrave: "he speaks leaning forward, his hands on the barrier before him; his delivery becomes like a series of pistol shots, each word out, each word reaching its mark. He is sociable as becomes a Dublin man and abundantly witty. His wit is a Dublin wit. It is founded on a very exact estimate of character. He can reveal character in a mordant phrase. Before his humour, before the phrase that springs up in his speech, pretensciousness of all kinds fall away"[22]. The Dail then adjourned to 10 February 1932.

Rememberance Ceremony at the Irish National War Memorial Islandbridge,
Dublin 2004.

GENERAL ELECTION 1932

The prerogative of dissolving the Dail and calling a general election rested with Cosgrave. This did not have to take place until October 1932. As in most elections, tactics are very important and correct timing vital. The budgetary outlook for 1932 was poor, with cutbacks the order of the day. Despite the fact that the government was bound to gain great popular kudos out of the forthcoming Eucharistic Congress, Cosgrave decided that it was better to go for the election, early rather than later. Indeed the advent of the Congress may have been a factor on his part, as he would not have wished that occasion to be marked by divisive politicking. The Eucharistic Congress was awarded to a different capital city every three years. Cosgrave had put a lot of personal effort into its awarding to Dublin, and the government had spent a very large amount of time and energy preparing for it. It would have been the crowning occasion for Cosgrave's association with the church. However, as it transpired, it was to be deValera who gained from the massive event.

On 10 January, speaking in Ennis Co Clare, Cosgrave made what appeared to be an election call to the people. Quoting Arthur Griffith, he said: " Let the people stand firm for the Free State. It is their national need and everyone's salvation. In his last, practically his dying political testament to the Irish people, Arthur Griffith enshrined in one vivid flash of thought, the ripe fruit of a political life, filled with arduous work for the Irish people. I call upon you Irish electors to stand firm for the Free State, with your votes and with your help, and to rally to the maintenance and defence of your Constitution: the same courage, industry, and clear national thought you brought so magnificently to their setting up"[1].

During the number of weeks before the election, Frank Gallagher, Editor of the *Irish Press* was standing trial before a Military Tribunal at Collins Barracks in Dublin, charged with seditious libel in that newspaper. The charge read that he "intended to bring the administration of the law into disrepute and to scandalise and vilify the government and the Garda"[2]. The relationship between the Garda and Fianna Fail was, not unexpectedly, problematic. As late as November 1928, Fianna Fail had criticised the Garda, accusing them of political bias, terrorising the countryside, not having enough work to do and there being too many of them.[2a]. The trial was a most unwise backdrop to an election campaign, as it could be seen as an attack on free speech in deValera's controversial new newspaper.

The result of the case, announced the day after polling, was a fine of £100 for Gallagher and the same for the newspaper.

Around that same time, Paddy McGilligan and the Irish High Commissioner in London, John Dulanty, met King George in Sandringham. The King expressed admiration for the way Cosgrave had fought so well, through such troubled times in Ireland. He hoped Cosgrave would be returned to power, casting doubt on whether deValera could even be classified as an Irishman[3].

On 29 January Cosgrave dissolved the Dail and announced 16 February as the election date, with 6 March the date for the new Dail to meet. The cabinet announced that the expected reduction of 5% in garda pay would not take place. That night a meeting was held at the Mansion House to launch the government election campaign. Thousands cheered Cosgrave from the street into the famous Round Room. Alfie Byrne chaired proceedings and spoke first. Then Cosgrave addressed the packed hall. He addressed many of the issues; no discrimination, respect for State institutions, the government record, good relations with Britain Ireland's best customer, emergence from chaos, ability to take decisions.

He said:

"We present the Irish people with the results of ten years work – national institutions soundly conceived and broad based upon equal opportunity for every citizen, regardless of their religion, creed or former political alliance.

We postulate that the State institutions shall be respected, and that due regard shall be had to the rights of the individual. We present you with a record of activity in every sphere of government, Education, Agriculture, Industry, Drainage, Housing, Social Services – with 50,000 more workers in insured employment today than there were in 1922, with a financial position which is the envy of the wealthier nations in Europe and across the Atlantic.

We present you with ordered social conditions and the reign of law, with peaceful and cordial relations, not alone with our near neighbour and greatest customer, but with every country in the world.

We found this country in chaos when we took office: we have it now in a better position than any other to face the world crisis, and to avail to the fullest of any amelioration which may take place in world conditions.

In commons with other countries, we in Ireland are faced with the immediate necessity of taking important and far reaching decisions. They require to be firmly and courageously acted upon. A government that has a clear mandate from the people, to take those decisions and to act upon them, can only do that safely and effectively.

That is what I ask tonight from the people of Ireland. We ask it, confident that the good sense which has characterised these decisions in the past, will guide them in this serious hour"[4].

The next day Cosgrave began a series of whirlwind tours of the country that was to bring him to all the large towns and cities. In Killarney he had lunch with the bishop of Kerry. He visited both Catholic and Church of Ireland bishops in Limerick.. He was welcomed from the altar at mass in Ennis by his friend Bishop Fogarty, who prayed for "divine protection and guidance for our great President WT Cosgrave, to whom we extend a cead mile failte to Ennis". Large-scale newspaper advertising of half page and full-page varieties occurred. One such example appearing on behalf of Cumann na nGaedheal appeared in the Irish Independent of 4 February 1932 and read:-

TO THE PEOPLE
OF THE
IRISH FREE STATE

THE Irish People fought for centuries to secure control over their destiny, to be able to develop an Independent, Cultural and Economic National Life, and so to contribute as a Nation to the Civilisation and Progress of mankind. Such has always been the aspiration of civilised oppressed peoples, and no people, once freed from oppression, has attempted to realise it by any other means than that of the organised State.

Through the instrumentality of the Treaty the Government have, in a brief space of time, constructed an ordered State. The framework of that State is wide enough to provide for the completest national development, cultural and economic, of the whole People of Ireland. That State is free from any external restraint whatsoever. The men who accepted the Treaty and who laboured to win from it all that is needed for the fullest development of the Nation's life have been eminently justified. With a tradition in which the Famine years were still vivid memories and in which an Ireland, oppressed and poverty-stricken for centuries, was the dominating factor, they knew that future generations would rightly hold them responsible if they did not seize the last chance of constructing a national life for the Irish People.

The State belongs to the people. On you depends its continued existence. On you depends the issue whether it shall continue to afford shelter to you and your children for the development of an ordered, prosperous, and God-fearing life, or whether it is to go down in a confusion of political experiments entirely foreign to Irish mentality, bringing with it for ever all hope of national or economic revival.

And that is the issue at the Coming Election.

The Members of the Government, having in their blood, like the vast majority of the plain People of Ireland, centuries of Irish history and Irish suffering, feel it to be their most solemn duty to save the State from those whose policy, if put into practice, would involve its destruction, and whose intentions, if realised, would ultimately throw us back to the dark despair and the grinding poverty which formed the normal life of our fathers only three generations ago. The Government's aim has been to preserve and strengthen the State so that its present citizens may live their lives in peace and happiness—so that the whole People of this Island may eventually find within it complete security for their fullest development on the basis of close friendly relations among themselves and cordial co-operation with the people of the neighbouring Island.

Our Nation has been built upon the spirit of sacrifice in the cause of the better things of human existence. That spirit has formed the essential fabric of its history and the main inspiration of its long struggle for Freedom. No other Nation has such a tradition of suffering and sacrifice in the cause of Religion as our Nation, and therein lies our strongest reason for pride in our past and our strongest hope for the future greatness of our People. No Nation can abandon its traditions without losing the essentials of nationhood.

We intend to continue to defend these traditions, as we intend to continue our work of enshrining once more in the Language which constitutes our only real hope of re-creating the living Irish Nation. We intend to shelter our national heritage from doctrines which are subversive of Religion, Home and Country, and we intend to use our utmost endeavour to prevent the occurrence in Ireland of the terrible things which are happening to-day in a country with a Spiritual tradition hardly less noble than our own.

On 11 February increases in unemployment figures for the current year in a variety of countries were published. They read:

France	566%
New Zealand	184 %
Latvia	124%
Belgium	118%
Irish Free State	3%[5]

On 13 February a forecast of the election results read:

Cumann na nGaedheal	76
Fianna Fail	75
Labour	20
Independents	14[6]

The New York Times found Cosgrave "cold and unromantic with no attraction for Irish youth", compared with the deValera campaign which it found "arousing emotions and enthusiasm, strangely like those Adolf Hitler is spreading through Germany. Only those with first hand knowledge of Cosgrave's difficulties can appreciate the greatness of this little tawny-headed man who has been in office longer than any other Prime Minister in Europe"[7].

The day before the election, consternation occurred as an ex-Cumann na nGaedheal T.D. Patrick Reynolds, and a detective, were shot dead at Foxfield near Ballinamore in Leitrim. For a brief period it was thought that the IRA had gone crazy, but luckily, it was soon discovered that the shootings were as a result of a local and personal feud. The country breathed a sigh of relief[8]. The election in the seven-seat constituency of Leitrim-Sligo was postponed until just before the Dail was scheduled to meet. Mrs Reynolds stood in her husband's place and won a seat. However Fianna Fail won a new seat there.

The election overall, passed off quite peacefully. The IRA, while having their differences with Fianna Fail, had no choice but to back deValera. Their slogan was, "Put Cosgrave Out"[9]. The forthcoming Eucharistic Congress on 20 June, had focussed the public's mind on the necessity for good order. An Imperial Economic Congress was scheduled for Ottawa on 21 July and an Irish government, with a solid mandate from the electorate, was important. The IRA was also very much on the defensive from the effects on it of Article 2A. If the IRA were to run an abstentionism campaign, they risked returning Cosgrave to power. The Army Council of the IRA changed its policy and allowed its members to participate in the Free State election, while emphasising to them that, "our objects cannot be achieved by the methods of politicans of the parties seeking election"[10]. According to Bowyer Bell, "IRA men participated in the time honoured fashion of multiple voting of emigrants, corpses and the poor man, who is slow to reach the booth", all on behalf of Fianna Fail, which provided it with the necessary voting lists. He states that some Volunteers voted as many as fifty times[11].

deValera being the cunning politician that he was, cut his cloth to suit his measure in the election campaign. He would abolish the oath. However, gone was any mention of the Republic or any thought of constitutional changes, without an additional mandate. He would abolish the land annuities and promote self-sufficiency on the land through he promotion of tillage. He would protect Irish industry by establishing tariffs on imports.

The result was not in any sense overwhelming in the circumstances, but it did offer the opportunity to "Put Cosgrave Out", by a little temporary manoeuvring with the Labour Party.

The Irish Times had little doubt as to which party, it wished to win the election, editorialising on Election Day:

" ...The fact that today the Free State can be numbered among the most prosperous countries in Europe, is a tribute to the devoted work that has been done against heavy odds by President Cosgrave and his colleagues". It spoke about the great diplomatic advances that had been made in recent years. Then it dealt with Fianna Fail, saying, " The party that is offering itself as an alternative, advances a policy of sheer negation...only constructive plank is high tariffs which will impoverish the country...there can only be one choice for an intelligent voter. Fianna Fail has an efficient organisation and will poll every available vote. Its policy appeals to younger and irresponsible elements".

By 18 February some results were in, with the figures for some leading personalities being compared with the two previous elections:

Name	1932	9/1927	6/1927
Cosgrave	18,125	17,395	-
deValera	12,507	13,903	13,025
Blythe	7,524	7,171	5,532
Redmond	7,276	6,633	7,687
Byrne Alfie	18,117	11,844	17,781
O'Kelly Sean T.	9,176	6,968	6,040
Lemass	10,426	11,240	8,582

On 19 February ninety-four seats were filled, with fifty-eight remaining.

Elected	C. Na nG.	F.F.	Ind.	Lab.	Farm
	36	46	8	5	2

On 20 February the list read;

46	62	11	7	3

On 22 February the list read;

49	65	13	7	4

The Irish Independent headline reported a, "Complex Political Situation", "Seeking Compromise to avoid effect of election Deadlock", "Mr deValera plans for Government". The indecisiveness of the Fianna Fail victory, assisted in calming the transitional period, between the election and the formation of the new government. The Completed list read:

57	72	13	7	4

Shortly before the take-over of power Fianna Fail, in the persons of deValera and Sean T. O'Kelly, met with Archbishop Byrne to ensure his good offices for the transition. Some of the party had opposed this meeting, on the basis that the bishops had been no friends of Fianna Fail. But deValera proved to be as keen as Cosgrave to have the hierarchy on side, and offer them full government consultation.

WT Cosgrave and his Ministers decided that their role would be in opposition. Cosgrave proposed to let Fianna Fail and Labour, who had been attacking his politics for the previous ten years, work for prosperity and better prices. He promised to assist them in every way he could and if they succeeded, he would take off his cap to them. He appeared completely unperturbed, and rather in high spirits by the situation. He hoped that the government would proceed in a regular way, if it desired to remove the oath, and negotiate with Great Britain on the matter. He offered to assist in every way in anything that would be of value to the people. Labour and Fianna Fail agreed a post-election programme.

1.   A maintenance scheme for 80,000 unemployed.

2.   Building of 40,000 houses.

3.   A pension scheme for widows and orphans[12].

Cosgrave thanked his constituents in Cork for re-electing him and said his services would be given in a different capacity. "The task of opposition in the Dail will, I sincerely hope, be characterised in the same sober and balanced judgement, as when we had administrative responsibility".

A not disinterested observer at the time, Conor Cruise O'Brien wrote, "I was fifteen then and rejoiced in the change…the idea of putting out a government which has been in as long as you can remember has natural attractions for a youth of fifteen… 1932 brought to most Irish people a new sense of legitimacy in the institutions of the new State. Up to 1932, the State and the pro-Treaty party had seemed one thing, and the idea of the State, and consequently the quality of Ireland's independence, seemed limited and tarnished thereby. When the government changed, through democratic elections, the citizens felt better about their State and about themselves"[12a].

COUP D'ETAT

Arrangements for the setting up of a new government appeared to be running smoothly, with Labour and Fianna Fail negotiating an understanding. Then, on the morning of 26 February, *The Irish Press* newspaper caused consternation, by editorialising on measures in hand by disaffected groups, to stage a coup d'etat, preventing Fianna Fail forming a government. The paper said:

"On Wednesday, commenting on the announcement that the members of the Government definitely intend to go into opposition, we expressed the hope that the decision would allay the rumour which has been in circulation about the activities of certain members of the outgoing government Ministry. Our hope has not been realised and are arousing considerable anxiety among a section of the public in Dublin. They are to the effect that two Ministers, a well-known member of the Cumann an nGaedheal party and some others, are engaged in a movement to obstruct the transfer of government to Fianna Fail. They are alleged to have formed a secret organisation for this purpose among Free State army pensioners, to whom they appeal, it is said, on the grounds that a Fianna Fail government would be committed to the revision of army pensions".

WT Cosgrave reacted immediately to the editorial deeming the suggestion, "grossly untrue...and clearly mischievous. Its origin can only be explained by a disordered imagination or a guilty conscience. The Ministers and army pensioners have given the best years of their lives to vindicating the right of the people of Ireland to choose the Government". Mr. Blythe called the editorial " utterly absurd and untrue". During the resumed election campaign in Leitrim-Sligo Mr. Hogan, Minister of Agriculture assured the electorate that undertakings had been given to Fianna Fail, that the Army, Civic Guard and ex-servicemen would be obedient servants of the established government.

On 10 February at Wynn's Hotel in Dublin, a meeting took place to organise an ex-army officers association. One week later a formal Army Comrades Association was formed[13].

It would indeed have been surprising, if the possibility of an attempt to prevent Fianna Fail coming to power had not occurred to some people, who had reason to fear such an eventuality. Britain certainly could not have welcomed the advent of their bete noir to power. David Neligan reported in 1970 that the unreliable Eoin O'Duffy had planned a coup in late 1931[14]. John Regan explores the possibility of certain officers and civil servants, who might have had personal reasons for fearing a Fianna Fail government, being involved in taking soundings about a coup[15]. But if so, there were few takers and an orderly transfer of power went ahead smoothly.

Gerry Boland had no doubt but that a coup was mooted by army and ex-servicemen and reported Fianna Fail men being armed in the Dail[16]. However Sean Lemass said about the guns," That is all nonsense". However Lemass was certain that there was a strong effort by a number of army officers, to prevent Fianna Fail taking over.

He said circulars went around with officers names attached, urging action. Lemass then said that, "Mr. Cosgrave must have known of these circulars and before we became ministers, we were given armed guards to protect us…It is a tribute to WT Cosgrave and to those associated with him, because there were some ministers who were mixed up with this idea of preventing a takeover, and they would have nothing to do with it. I suppose it is a remarkable thing that ten years after the Civil War that the Party that lost the war, had by peaceful process, acquired political power and became the government of the State"[17].

Some years earlier Lemass was being criticised for his mode of public speaking, he adopted Cosgrave's style, clipped and direct without long rambling sentences[18].

Cosgrave told the *New York Times* during the interregnum, that he would have preferred as President one of deValera's lieutenants, like Sean Lemass, whom he regarded as a practical politician, rather than deValera, whom he looked upon as an impractical dreamer and a coiner of dangerous phrases[19]. John Horgan wrote, "The Cosgrave government's approach to the 1932 election was marked by an extraordinary tendency to embrace policies guaranteed to bring about defeat"[20].

When the new Dail met on 9 March, Labour, two Farmer T.D's and one Independent supported the election of deValera as President. A vote was called when Cosgrave challenged the motion. The vote was 81 to 68:

FOR:

Aiken, Frank
Allen, Denis
Bartley, Gerald
Beegan, Patrick
Blaney, Neil
Boland, Gerald
Boland, Patrick
Bourke, Daniel
Brady, Bryan
Brady, Seán
Breathnach, Cormac
Breen, Daniel
Briscoe, Robert
Browne, William Frazer
Carney, Frank
Carty, Frank
Clery, Michael

FOR: cont.

Colbert, James
Cooney, Eamonn
Corish, Richard
Corry, Martin John
Crowley, Fred Hugh
Crowley, Tadhg
Curran, Patrick Joseph
Davin, William
Derrig, Thomas
De Valera, Eamon
Dillon, James M.
Dowdall, Thomas P.
Everett, James
Flinn, Hugo V.
Flynn, John
Flynn, Stephen
Fogarty, Andrew

FOR: cont.
Geoghegan, James
Gibbons, Seán
Gormley, Francis
Gorry, Patrick Joseph
Goulding, John
Harris, Thomas
Hayes, Seán
Hogan, Patrick (Clare)
Humphreys, Francis
Jordan, Stephen
Kelly, James Patrick
Kennedy, Michael Joseph
Keyes, Raphael Patrick
Kilroy, Michael
Kissane, Eamonn
Lemass, Seán F.
Little, Patrick John
Lynch, James B.
McEllistrim, Thomas
MacEntee, Seán
Maguire, Ben
Maguire, Conor Alexander
Moane, Edward

FOR: cont.
Moore, Séamus
Moylan, Seán
Murphy, Patrick Stephen
Murphy, Timothy Joseph
Norton, William
O'Grady, Seán
O'Hanlon, John F.
O'Kelly, Seán Thomas
O'Reilly, Matthew
O'Reilly, Thomas J.
O'Rourke, Daniel
O'Shaughnessy, John Joseph
Powell, Thomas P.
Rice, Edward
Ruttledge, Patrick J.
Ryan, James
Ryan, Robert
Sexton, Martin
Sheehy, Timothy
Sheridan, Michael
Smith, Patrick
Traynor, Oscar
Walsh, Richard
Ward, Francis C. (Dr.)

AGAINST:
Alton, Ernest Henry
Anthony, Richard
Beckett, James Walter
Bennett, George Cecil
Blythe, Ernest
Bourke, Séamus A.
Brasier, Brooke
Broderick, William Jos.
Brodrick, Seán
Burke, Patrick
Byrne, Alfred

AGAINST: cont.
Byrne, John Joseph
Coburn, James
Collins-O'Driscoll, Mrs. Margt.
Conlon, Martin
Cosgrave, William T.
Craig, Sir James
Davis, Michael
Desmond, William
Dockrell, Henry Morgan
Doherty, Eugene
Doyle, Peadar Seán

AGAINST: cont.
Duggan, Edmund John
Esmonde, Osmond Grattan
Finlay, Thomas A.
Fitzgerald, Desmond
O'Higgins, Thomas Francis
O'Leary, Daniel
O'Mahony, The
O'Neill, Eamonn
O'Reilly, John Joseph
O'Sullivan, Gearóid
O'Sullivan, John Marcus
Redmond, William Archer
Good, John
Gorey, Denis John
Hassett, John J.
Hayes, Michael
Hennessy, Thomas
Hennigan, John
Hogan, Patrick (Galway)
Keating, John
Keogh, Myles
Kiersey, John
Lynch, Finian

AGAINST: cont.
McDonogh, Fred
MacEoin, Seán
McGilligan, Patrick
McMenamin, Daniel
Minch, Sydney B.
Mongan, Joseph W.
Morrissey, Daniel
Mulcahy, Richard
Murphy, James Edward
Myles, James Sproule
Nally, Martin
O'Brien, Eugene P.
O'Connor, Batt
O'Donovan, Timothy Joseph
O'Hara, Patrick
Reidy, James
Reynolds, Mrs. Mary
Roddy, Martin
Shaw, Patrick Walter
Thrift, William Edward
Vaughan, Daniel
White, John
Wolfe, Jasper Travers

The new President named his cabinet:
The President,
(Department of External Affairs)
Deputy Seán T. O'Kelly, Vice-President,
(Department of Local Government and Public Health)
Deputy Thomas Derrig, (Department of Education)
Deputy Patrick J. Ruttledge, (Department of Lands and Fisheries)
Deputy Seán F. Lemass, (Department of Industry and Commerce)
Deputy Seán MacEntee, (Department of Finance)
Deputy James Ryan, (Department of Agriculture)
Deputy Frank Aiken, (Department of Defence)
Deputy James Geoghegan, (Department of Justice)

One of the first actions taken by the new government was the immediate release of twenty prisoners from Mountjoy Jail. Frank Aiken with the Minister for Justice, James Geoghegan, went to Arbour Hill prison to consult with IRA leaders. Those released included Frank Ryan and George Gilmore. Within a few days, for the first time in many years, several battalions of IRA men marched through Dublin to a large demonstration at College Green, to welcome home the prisoners. Leaders of both the IRA and Saor Eire addressed the large and enthusiastic crowd. Towards the end of the proceedings, Sean MacBride, who was on the platform party with his mother[21], cautioned against the euphoria of the occasion, saying, "We must remember that while the day of coercion has passed, for a time, the task we have set ourselves has not yet been achieved". Two days later de Valera made it clear in the Dail that there would only be one army in the State and he expected the IRA to obey that law. He announced plans to end the oath, end the payment of land annuities and revoke Article 2A. He declared that the country was too small for partition to remain.

Suddenly membership of the IRA became fashionable and it was inundated with new recruits. Many felt that it would be incorporated into the national army. Frank Aiken offered Sean MacBride a commission in the army. MacBride felt insulted and rejected the offer immediately[22]. However he soon accepted a job as sub editor in *The Irish Press*. Within a few months MacBride's mother, Maud Gonne MacBride, felt that de Valera was reneging on his promises, spying and arresting members of the IRA. She reinstated her street activities, protesting against the holding of political prisoners, in her Women Prisoner's Protection League.

De Valera introduced a Bill to abolish the oath of allegiance on 22 March. Cosgrave described the Bill as one of the greatest pieces of political chicanery in history, saying that the Treaty was based on the confidence of mutual respect in each other's good faith. Two of the greatest Irishmen who ever lived signed it and never believed that their signatures would be repudiated. Cosgrave added that the presence on the opposite benches of over 70 T.D.'s, was ample proof for him personally, and the late administration that their persuasive methods bore fruit. He acknowledged that it had been open to his government to enact this measure unilaterally, but though it would have been legal, it would have been dishonourable and a breach of faith. He declared that the British Commonwealth of Nations was as far removed from the British Empire of his boyhood, as they were from the battle of Waterloo. If he was offered the unity of the country with even less powers than they currently had, or a Republic for the Free State, he would plank for the former. He believed that one could advance with a united State, however different the views politically may be; but if such a division was made, as would forever divide off a very important portion of our country, then what do Irish national aspirations mean? He did not see that the economy of the country was going to be assisted by the measure. Britain purchased £30 million worth of goods annually and took 90% of exports. That trade was vulnerable. Britain provided a great market for tourism. In the election Fianna Fail promised a plan and a solution for unemployment. Cosgrave said that all other governments, including that of Hindenburg, Hoover, Britain, France and even Signor Mussolini, the Duce, had failed to cure it.

One of deValera's earliest decisions was to announce a reduction in salaries for the government personnel. His salary was reduced from £2,500 to £1,500 and that of his ministers from £1,700 to £1,000. The equivalent figures payable in the North were £3,200 and £2,000.

On 22 March deValera introduced a Bill to remove the Annuities. In June he announced the unilateral withholding of the land annuities. This led to the British imposing a twenty per cent duty on most Irish exports to Britain. deValera responded in like measure to British imports, initiating what came to be called 'the economic war'.

Many people have written about the almost inevitability of Cosgrave's defeat, even without the IRA working so assiduously for Fianna Fail. The election campaign has been described as, " the most appallingly inefficient campaign in living memory". Cosgrave's motives are not doubted, but his political acumen is. The reduction of old age pensions and salaries of teachers and gardai, and the prohibition on married women teachers allied to the fact of 100,000 unemployed, did not help. Both the rich and the poor had good cause to fear a revolution. Cumann na nGaedheal fought the election on the 'Red Scare' and the untrustworthiness of Fianna Fail. They promised more of the same, stable government and austerity measures. Their national organisation remained amateur compared to the 1,404 Fianna Fail Cumainn. The division between the elite government cadres and the party membership remained distant. Even the party's T.D's had been poor attendees in the Dail. The pressure exercised by the party on the elite had lessened greatly when John Marcus O'Sullivan became Chairman of the party, after JJ Walsh left in 1927. Thus the elite professional class of Cumann na nGaedheal throughout the country remained intact but could not deliver mass votes, despite their local respectability and association with the church and ex-unionists Another element within the party, relished the advent of Fianna Fail to office on constitutional grounds, so that they would experience the harsh facts of economic management and fail therein. The elite of Cumann na nGaedheal still saw themselves, not as politicians but as guardians of the State and tied bound by that, into believing that the people would continue to thank them for that task. Cosgrave saw the average man in the street as getting a sense of responsibility, an emotional and spiritual satisfaction out of independence and self-government. He saw the future as, "in the hands of the people themselves. They put us in to look after their interests. If they are satisfied that we are doing for Ireland what they want us to, the good work will go on"[23.]

Padraic Colum wrote in *The Commonweal* on 23 March 1932, "Mr. Cosgrave leaves to his successor in the Presidency, an administration which has no taint of graft or inefficiency and an array of National Institutions, which are practically fool-proof.

After ten years in office, he is displaced by sixteen votes, which shows that objections to men who have the courage to be honest with the people, is not widespread".

As Joe Lee so correctly writes, "Cosgrave's place in history, does not ultimately depend on his performance as a vote-getter, but on his performance as a state builder"[24]. He came to power unexpectedly, in appalling circumstances. The sole surviving charismatic leader remained on the side of the enemy, which threatened murder and mayhem to all who manned the uncertain ship of state. There were divisions among the crew and some abandoned ship or were lost at sea. Only a steady hand, a firm captain, could have prevailed against the odds. The ship did not founder. It moved slowly yet surely into calmer waters. Other ships duly acknowledged it as a fellow mariner. The charismatic leader wished to come aboard and sail the ship himself. Eventually, after some skirmishing, he was allowed to do so and welcomed. Though eager to sail the ship immediately, he was forced to become an apprentice sailor. When he did assume control, he marvelled at how well the ship had been maintained by the founding captain".

Tim Pat Coogan summarised the achievements of Cosgrave and his team as creating "a democratic, legal and political stability out of chaos. They had replaced the RIC with an unarmed police force. Their Local Appointments Commission which went far to achieving what was in the existing Irish circumstances, a contradiction in terms – ethical and professional standards in State appointments"[24a].

deValera said to his son Vivian, who was propounding the traditional negative comments on the Cosgrave governments, "Yes, yes, we said all that, I know, I know. But when we got in and saw the files… they did a marvellous job, Viv, they did a magnificent job"[25].

TD Williams wrote of Cosgrave in *The Irish Times* of 1956:

"The Irish tradition is a mixed one; it has been influenced by ingredients deriving from Protestantism and Catholicism, republicanism and Monarchism…It was Cosgrave's achievement that, right at the very beginning, he understood the mixed nature of Irish society; and appreciated the role played by Irishmen of different racial origins and possessing varied religious and intellectual convictions. To set the ship in motion, it was necessary to achieve reconciliation"[26].

However Cosgrave himself, writing to a colleague in July 1944, was to concede that: "We must be candid – in the sphere that we considered the least important but which was the most important we failed – Viz: to retain popular support. It should not and I believe it is not beyond the capacity of able men to discover a way to the people's confidence and having found it, to keep it"[27].

The term 'elites' has been used frequently throughout the text, particularly in relation to the leaders of the Irish Free State. This 'Irish elite' founded the political system, which like in other democratic countries, after ten years in operation, led to structures, which crystallised and became relatively permanent. This reality was inherited by deValera, who tried anxiously to transform after his own ideas and in a way, after himself. As Tom Garvin argues, deValera himself became the ultimate Free Stater in this ineffective pursuit. "Furthermore, the electorate permitted its reluctant servant to get away with this rebaptism and become its leader and eventually, obedient servant"[27a]

In his poem, "Parnell's Funeral", WB Yeats wrote imaginatively and astutely about the possible influence of Parnell's heart might have had on deValera, WT Cosgrave and Kevin O'Higgins:

> The rest I pass, one sentence I unsay.
>
> Had de Valera eaten Parnell's heart
>
> No loose-lipped demagogue had won the day,
>
> No civil rancour torn the land apart.
>
> Had Cosgrave eaten Parnell's heart,
>
> The land's Imagination had been satisfied,
>
> Or lacking that, government in such hands,
>
> O'Higgins its sole statesman had not died[28]

The Yard in Kilmainham Jail Dublin,
site of executions after 1916 Rebellion.

EPILOGUE

The defeated ministers saw their income and associated perks reduce drastically. Several had careers to return to, and did so. Cosgrave was able to continue to derive an income from his lands at Templeogue. Mulcahy alone remained solely dedicated to the party.

The IRA made a lot of the early running in party political functioning during 1932, when essentially, as Frank Ryan declared their attitude to Cumann na nGaedheal was, "No matter what anyone says to the contrary, while we have fists, and boots to use, and guns, if necessary, we will not allow free speech to traitors". In May 1932 Cosgrave was shouted down at a meeting of his election workers in Cork. Patrick Lindsay writes on page five of his autobiography *Memories*, "If it had not been for the presence and support of the Blueshirts, public meetings organised by Cumann na nGaedheal and the Centre Party could not have been held in 1932 and 1933, such was the ferocity of the organised conspiracy against these meetings. The supporters of Fianna Fail and the IRA, many of the latter just recently released from jail, some of whom had been convicted of very serious offences, set out deliberately and with malice to smash up these meetings, to howl down men like WT Cosgrave, Paddy McGilligan and Patrick Hogan who had given the best years of their lives to establishing a strong democracy in this country. DeValera like the Pontius Pilate he could be, made no attempt to stop this happening"[1].

Cumann na nGaedheal people felt obliged to establish their own protective organisation to defend their supporters from the IRA harassment. A brother of Kevin O'Higgins became head of the Army Comrades Association. From the summer of 1932 Cumann na nGaedheal looked to the ACA as the guardians of the people and every threat to their freedom, whether it took the form of mob-rule, Communistic tyranny, or a deValerian dictatorship. Conor Cruise O'Brien has written, "The respect for the democratric process shown by Mr. Cosgrave's government was, in the circumstances, rather remarkable. It was, indeed, too remarkable to please many members of the fallen party, and some of these set about organising a para-military movement, on the Fascist model, for the intimidation of their opponents and the recovery of power…Yeats took part in the launching of this movement and wrote songs for it"[1a]

deValera called a snap election in January 1933 and returned with a clear majority.

	% vote	Seats won
FF	50%	76
C na nG	31	48
Centre	9	11
Labour	6	8
Ind	5	9

The ex- Garda Commissioner, Eoin O'Duffy was summarily dismissed by deValera in February 1933. Cosgrave challenged President deValera in the Dail on 1 March to, "state the reasons for the removal" and indicate whether any charges were pending. deValera replied that the dismissal was in the national interest and refused to give any further explanation, though he did clarify that no charges were to be made against O'Duffy.

The latter became leader of the Army Comrades Association on 20 July 1933, and renamed it the National Guard. The wearing of a blue shirt had been adopted in March and in May the stiff-arm salute was introduced. O'Duffy had a long pedigree in the national movement, as a man who got things done and would be capable of confronting the enemy

The sudden change in circumstances of the Cumann na nGaedheal front bench, led to a deterioration in their attendance at the Dail and at Parliamentary meetings. Cosgrave sought Mulcahy's intervention to stop the slide into oblivion, writing to him on 22 May 1933. He said, "there is a very general and growing belief that Cumann na nGaedheal is finished. This belief has been brought home to me in an intensified form over the weekend and again this morning. We have ten collectors working in Dublin City North, South and County. Their collections are much weaker than last year and the incline is downwards…The subscriber says – What's the use in subscribing; there is no effort in the party; look at the majority in the Dail every day, forty and fifty; you are not able to beat them and evidently your Party thinks this too. At a convention in Dungarvan last Sunday, friendly criticism was, the country is watching the Dail. They want to see Cumann na nGaedheal fighting by voice and vote and you're not[2]. Thus the party was almost irrelevant and the Army Comrades Association became the only adjunct of the organisation that appeared to have vibrancy and the will and muscle, to fight Fianna Fail and the IRA.

In 1933 Cumann an nGaedheal amalgamated with the Centre Party, which was essentially the old Farmer's Party to form Fine Gael, with O'Duffy as leader. After two general election defeats, Cosgrave was no longer seen as an electoral asset. Maurice Manning writes that James Dillon was influenced in part by Cosgrave to accept O'Duffy as leader[3]. Stephen Collins finds Cosgrave's agreement to O'Duffy's leadership "puzzling"[4]. Terence deVere White writes that "The quality which finally destroyed him was modesty: with a humility as praiseworthy as it was misguided, the experienced Cosgrave stood down for this futile person who had won local celebrity as chief of police"[5].

There was much confrontation at political rallies and renewed talk of coup d'etats from either side. Fine Gael felt it needed a strongman to survive. However, O'Duffy proved a disastrous leader, with clear fascist leanings, which were very common in Europe at the time. deValera was able to portray himself as the upholder of law and order in the State. In 1934 O'Duffy resigned, as opposition to his unconstitutional methods grew. WT Cosgrave then became leader of Fine Gael.

The economic war, caused by deValera reneging on the annuities to Britain, was causing great difficulty to the livelihood of the people.

On 29 March 1935 deValera, speaking in the Dail, expressed his disappointment that the IRA had not accepted peaceful government by majority rule. Political murders and intimidation had continued as before. Sean MacBride had had several meetings with deValera on behalf of the IRA. MacBride found those meetings of little value. MacBride said that deValera saw himself as the embodiment of the State declared by his comrades in 1916, and believed all true republicans should row in behind him and accept majority rule then. When MacBride challenged the inconsistency of deValera's position, he would "then put his integrity and judgement against my argument"[6]. In 1934 deValera wrote to Joe McGarrity explaining why he had to act against the IRA, "We have undertaken a responsibility to the people at present living, to the future and to the dead. We will not allow any group of individuals to prevent us carrying it out"[7].

In 1936 the IRA was again declared illegal and the annual march to Wolfe Tone's grave at Bodenstown was banned. In 1937 the Army Comrades Association was banned and Military Tribunals re-instated. Cosgrave must have had a strong sense of *déjà vue* as deValera took on the IRA using Military Tribunals.

DeValera brought in a new constitution in 1937, which Cosgrave opposed as granting the Taoiseach dictatorial powers. He felt that the leader of government should still be a Chairman rather than a Chief. One of deValera's close advisors on the constitution was his good friend, Archbishop John Charles McQuaid of Dublin. The constitution gained a relatively small majority of 56% in the referendum, being opposed vociferously by many women. deValera had also called a general election for the same day, in which Fianna Fail lost eight seats. This resulted in it becoming a minority government again, relying on Labour for support.

The economic war ended in 1938 when the Anglo-Irish Trade Agreement was signed. That year too saw Doughlas Hyde, on the recommendation of Cosgrave, become President of the country. During the 1938 general election, deValera no longer thought it necessary to break from the British Commonwealth in order to establish freedom[8]. *The Irish Times* welcomed this conversion.

The war years further isolated the country. When Churchill became Prime Minister he railed against deValera over access to the Treaty ports. These had remained under the British at the Treaty, but to Churchill's horror, were handed over by Neville Chamberlain in 1938. However most of the country backed deValera's handling of the issue in a benign neutrality. One politician, who did not, was James Dillon, the Deputy leader of Fine Gael. Without any advance notice to his party colleagues, he broke ranks in the Dail on 27 July 1941, decrying Ireland's isolationist stance in dramatic terms. Cosgrave was furious and told the Dail that his party had not debated the issue. He continued, "We are not bound to take part in a conflict of this kind. It is no part of the Christian religion or the Catholic faith to insist in our taking part in it. The duty and responsibility of everyone in public life…lies in ensuring due security and stability and integrity of this country. If that is better served by a policy of neutrality, then it is our duty to accept and adopt that policy. In times of crisis it is advisable- it is necessary - to make up your mind rapidly, to make it up correctly and , having made it up, to stick to it like a man and to do what you can towards preserving, improving and exalting the country, which it is our duty to serve"[9].

Dillon handed in his resignation to Cosgrave, who asked him to withdraw it. This he was glad to do. The matter was then closed until on 10 February 1942, Dillon gave a passionately pro-American speech at the Fine Gael Ard Fheis. At that stage Cosgrave accepted Dillon's resignation. Dillon wrote, " I know it is unnecessary for me to assure you of my continued sincere admiration and warm personal regard for yourself and the colleagues"[10.].

deValera won another general election in 1943. That election saw WT Cosgrave's son Liam T. Cosgrave, join his father in the Dail;. deValera called another snap election within the year. WT Cosgrave resigned from politics before that 1944 election. General Richard Mulcahy succeeded him as leader. In his announcement to Cumann na nGaedheal, Cosgrave may well have given the ultimate evidence of his attitude to the party, with which he had been for so long been associated in a semi-detached way. He told them that he found himself incapable of making the physical effort called for, in the office of leader of the party. He added that, "he was gratified by the fact that his relations with the party were never more cordial"[11]

When the Dail was debating the United Nations in July 1946, the question of raising partition there came up. Cosgrave's attitude was, "Partition should never be absent from our minds or from the consideration of this country, either at the United Nations or elsewhere…so long as Partition continues, harmonious, cordial and friendly relations between this country and Great Britain can never be established on the basis on which they might, if Partition ceased to exist…I think as soon as the opportunity presents itself this country will raise the matter of Partition..". Deirdre MacMahon comments that, "While most of the Fine Gael front bench agreed that it was better not to raise partition, it was interestingly the former party leader, who judged otherwise"[12]

In retirement Cosgrave devoted himself to bloodstock and dairy shorthorn cattle farming on his land[13]. He became a member and later Chairman of the Racing Board.

WT Cosgrave kept in touch with Oliver Gogarty, who had moved to live in the USA. When he heard that Gogarty was thinking of retiring he wrote on 5 November 1956, advising, possibly from personal experience, " …Don't! Everyone who does, steps over a canyon making it impossible to retrace; then they find it lonesome and are prone to lose interest in men and things"[14]. When Gogarty died in New York in September 1957, he was buried in Renvyle, with WT Cosgrave in attendance. In 1959, WT's wife Louisa died and was buried in Goldenbridge cemetery. He and his wife and had earlier moved to a small house, and he now returned to join his son Liam in the family home, Beechpark.

The Irish-American President of the USA, John Fitzgerald Kennedy visited Ireland in the summer of 1963. He was invited to address the Oireachtas. The Dail chamber had been almost packed for a half hour before the President was due to arrive. In the lobby sat distinguished visitors and members of both Houses. All stood and clapped when Mr.WT Cosgrave entered, accompanied by his son, Liam T. Cosgrave T.D. He bowed to the applause and took his seat in the lobby. A few minutes later the tribute was renewed when Mr. Sean T. O'Kelly,ex President, entered. As the white haired former President passed though the lobby, he paused for a moment to place his right arm around the shoulders of Mr. Cosgrave, and the two former comrades-in-arms and statesmen, shook hands warmly and spoke together for a moment[15].

WT Cosgrave died on 16 November 1965. He had served mass that morning for a visiting American priest at Mount Argus in Kimmage, where he often went to hear mass. He received a state funeral, in the presence of President deValera, the cabinet and other dignitaries. At the request of his family the National Flag was not draped over the coffin, which was carried on a gun carriage and received a 21gun salute. The cortege halted at the former South Dublin Union opposite his former home on James' St. He was buried alongside his own mother and father. The headstone reads:

WT COSGRAVE

DIED 16th NOVEMBER 1965

LOUISE COSGRAVE

DIED 16th JUNE 1959.

In the Dail, Sean Lemass said:

"Although William T. Cosgrave has left us, the work he has done for Ireland endures. The generosity of his youthful response to the call to serve Ireland, the privations and the sacrifices that he endured so that the national freedom might be ours, the capacity he displayed in presiding over the administration while responsibility was his, the grace with which he handed over responsibility when the people so willed, the dignity with which he carried out his duties as leader of the Opposition and later as a private member of this House, the generosity of spirit with which he lent his hand to the defence of the State in a time of national danger, the readiness with which, even in retirement from active public life, he gave of his counsel in the sphere of national development which was dear to him and, finally, the exemplary character of his long life, these are elements of a legacy which we in Ireland and indeed the people who value freedom and democracy everywhere will forever cherish".

Richard Mulcahy, leader of Fine Gael said, "It is in terms of the Nation and its needs and its potential that I praise God who gave us in our dangerous days the gentle but steel-like spirit of rectitude, courage and humble self-sacrifice, that was Liam T. Cosgrave".

CENTENARY OF BIRTH OF W.T. COSGRAVE

On the 6th of June 1980 the centenary of WT Cosgrave's birth was celebrated in Dublin. It was a low key, non-political affair, with the public informed by an advertisement in the press. Mass was said in St. James' Church, James' St., by Fr. Patrick Tuohy PP, Rathfarnham, who had been a former chaplain to the Cosgrave family. Dr. Patrick Hillery attended on the personal invitation of Dr. Garret Fitzgerald, leader of Fine Gael. No invitations were issued to members of the Government, or the Labour Party, to avoid any embarrassment. The Deputy leader of Labour, Mr. Michael O'Leary attended with the Fine Gael front bench, the Lord Mayor, the General Officer Commanding the army, Lt. Col, Carl O'Sullivan. Patrick and Pauline Cosgrave, first cousins of WT. from Castledermot Co. Kildare, attended. After the mass a plaque was unveiled on number 174 James' St, the birthplace of WT Cosgrave. Dr. Fitzgerald spoke and identified WT as the first leader of the Irish Free State and the man who "established the standards of Irish democracy". Though it was a non-political occasion, the *Irish Independent* commented, "We are not yet out of the woods of Civil War politics, for no prominent figure of Fianna Fail attended on a personal basis. This despite the fact that WT Cosgrave took part in the 1916 Rising, was court-martialled and sentenced to death, later commuted to life imprisonment". The plaque on what was then Kenny's public house, read:

"WT Cosgrave. Born here 6th June 1880. Died November 1965". . .

The Grave of W.T. Cosgrave and his wife Louise,
in Goldenbridge Cemetery, Dublin.

BIBLIOGRAPHY

Bew P., Gibbons, P. and Patterson, H., *The State of Northern Ireland 1921-72 Political forces and social classes*, Manchester 1979.

Bowyer Bell, J., *The Secret Army; a history of the IRA, 1916-1979*, Dublin 1980.

Collins S. *The Cosgrave Legacy*, Dublin 1996.

Coogan Tim Pat *Michael Collins*, London 1969.

Eamon deValera, London 1995.

Curran J. M. *The Birth of the Irish Free State*, Alabama 1980.

DeVere White, T. *Kevin O'Higgins*, Tralee 1966.

Doorley M *Irish American Diaspora Nationalism*, London 2005.

Fanning R. *The Irish Department of Finance*, Dublin 1978.

Farrell B. *Chairman or Chief? (The Role of the Taoiseach in Irish government*, Dublin 1971).

Feeney B. *Sinn Fein*, O'Brien. 2002.

Gallagher M. *Politics in the Irish Republic*, Routeledge 2005.

Garvin Tom. *The Birth of Irish Democracy*, Gill & MacMillaan 2006.

Gaughan JA. *Austin Stack*, Kingdom Books. 1977.

Gwynn D. *John Redmond*, London 1932.

Hand GJ. *Reports of the Irish Boundary Commission*, Shannon 1969.

Jordan A. *Churchill A Founder of Modern Ireland*, Dublin 1995.

Sean – A Biography of Sean MacBride, Dublin 1993.

Major John MacBride Dublin 1991.

Kennedy M. *Ireland and the League of Nations*, Irish Academic Press. 1996.

Keogh DF. *The Vatican, the bishops and Irish politics 1919-1939*, Cambridge 1986.

Kiberd Declan. *Inventing Ireland*, Vintage 1996.

Kotsonouris Mary. *Retreat From Revolution*, Irish Academic Press. 1994.

Laffan M. *Resurrection of Ireland*, London 2005.

Lee JJ. *Ireland 1912-1985 Politics and Society*, Cambridge 1989.

MacArdle D. *The Irish Republic*, Dublin 2005.

Manning M. *The Blueshirts*, Dublin 1970.

Ó'Broin L. *WE Wylie and The Irish Revolution*, 1989.

Ó Grada C. *Ireland; A New Economic History 1789-1939*, Clarendon Press. 1994.

O'Halloran C. *Partition and the Limits of Irish Nationalism*, Dublin 1987.

O'Neill TP, and Lord Longford. *Eamon deValera*, Dublin 1970.

O'Sullivan D. *The Irish Free State and its Senate*, London 1940.

Pakenham Tom. *Peace By Ordeal*, London 1935.

Regan John. *The Irish Counter Revolution 1921-1936*, Gill 1999.

Ryle Dwyer T. *Eamon deValera*, Dublin 1980.

Townshend C. *Easter 1916*, London 2005.

Valiulus M. *General Richard Mulcahy; Portrait of a Revolutionary*, Dublin 1992.

Whyte JH. *Church and State in modern Ireland 1923-1970*, Dublin 1971.

FOOTNOTES

Introduction

[1]. Collins Stephen, *The Cosgrave Legacy*, Blackwater 1996. p. 32

[2]. O'Connor Frank, *The Big Fellow*, Thomas Nelson 1937..

[3]. Valiulis Maryann Gialanella, *General Richard Mulcahy*, Irish Academic Press, 1992. p. 172.

[4]. Farrell Brian, *Chairman or Chief; The R ole of Taoiseach in Irish Government*, Dublin 1971 p. 19.

[5]. Jordan Anthony, *Sean A Biography of Sean MacBride*, Blackwater 1993. p. 61.

[6]. Dail Debates

[7]. Dail Debates, 1922/1942 Col. 1878.

[8]. Farrell, p. 21.

[9]. Garvin Tom, *Birth of Democracy*, Gill 2005, p. 175.

[10] *Irish Press and Irish Times*.

[11]. Manning Maurice, *James Dillon*. Quoting from unpublished memoir of James Burke p. 45.

[12]. *New York Times*, 19 August 1928.

[13]. ibid, 21 February 1932.

[14]. In conversation with author at Conference on *Eamon deValera 30 Years On* at UCD, October 2005. The Fianna Fail Party in part, sponsored this conference. Ex-President Patrick Hillery, Minister Eamon Ó'Cuív TD, Ex-Taoiseach Garret Fitzgerald, Ex-Senator Michael Yeats, Senator Martin Mansergh, Maire O'Kelly, the ex-secretary of deValera, and a panel of eminent historians attended. It was stated that around fifteen biographies of Eamon deValera had been published. A lengthy article in the *Irish Times* also marked the anniversary. The 40th anniversary of the death of WT Cosgrave occurred the following month and passed without any public notice.

[15]. WT Cosgrave Papers, National Archives Ireland [NAI], 1194-14.

Chapter 1.

[1]. WT Cosgrave Papers, 1194-15. NA.

[2]. ibid

[3]. Thom's Directories.

[4]. Collins, p. 5.

[5]. ibid.

[6]. Feeney Brian, *Sinn Fein*, O'Brien 2003. p. 29.

[7]. Jordan Anthony, *Major John MacBride*, Westport Historical Society 1991, pp.37-42.

[8]. Bureau of Military History; Document No. 268; Witness, Mr. Liam Cosgrave, Lieut. 4th Battalion Dublin Brigade, Irish volunteers, 1916.; Ex-President Executive Council Saorstat Eireann. Hereafter, BMH. WS 268

[9]. Feeney, pp. 37-39.

[10]. ibid. p. 50.

Chapter 2.
1. O'Higgins used this title to describe Cosgrave when he was chosen as Chair of the Provisional Government.
2. Reference number to items of business.

Chapter 3.
1. Feeney, p. 55.
2. BMH. WS 268
3. Jordan, *Major* John *MacBride*, p. 105.
4. Gwynn Denis, *John Redmond,* Harrap, London 1932 p. 450 passim.
5. BMH. WS. 268. p. 1.
6. ibid.
7. MacArdle Dorothy, *The Irish Republic,* Wolfhound 2005. p. 114-5.
8. BMH. WS 268.
9. ibid.
10. ibid.
11. Collins, pp. 8-9.
12. BMH. WS. 268
13. *The Catholic Bulletin,* March 1918 p. 153.
14. BMH. Burke Place, at Ceannt Fort is named after Frank Burke.
14a. Manuscript 23,576, National Library of Ireland (N.L.I.).
Brugha later wrote to Thomas Ashe, "Tell Willie Cosgrave that I can never forget the extreme kindness I received from himself and one or two others".
15. Townshend Charles, *Easter 1916,* Allen Lane 2005. *p.* 231. and Ryan Annie *Witnesses Inside the Easter Rising,* Liberties Press, 2005, p. 142.
16. BMH. WS 268.
17. ibid.
16. ibid.
17. ibid
18. Mac Lochlainn Piaras, *Last Words,* Office of Public Works, 2005. pp. 131-2.
19. BMH. WS. 268.
20. ibid.
21. O'Broin Leon, *WE Wylie and the Irish Revolution,* 1989, p. 22.
22. Gwynn, p. 474.
23. Jordan, *Major John MacBride,* p. 124.
23a. O'Broin Leon p. 25.
24. BMH. WS. 268.
25. 1194. National Archives.
26. ibid.
27. Laffan Michael, *The Resurrection of Ireland,* Cambridge 2005, p. 65.
28. Gwynn, P. 481.
29. ibid. p. 477.
30. ibid. p. 477.
31. ibid. p. 486.
32. ibid. p. 470.
33. Mac Lochlainn, p. 136.
34. *Irish Times,* 28 January 2006

Chapter 4.
1. Coogan Tim Pat, *Michael Collins,* Arrow 1969, p. 69.
2. *Kilkenny Journal* 28, July 1917.
3. ibid. 10 August 1917.
4. *Kilkenny Journal,* 15 August 1917.
5. BMH. WS 238.
6. Coogan Tim Pat, *deValera,* Arrow, 1995 p. 100.
7. ibid. p. 110.
8. *The Times,* 1918.
9. Feeney, P. 103.

Chapter 5.
1. Feeney. P. 121.
2. ibid. p. 122.
3. Coogan, *deValera,* p. 132.
4. O'Connor Ulick, *Oliver St. John Gogarty,* O'Brien, 2000 p. 37.
5. O'Connor Ulick, *Diaries,* John Murray, 2001, p. 15-16.
6. ibid. p. 159.
6a. In a Dáil debate on 1/3/1922 on the language in which births, marriages, and deaths should be registered. Cosgrave said that his own marriage and the birth of his son had been registered in Irish.
7. Valulis. P. 40.
8. Doorley Michael, *Irish-American Diaspora Nationalism,* Four Courts, 2005. p. 92-96.
9. ibid. p. 105-121.
10. Feeney,. P. 124.
11. BMH. WS 268.
12. Garvin Tom, *Birth of Democracy,* Gill & MacMillan, 1922, p. 66.
13. Coogan, *Michael Collins.* P. 20.
14. BMH. WS. 268.
15. Collins. P. 19.
16. Ó'Gráda Cormac, *Ireland: A New Economic History 1789-1939,* Clarendon Press 1994, p. 372.
17. ibid. p. 375.
18. Ferriter Diarmaid, *Lovers of Liberty, Local Government in 20th Century Ireland,* National Archives, P. 54.
19. Dail Eireann File, 2/84 3 May 1921 NA.
20. Garvin, P. 68.
21. ibid. p. 70.
22. NAI, 23/ Nov. 1921. 22/18.
23. NAI,. 30 Nov + 15 Dec. 23/14.
23a. NAI,DELG, 16/19, 6Sept. 1922.
24. BMH. WS. 268.
25. NA. 1194.

Chapter 6.

1 . BMH. WS. 268.
2 . Jordan Anthony, *Churchill; A Founder of Modern Ireland,* Westport Books, 1995, p.p. 70-75.
3 . Mitchell and Ó'Snodaigh, *Irish Political Documents,* 1985. pp. 84-5.
4 . BMH. WS. 268.
5 . deVere White Terence, *Kevin O'Higgins,* Tralee 1966. passim.
5a . Jordan Anthony *Yeats Gonne MacBride Triangle,* Westport Books, 2000, p. 111.
6 . Jordan Anthony, *Yeats Gonne MacBride Triangle,* Westport Books, 2000, p. 133.
7 . Mitchell Arthur, *Revolutionary Government in Ireland, Dail Eireann 1910-1922,* Dublin 1995.
8 . Neligan David, *The Spy in the Castle,* Prenderville, 1998, p. 96.
9 . Coogan, *Michael Collins,* p. 96.
9a . Lee. p. 66.
9b . Gaughan J. Anthony, *Austin Stack Portrait of a Separatist,* Kingdom books, 1977. p. 275-6. note 8.
10. Collins, P. 21.
11 . ibid. p. 21.
12 . *Irish Times,*17 November 1965.
13 . House of Commons Statement, 22 May 1921.
14 . Pakenham Frank, *Peace By Ordeal,* Pimlico 1992. p. 66.
15 . Jordan, *Churchill,* pp. 68-9.
16 . Hopkinson Michael, ED. *The Last Days of Dublin Castle; Diaries of Mark Sturgis* Irish Academic Press. 1999.
17 . Beaslai Piaras, *Michael Collins and the Making of a New Ireland, Vol II* . p. 236..
18 . Pakenham, P. 68.
19 . MacArdle, P. 857.
20 . Pakenham, P. 80.
21 . Regan John, *The Irish Counter-Revolution, 1921- 1936,* Gill. 1999. p. 10.

Chapter 7.

1 . Jordan, *Churchill,* pp.80-86
2 . Pakenham, P.72.
2a . Gaughan J. Anthony, *Austin Stack Portrait of Separatist Kingdom Books* 1977. p. 157.
2b . Ryle, Dwyer T, *deValera,* Poolbeg. 1991, p. 58.
2c . Gaughan, p. 158.
3 . Private Session Dail Eireann, 14 September 1922, p. 95.
4 . Collins, P. 23.
5 . Jordan, *Churchill,* P. 86.
6 . ibid. pp. 62-105.
7 . Blythe Ernest, *Irish Times,* 18/11/1965
8 . Pakenham, P. 198
8a . Gaughan, P. 163.

8b . Lee, p. 97.
8c . Gaughan, p. 167.
8d . ibid.
9 . ibid. p. 198.
10 . NAI. 304/21, December 1021.
11 . Dail Eireann, September 1923.
12 . Jordan, *Churchill*, Pp. 93-103.
13 . Gilbert Martin, C*hurchill, Vol IV*, Heinmann 1980, p. 676.
14. . Information from Dr. Risteard Mulcahy.
15 . Pakenham. p. 262.
16 . ibid. p. 263.
17 . ibid. pp. 263-4.
18 . ibid. 264
19. Hart Peter, *Mick*, MacMillan, 2005. p. 326.
20 . Longford & O'Neill, *deValera*, Dublin 1970. P. 168/
21 . Moynihan M, *Speeches and Statements by Eamon deValera, 1917-73*. Dublin 1980. p. 86.
22 . Ryle Dwyer T, *deValera*, Dublin, 1980. P. 64.
23 . Longford & O'Neill, p. 175.

Chapter 8.
1. Collins, P. 25.
2 . ibid. p. 26.

Chapter 9.
1 . Collins. p. 29.
2 . Gilbert Martin, *Churchill, Vol IV* Heinemann 1980 p. 727.
3 . Jordan, *Churchill*, P. 124.
3a . PRO DO 34/397.10. p. 33.
4 . Jordan, *Churchill*, p. 127-132.
5 . ibid. pp. 125-6.
6 . Garvin Tom, *The Birth of Irish Democracy*, Gill 1996. p 129.
7 . O'Malley Notebook,17/B/94, Liam Tobin interview with Ernie O'Malley.
8 . NAI. D/TS, 6695 note 93.
9 . Jordan, *Churchill*, Pp. 133-138.
10 . ibid. p. 125.
11 . Jordan Anthony, *Sean*, P. 34. & Cullen Rosemary. *Social history of Women in Ireland 1870-1970*. Gill 2005. p. 4..
12 . Hart, P. 401.
13 . Valulis, Pp. 160-163.
14 . Collins, P. 32.
15 . Countess of Fingal, *Seventy Years Young*, Lilliput 1994 p. 409.
16 . Valulis, p. 168.
17 . NAI, 1194.
18 . O'Connor Frank, p. 295-6.

19. Regan, P. 78.
20. ibid. p. 83.
21. Valulis, p. 172. *'A Nation Once Again'* was written by AM Sullivan (Senior), Uncle to Tim Healy, Kevin O'Higgins and Serjeant Sullivan. It was the anthem of the Irish Parliamentary Party.
22. NAI. 1194.
23. Gilbert, ibid. p. 142.
24. ibid, Cope was an ex-Excise policeman, confidante of Lloyd George, Head of M15 in Ireland and well aware that the South would get some kind of Dominion/Home rule eventually.
25. ibid. p. 147.
26. ibid. p. 143.
27. Valulis, p. 173.
28. ibid. p. 173.
29. O'Connor, Frank, p. 296.
30. *Irish Times* Interview, 18 November 1965.
31. ibid.
31a Dail Debates, 6 December 1922. Col 17.
32. Dail Debates, Vol 2. 12 December 1922.
33. Regan, P. 83.
34. Valulis, p. 176.
35 Garvin, P. 91.
36. Macardle, P. 811.
36a. Archbishop Byrne Papers, Diocesan Archives, Drumcondra, Dublin.
36b ibid.
37. ibid. p. 813.
38. ibid. p. 814.
39. Dail Debates, November 1922.
39a Archbishop Byrne Papers, Diocesan Archives, Drumcondra, Dublin.
40. Regan p. 113.
41. Keogh Dermot, *Vatican,* Cambridge, 1986 p. 98
42. Foley Conor, *Legion of the Rearguard,* Pluto 1002
42a .Mulcahy Papers, P,P7/B/85
43. Greaves Desmond, *Liam Mellowes,* London, 2004 p. 373.
44 Curran JM, *The Birth of the Irish Free State,* Alabama 1980 p. 253
45. Foley, P. 30.
46 Keogh, p. 98.
46a .Garvin, p. 216.
46b Archbishop Byrne Papers, Diocesan Archives, Drumcondra, Dublin.
47. Gilbert, P. 748.
48. Papers, p7/B/107 26 January 1923.
49. ibid.

[50] . ibid. p7/B//284 .
[51] . ibid.
[52] . Garvin, p. 164.
[53] . ibid.
[54] . Lee Joseph, *Ireland 1912-1985*. Cambridge 1995. pp. 69-70.
[55] . ibid. p. 75.
[56] . Keane Vincent, *Joseph MacBride's Undercover visit to Achill in 1923,* Cathair na Mart, vol 24. 2004-5.
[57] . Toomey Maurice, Papers Ms. P/69/52.
[58] . McCoole Sinead, *No Ordinary Women,* O'Brien 2005 P. 97.
[59] . Jordan Anthony, *Sean,* P. 55.
[60] . Keogh Dermot, *Vatican,* pp. 108-121.
[61] Macardle, pp. 851-3.
[62] . Gaughan Anthony Ed, *Memoirs of Senator James Douglas & Senate Debates* 1923.
[63] . Garvin, p. 166.
[63a] Archbishop Byrne Papers, Diocesan Archives, Drumcondra, Dublin.
[64] . Macardle, P. 897.
[65] . NAI, 1194.
[66] . Garvin, p. 159.
[67] . Dail Debates, September 1923.
[68] . Kleinricheet Denise, *Republican Internees and the Prison ship Argenta,* IAP 2005.
[69] . NAI. S5 760/16 (WT Cosgrave to Minister of Defence, 19 October 1923).
[70] . Lee, p. 68.
[71] . Ryle, Dwyer T, *deValera,* Poolbeg, 1991 p. 58.

Chapter 10.
[1] . Lee, P. 100.
[2] . Valulis, p. 204.
[3] . ibid. p. 206.
[4] . ibid. p. 209.
[5] deVere White Terence, *Kevin O'Higgins,* Tralee 1966. pp.159-160.
[6] . Lee, P. 96.
[7] . Dail Debates, Vol 6. col. 1996-2001 12 March 1924.
[8] . *Irish Times,* 13 March 1924.
[9] . Mulcahy Papers, P7/D/78.
[10] . McGarry Ferghal, *Eoin O'Duffy,* Oxford. 2005. p. 134.
[11] . Ibid. p. 215.
[12] . Regan, P. 184.
[13] . McInerney Michael, *A Political Profile of Ernest Blythe, Irish Times,* 5 January 1975.
[14] . Dail Debates, Vol 6. 19 March 1924. Passim.
[15] . Regan. P. 179.
[16] . NAI. CAB. 2/69 19 March 1924 & 2/72 21March 1924.
[17] . Mulcahy Papers, P7/C/99 20 November 1924.

[18] . McGarry. P. 135.
[19.] Minutes, National Executive Cumann na nGaedheal, 13 May 1924. P/39/1/1.
[20] . Regan, p. 216.
[22] . Lee, p. 103.

Chapter 11.
[1] . Regan, P. 141.
[2] . Mulcahy Papers, P7/B/325.
[3] . ibid. P7/B/322. 18 May 1923.
[4] . deValera Conference UCD, October 2005.
[5] . Burke Memoir, P. 328-9. Quoted in Regan. p. 133.
[6] . Minutes, Nat. Executive Cumann na nGaedheal, 3 December 1923.
[7] . Coakley John, & Gallagher Michael, Eds, *Politics in the Irish Republic*, Rentledge 2005, *The Party System*, Mair Peter, & Weeks Liam. P. 141.

Chapter 12.
[1] . Pakenham, p. 221.
[2] . Dail Debates, Vol. 8. Col. 2502.
[2a] . Lee, p. 55.
[3] . O'Halloran Clare, *Partition and the Limits of Irish Nationalism*, Gill 1987. p. 111.
[4] . Blythe Papers, P24/171.
[5] . Ferriter, *The Transformation of Ireland 1990 -2000, profile 2004* p. 282.
[5a] . Manuscript, 22,496, N.L.I.
[6] . *The Times,* 23 November 1925, p. 13.
[7] . Ferriter, *Transformation, p. 294.*
[8] . Bew, Gibson, Patterson, *Northern Ireland 1921-94. Political Forces and Social Classes.* London 1994. p. 17.
[9] . ibid. p. 112.
[10] . Jordan, *Churchill,* p. 156.
[11] . ibid. pp. 156-8.
[12] . Dail Debates, Vol. 12, col. 1313.
[13] . *Belfast Telegraph,* 4 December 1925.
[14] . Hand GJ, *The Scholar Revolutionary Eoin MacNeill,* Irish University Press. 1973. p. 211.
[15] . Hand. GJ, Ed. *Report* of *the Boundary Commission,* 1925, Irish University Press 1969.S/10
[16] . Hand, *Eoin MacNeill* p. 216. & Lee. P. 704.
[17] . Dail Debates, 19 December 1925. Col. 1541.
[18] . Fanning Ronan, *Independent Ireland,* Dublin 1983. p. 180.
[19] . O'Halloran, p. xv.
[20] . Dail debates, 24 October 1929.
[21] . Jones Tom, *Whitehall Diary 3;* p. 138,240. Oxford 1971.
[22] . Hand, p. 272.

Chapter 13

1. NAI. DFA 2/3, 2/314. 4 March 1921.
2. O'Sullivan Donal, *The Irish Free State and its Senate*, Faber and Faber 1959. p. 90.
2a. BMH WS 268.
2b. ibid
3. O'Sullivan, p. 94.
4. ibid. pp. 102-108.
5. *Irish Independent*, 12 February 1923; from interview in *Daily Mail*.
6. Senate Debates, Vol 1.
7. ibid Vol 1. 155.
8. NAI. DFA 98/1 June 1923.
9. Jordan Anthony, *WB Yeats,* Westport Books 2003. pp. 163-7.
10. ibid. pp. 154-167.
11. O'Connor Ulick, *Oliver St. John Gogarty,* O'Brien 2000 p. 187.
12. ibid. p. 220.
13. ibid. p. 225.
14. Ferriter Diarmaid, *Transformations 2000,* p. 301; from MA thesis by Charlotte Fallon 1980.
15. MacBride Anna, & Jeffares A. Norman, *Gonne Yeats Letters* Pimlico 1993 p. 434.
16. Jordan Anthony, *Sean.* pp. 46-7.
17. MacBride Anna, p. 438 4 October 1927.
18. Senate Debates, 30 February 1927.
19. Senate Debates, Vol X 193-227.
20. Dail Debates, XX11, 140.
21. McCoole Sinead. *Hazel Lavery,* Lilliput 1996. p. 111.
22. Lavery John, *The Life of a Painter,* P. 232.
23. Foster Roy, *WB Yeats; A Life the Arch-Poet.* Oxford 2003. p 434.
23a. Bodkin was Director of National Gallery of Ireland.
24. NAI. Ms. S9987 9 December 1929.

Chapter 14.

1. Maguire Conor, '*The Republican Court',* Capuchin Annual 1968.
   The case went against the small claimants, with whom Tom Maguire was in sympathy.
   He had to be persuaded to uphold the verdict.
1a. Macardle p. 771.
2. Kotsonouris Mary, *Retreat From Revolution; The Dail Courts.* IAP.p. 87.
3. ibid. p. 86.
4. Macardle, pp. 772-4.
5. ibid. p. 771.
6. Kotsonouris, P. 88 & p. 151 note 65.
7. Dail Debates, Vol 1. col. 288-9 September 1922.
8. Kennedy Papers.
10. Senate Debates, 3 April 1924 col. 614-5.

11 . Kotsonouris, P. 117.
12 . Ibid-p. 119.
12a Lee, p, 128
13 . Fanning Ronan, *The Irish Department of Finance*, Dublin, 1978 p. 41.
14 . NAI. S1932
15 . Lee. p. 119.
16 . Dail Debates. Vol. 9. col. 562. 30 October 1924.
17 . Collins. P. 45.
18 . NAI. 1194-5.
18a .Archbishop Byrne Papers, Diocesan Archives, Drumcondra, Dublin.
18b ibid.
19 . Collins. P. 46.
20 . Whyte John, *Church and State in Modern Ireland 1923-70*. Dublin, 1971. p. 60.
20a .Archbishop Byrne Papers, Diocesan Archives, Drumcondra, Dublin.
21 . Keogh, p. 60.
22 . *Irish Times,* 22 June 1929.
23 . Keogh Dermot, *The Vatican, the Bishops and Irish Politics,* Cambridge, 1986 p. 196.
24 . O'Connor Ulick. *Diaries,* p. 17.
25 . Cooney John, J*ohn Charles McQuaid,* O'Brien. P. 62.
26 . Senate Debates, Vol !3. col. 1759. 20 June 1930.
27 . Kiberd Declan, *Inventing Ireland,* Vintage, 1996. p. 263.

Chapter 15.
1 . NAI. S 3332, 15 September 1922.
2 . Fitzgerald Papers, P/80/5127
3 . Kennedy Michael, *Ireland and the League of Nations,* IAP. 1996. p. 30.
4 . NAI. 1194-2.
5 . PRO CO, 739/4/49361 Curtis to Devonshire 5-10 September 1923.
6 . Dail Debates, Vol 5. col. 139.
7 . Kennedy, pp. 60-63.
8 . Dail Debates, Vol 33. col. 2050-2167 & 2195-2330.
9 . ibid. Vol. 28. col. 277-320. & 334-374.
10 . NAI, S6051 !7 July 1930.
11 . O'Sullivan, p. 251-2.
12 . ibid. p. 252.
13 . Dail Debates, Vol. 36. Col. 2290-2332 & 2334-2362.
14 . House of Commons Debates, cylix, 1193-4 & 1205.
15 . Gilbert Martin, *Churchill,* Vol V Heinemann 1981, p. 375.
16 . House of Commons Debates, Clix, 311.
17 . Gilbert, p. 420.
18 . Jordan, *Churchill,* pp. 160-2.
19 . Senate Debates, Vol. 15. Col. 938.
20 . Regan, P. 382.

Chapter 16.

1 . *Connacht Telegraph*, 3 January 1931.
2 . *Standard*, 13 December 1930.
3 . *Connacht Telegraph*.
4 . NAI. S2547A, Cosgrave to O'Hegarty, 10 January 1931.
5 . NAI. S2547A.
6 . ibid.
7 . *Irish Press*, 2 January 1932.
8 . NAI S2547B
9 . Butler Hubert, *In the Land of Nod*. Dublin, 1996 pp. 22-6.

Chapter 17

1 . *Irish Independent*, 11 March 1926.
2 . Boland Gerry, *Irish Times*, 10 October 1968.
2a . Garvin Tom, P. 175.
3 . McCoole, Sinead *Women's History No 3. 2004* p. 145.
4 . Macardle, p. 986.
5 . Coogan, *deValera*, p. 398.
6 . Dail Debates. Vol. xx, vol 11-15.
7 . Keogh Dermot, *Twentieth Century Ireland: Nation and State*, Dublin 1994. p. 47.
7a . Archbishop Byrne Papers, Diocesan Archives, Drumcondra, Dublin.
8 . Dail Debates Vol. xli col. 1101-1102.
9 . Bowyer Bell J, *The Secret Army*, Anthony Blond, 1970. p. 63.
10 . *Irish Independent*, 12 September 1927,
10a .Lindsay Patrick, *Memories*, Blackwater, 1992. p. 32.
11 . *Irish Press*, 24 January 1969.
12 . *Irish Times*, 10 October 1968.
13 . Keogh, *Twentieth Century Ireland, p. 34.*

Chapter 18.

1 . *Irish Times*, 20 January 1928.
2 . ibid. 23 January 1928.
3 . ibid. 5 February 1928
4 . *Irish Independent*, 24 January 1928
5 . *Irish Times*, 5 February 1928.
6 . *New York Times*, 29 August 1928 & *Irish Times*, 18 November 1965.
   Interview with Ernest Blythe.
7 . *Irish Independent*, 3 February 1928.
8 . Lee, p. 120.
9 . O'Gráda, p. 396.
10 . Blythe Papers, P/24/488 22 January 1931.
11 . Jordan Anthony, *Sean*, pp. 51-53.

[12] . Dail Debates, 4 September 1931.
[13] . NAI. S5864B 10 September 1931.
[13a]. Archbishop Byrne Papers, Diocesan Archives, Drumcondra, Dublin.
[14] . Dail Debates, Vol 40. Col 325.
[15] . MacRory Papers, 19 October 1931, Archdiocesan Archives Armagh.
[16] . Coogan, *deValera*, p. 415.
[17] . Dail Debates, XL 34-6 1931.
[18] . ibid. Col 51 & 54.
[19] . *Irish Independent*, 19 October 192?
[20] . Jordan, *Sean*, p. 56.
[20a]. Lynch Patrick, M. Litt Treatise on National War Memorial
[20b]. *Irish Independent*, 12 Novemner 1928.
[20c] .Lynch Patrick.
[20d]. *Republican File*, January 1931.
[20e] .Lynch Patrick.
[21] . *Connacht Telegraph*, 11 February 1931.
[21a] Horgan John, *Sean Lemass*, Gill 1997 p. 59.
[22] . Collins. P. 36.

Chapter 19.

[1] . *Irish Independent*, 11 January 1932.
[2] . ibid. 26 January 1932.
[2a] . ibid 1/11/1928.
[3] . NAI. DFA P35B/115 18 Dulanty to Walsh.
[4] . *Irish Independent*, 30 January 1932.
[5] . ibid.
[6] . ibid.
[7] . *New York Times*, 12 February 1932.
[8] . *Irish Independent*, 15 February 1932.
[9] . *A Phoblacht*, January 1932.
[10] . Bowyer Bell, *Secret Army*, p. 92
[11] . ibid. p. 93.
[12] . Keogh, *Twentieth Century Ireland*, p. 62.
[12a]. Cruise O'Brien Conor, *States of Ireland*, Panther 1974. P. 114
[13] . ibid.
[14] . Brady Conor, *Guardians of the Peace*, Dublin 1974. pp. 167-8.
[15] . Regan. Pp. 291-7.
[16]. *Irish Times*, interview 1965.
[17] . *Irish Press*, interview 24 January 1968.
[18] . Horgan John, *Sean Lemass*, Gill 1997. p. 59.
[19] . *New York Times*, 21 February 1932.
[20] . Horgan, p. 60.

21. Jordan, *Sean.* p. 59.

22. ibid. p. 59.

23. *Sunday Chronicle,* 15 February 1932.

24. Lee, p. 171.

24a .Coogan TP, *deValera,* Hutchinston, 1997 p. 427.

25. ibid. p.426.

26. Keogh, *Twentieth Century Ireland.* P. 63.

27. Hayes Papers, P53/258 3 July 1944.

27a .Garvin, pp. 200-204.

28. Yeats WB, *Collected Poems,* Macmillan 1969. p. 320.

Epilogue.

1. Lindsay. p. 53.

1a. Cruise O'Brien, Conor. *Passion and Cunning.* Paladin 1990. p. 54-55.

2. Mulcahy Papers, P7B/96/13

3. Manning, P. 105.

4. Collins, P. 57.

5. DeVere White, *A Frightful Midge*

6. Jordan, *Sean,* p. 62.

7. Cronin Sean, *Frank Ryan.* Repsol 1980. p. 64.

8. Lee, p. 202.

9. Dail Debates, 27 July 1941. Col. 1878.

10. Manning. P 170.

11. *The Times,* 19 January 1944.

12. MacMahon Deirdre & Michael Kennedy Eds, *Obligations & Responsibilities: Ireland and the United Nations, 1955-2005.* IPA. P. 141.

13. NAI. 1194.

14. Lyons JB, *Oliver St. John Gogarty,* Blackwater 1980. p. 287.

15. *Irish Independent,* 29 June 1963.

INDEX

MacCurtain Tomas, 18,53
MacDermott, Sean 12,35
MacDonagh Joe, 81
MacDonagh Thomas, 25,29,32,35
MacDonald Malcolm, 124
MacDonald, Ramsay, 10,124,140
MacEntee Sean, 180
MacEoin Sean, 124
MacMahon Deirdre, 188
MacNeil Eoin, 23-4,26,37,39,45,69,
75,104,112-115,126,152
MacNeill John, 25,31,97,131
MacNevin William, 160
MacReady Gen., 55
MacRory Cardinal, 91,132, 147, 164
MacSweeney Mary, 67,85-6,99
MacSweeney Terence, 53
Magennis John, 40
Magician of Political Metaphysics, 80
Maguire Conor, 125
Maguire Tom, 125
Mahon Bryan Sir, 42-3, 118-9, 123
Majority Rule, 1611-2
Malahide Road, 24
Mallin Jas., 32
Manning Maurice, 8
Mansergh Martin Sen., 192
Mansion House, 15,45,64,76,108
Manorhamilton, 50
Marckievcz Countess, 20,39,43,75
Markets Committee, 15
Marrowbone Lane, 56
Mater Hospital, 42
Martial Law, 18
Martyn Edward, 11
Maxwell Gen., 32,37-8
Mayflower Hotel, 155,159
Maynooth, 55,167
Maynooth Statutes, 146
Mayo, 143, 165
Mayo County Council, 144,147-8
Mayo County Library, 143
Mayo Papers, 122
Mayo Senator, 119
McArdle Dorothy, 93
McCartan Patrick, 44,46,60

McCarthy Eugene, 36-7
McCullagh Music Shop, 119
McGarrity Joe, 47,88,187
McGarry Fergal, 105
McGarry Sean, 33,119
McGilligan Paddy, 55,105,114-
5,129,137,162,172,185
McGrath Joe, 75,81,87, 101-2, 105-6,171
McGrath Patrick, 90
McGuiness Joseph, 39,50
McKee Dick, 54
McKelvey Joe 87
McLoughlin Alf, 8
McQuaide Archbishop 132, 187
Meath, 50
Mellows Liam, 37
Messines, 39
Metropole, 136
Meyer Kuno, 16-17
Milroy Sean, 39,141-2
Military Service Bill, 43-4
Military Tribunals, 189,171,187
Ministers & Secretaries Act [1924], 129
Monaghan,
Montreal, 160
Moore Maurice, 119-120
Morahan TJ., 144
Moral Handicap, 162
Morning Post, 112
Mount Argus, 189
Mount Vernon, 189
Mulcahy General Richard :
  Active in Cumann na nGaedheal, 107,185
  Consulted by Cosgrave on Party Future, 186
  Cosgrave On, 189
  Fine Gael Leader, 188
  Isolated by Collin's Death, 82
  Old IRA Fights, 101-6
Mulligan Buck, 149
Mutinous Officers, 104
Munster & Leinster Bank, 48
Mussolini , 130,182
O'Connor Frank On, 83
Signs Execution Warrants, 89
Suspected by Civilians in government, 89

Royal College Surgeons, 118
Royal Dublin Society, 100,162
Royal Hibernian Academy, 123
Royal Hospital Kilmainham, 28-9,100
Royal Irish Academy, 16
Royal Irish constabulary [RIC], 44-5,53
Royal Republican A, 69
Roynane John BL., 24,33
Rules of Court, 127
Russell Charles Col., 96
Russell Dr. MOH, 24
Russell George, 23,120
Russian Communists, 164
Russian Soviet Republics, 167
Ruttledge Patrick. TD., 148, 180
Ryan Fr. TW. CC., 32
Ryan Frank, 166,181,185
Ryan James Dr., 50,169,180
Ryan Michael, 47

S
Salary Reductions, 129,182
Salisbury Lord, 118
Salthill Hotel, 60
Sandringham, 171
Sandymount, 149
Saor Eire, 164,166-7,181
Scala Theatre, 149
Second Dail, 58,126
Senate, 117-124
Senate Elections, 123
Senators, Names, 118
Senate Powers of, 123
Seskin Co. Tipperary, 10
Sexuality, 163
Shannon Hydroelectric Scheme, 162
Shaughran The, 143
Shaws Bernard The, 80
Shelbourne Hotel, 121
Sherlock Councillor, 18,33-4
Sigerson Dr., 119
Sinn Fein, 6,10-13,18,23,25,36,39,40,42-3,45,48,53,58,91,96,106-7,150
Sinn Fein Ard Fheis, 47,76-7,149
Sinn Fein on Dublin Corporation, 13-21
Six counties, 114,145

Sligo, 155
Smylie RM., 155
Smith O'Brien, 69
Smuts Gen. 57
Snap Election 1933, 185
Social Values, 131
Solohead Ambush, 45
South Africa, 19,35-6,557,65,107,112,137,140
South Armagh,,112
South Circular Road, 29
South Dublin Union, 9,13,18,26-7,31,33-4,43,189
Southampton, 160
Soldier's Song, 31
Speaker the, 71
Special Courts,153
Stack Austin, 42,49,56,58,60-4,125
Staines Michael, 88
Standard of Living, 90
Standard The, 144
Standing Committee Cumann na nGaedheal, 108
Star The, 148
State funeral, 189
St. Columbanus, 136
St. Michael & John Church, 25
St. Patrick's Park, 31-2
St. Patrick's Society, 169
Sturgis Mark, 57
Suffolk St., 86
Sugar Beet Factory Carlow, 162

T
Tallon Laurence, 28
Taoiseach, 187
Templeogue,
Tenements, 69
Terenure, 152
Third Dail, 77
Third Royal Irish, 28
Thomas St., 31
Thompson William Hale, 159
Tipperary, 7
Tories, 63
Tobin Liam Gen., 101-2
Tokyo, 136

Tone Wolfe, 56,166,187
Train Crash in Canada, 160
Transitional [Provisional] Government, 75
Traynor Oscar, 28
Treasonable Offences Bill, 150
Treaty, 7
Treaty Article 1, 65
Treaty Cabinet vote on, 64
Treaty Dail vote on, 71
Treaty Debates, 6,67-74
Treaty Delegates, 60-1
Treaty Draft, 62
Treaty Negotiations, 61-3,123
Treaty Ports, 187
Treaty Signatures, 66
Treaty Ultimatum, 62
Truce Moves [1921], 57,59
Tuam, 146
Tuohig Richard, 85
Tuohy Patrick Fr., 190
Twenty Six Counties, 167
Two Thousand Guineas Race [1927], 155

U

Ulster, 15,23,57,78,84,120
Ulster Unionist Council, 23
Ulster Unionists, 43,57
Ulster Volunteer Force, 23,113
Ultimate Freestater, 184
Ulysses, 121
Unconditional Democrats, 88
Unemployment Figures, [1932], 174
Unionist Association Dublin, 15
United Ireland, 109,115
United Irishman, 107
United Kingdom, 131,140
United Nations, 188
United States Embassy, 18
University College Dublin, 67
Up deValera, 159

V

Vane Richard Sir, 43
Vatican, 91,130,136,168
Versailles Treaty, 47
Victoria Hotel, 40
Virgin Mary, 14

Visitor's Book, 80,113
Vocational Education Act, 132
Volunteers The, 25,2-9,32
Volunteers-IRA, 45,53
Volunteer Split, 24

W

Wall St. Crash, 162
Walker Mayor, 159
Walsh Frank, 47
Walsh JJ., 50,97,109,159,182
Walsh Joseph, 136,168
Ward Union Hunt, 162
War of Independence, 47,57
Warrington Capt., 28
Washington, 46,159
Washington's Tomb, 46,160
Water Bailiff, 15,18
Waterloo, 181
Watling St. Bridge, 132
Werburgh St., 31
Westland Row Church,. 151
Westmeath, 33,50
Westminster, 39,4-4, 107
Westport, 90
Westropp Sen.,132
Wexford, 119
Whitefriars St. Church, 87
White House, 159
Williams TD., 183
Wilson President, 20,46-7
Wilson Henry Sir, 77
Wilson Volunteer, 31
Women's International League for Peace &
Freedom, 150
Women's Prisoners Protection League, 181
Women Republicans, 122
Women's Rights, 122
World League of Nations, 41
Whyte John, 131
Wynn's Hotel, 177
Wyse-Power, Charles, 36
Wyse-Power Mrs, 118-120, 122

Y

Yeats Michael, 192
Yeats WB., 100,122-3, 185

ᴸ

BOOKS BY ANTHONY J. JORDAN AVAILABLE

From
westportbooks @yahpp.co.uk

CHRISTY BROWN'S WOMEN
A BIOGRAPHY
ISBN 0952444739 €10.00

WB YEATS; VAIN, GLORIOUS, LOUT.
A MAKER OF MODERN IRELAND

ISBN 0952444720 €12.00

BOER WAR TO EASTER RISING
WRITINGS OF JOHN MACBRIDE

ISBN 0952444763 €14.00